Imagining the Plains
of Latin America

Environmental Cultures Series

Series Editors:
Greg Garrard, University of British Columbia, Canada
Richard Kerridge, Bath Spa University

Editorial Board:
Frances Bellarsi, Université Libre de Bruxelles, Belgium
Mandy Bloomfield, Plymouth University, UK
Lily Chen, Shanghai Normal University, China
Christa Grewe-Volpp, University of Mannheim, Germany
Stephanie LeMenager, University of Oregon, USA
Timothy Morton, Rice University, USA
Pablo Mukherjee, University of Warwick, UK

Bloomsbury's *Environmental Cultures* series makes available to students and scholars at all levels the latest cutting-edge research on the diverse ways in which culture has responded to the age of environmental crisis. Publishing ambitious and innovative literary ecocriticism that crosses disciplines, national boundaries and media, books in the series explore and test the challenges of ecocriticism to conventional forms of cultural study.

Titles Available:

Bodies of Water, Astrida Neimanis
Cities and Wetlands, Rod Giblett
Civil Rights and the Environment in African-American Literature, 1895–1941, John Claborn
Climate Change Scepticism, Greg Garrard, George Handley, Axel Goodbody and Stephanie Posthumus
Climate Crisis and the 21st-Century British Novel, Astrid Bracke
Colonialism, Culture, Whales, Graham Huggan
Ecocriticism and Italy, Serenella Iovino
Fuel, Heidi C. M. Scott
Literature as Cultural Ecology, Hubert Zapf
Nerd Ecology, Anthony Lioi
The New Nature Writing, Jos Smith
The New Poetics of Climate Change, Matthew Griffiths
This Contentious Storm, Jennifer Mae Hamilton

Climate Change Scepticism, Greg Garrard, Axel Goodbody, George B. Handley
and Stephanie Posthumus
Ecospectrality, Laura White
Teaching Environmental Writing, Isabel Galleymore
Radical Animism, Jemma Deer
Cognitive Ecopoetics, Sharon Lattig
Digital Vision and Ecological Aesthetic, Lisa FitzGerald
Environmental Cultures in Soviet East Europe, Anna Barcz
Weathering Shakespeare, Evelyn O'Malley
The Living World, Samantha Walton
Ecocollapse Fiction, Sarah E. McFarland

Forthcoming Titles:

Contemporary Fiction and Climate Uncertainty, Marco Caracciolo
Ecocriticism and Turkey, Meliz Ergin

To Latin America, its lands and peoples, to them belongs this book.

To Gabriela and Ignacio, for my writing without them is incomplete.

Contents

Acknowledgements	x
Notes on translations	xii
Introduction: The continental imaginaries of Latin America	1
1 The empty desert of the Pampas	19
2 The ruined lands of the Altiplanos	39
3 Predation in the Orinoco Llanos	65
4 Naming the Pantanal wetlands	93
Conclusion	123
Notes	131
References	155
Index	164

Acknowledgements

I distinctly remember my arrival in Mexico City in 2007 to undertake a year abroad as a student at the Faculty of Philosophy and Letters in the Universidad Nacional Autónoma de México (UNAM). Whereas most of my classmates back in Spain chose to pursue academic exchanges in Europe, I was convinced that part of my training had to take place in Latin America. In many ways, I began the long journey of writing this book that same year. Particularly vivid in my mind are Enrique Dussel's lectures on the politics of liberation. In one particular lecture, he explained to a class filled to the brim with students what he meant by the 'exercise of a critical ethics that affirms the negated life of the victim, the oppressed or the excluded'. He said that to affirm the life of the oppressed is to struggle against the institutions that would drown them, violently shaking off the hands that smother them in the water as they gasp for air. I was and continue to be shaken to my very core by that powerful image. Years later I would read Gloria Anzaldúa's *Borderlands/La Frontera*, and her essays on the struggles of Chicanx would resonate not only with my ideas on decolonization but also on a personal level concerning my experiences as a Hispanic adolescent growing up in the United States, in Florida. Both Dussel and Anzaldúa have shaped who I strive to be; they are the source of much of my work on Latin America to this day.

This book has been the result of many years of research that could not have been possible without all the people and institutions that supported my ambitious project of tracing the literatures of the plains throughout the Americas. A significant part of my research was made possible by the generous support of the Izaak Killam Trust and the University of Alberta. My years in Canada were crucial in developing my ideas. Odile Cisneros was always ready to challenge my claims to push me further along in my research, and I would not be where I am today if it wasn't for her unremitting intellectual rigour and support. Laura Beard was also very supportive of my project from the beginning, and her insistence of addressing the role of Indigenous cultures in portraying the plains has become central to my intellectual and personal views of Latin America. Other colleagues were also incredibly supportive in the five years I spent in Canada: Ann de León, Stefano Muneroni, Kim Noels, Xavier Gutiérrez, Lars Richter, Marine Gheno,

Jérémie Pelletier-Gagnon, Mimi Okabe, Stephen Cruikshank and Jay Friesen. To all my Brazilian colleagues in Paraná and São Paulo, I am very grateful for always lending an ear to my ideas and offering reading suggestions. To all my colleagues and professors in Mexico City – some who unfortunately are no longer with us, but whose lectures I carry with me – I am thankful for their guidance: Rodolfo Mata, Ambrosio Velasco, Bolívar Echevarría and Adolfo Sánchez Vázquez. I would also like to thank Antolín Sánchez for his support all these years, always welcoming me into his office at the Spanish National Research Institute to discuss research. Having arrived at Durham University in 2018, I have had the opportunity to work alongside some brilliant colleagues who continue to drive my research into the environmental humanities: Francisco J. Hernández Adrián, Kerstin Oloff and Joanna Allan.

Translations

All translations of the canonical fictions of Latin America that appear in the chapters of this book are the author's. I have only included the original texts in the longer citations so as to make the overall argument more accessible to the general reader. In Chapters 1 and 2, I have translated directly from the originals so as to best capture the nuances in the portrayals of the plains. In Chapter 3, I compared my translations with those of Robert Malloy for the English edition of *Doña Bárbara* in Chicago University Press, while directly translating the Spanish texts in *La vorágine*, although an excellent English translation of the novel is now available in Duke University Press by John Charles Chasteen. In Chapter 4, I directly translated from the original Brazilian Portuguese, given that none of the works are available in English.

Introduction

The continental imaginaries of Latin America

In the twentieth century, Brazilian writer Érico Veríssimo began publishing what would become a three-volume historical narrative of Rio Grande do Sul, the southernmost state of Brazil that shares borders with Uruguay and Argentina. In grand style, each book in the trilogy *O tempo e o vento* traces the life of the Terra-Cambará family in the city of Santa Fé since the establishment of the Jesuit missions at the limits between the Spanish and Portuguese empires. More than a set of regional novels, Veríssimo's trilogy attempts to compare the 'incipient South American civilisation with that of Europe'.[1] It narrates the formation of Brazil as a nation state through the perspective of rural landowners in its southern state.[2] The first book is titled *O Continente* (1949) and tells of the settlers that arrived in that 'immense green desert of the Continent', founding several of the cities in Rio Grande do Sul. One of these cities is Santa Fé, where the Terra-Cambará family is caught in the middle of the Federalist Revolution.[3] The following two books continue that initial saga as it unfolds well into the 1950s: the second book is *O Retrato* (1951) and the third is *O Arquipélago* (1962). The 'immense green desert' of the first volume refers to the flat grasslands that cover most of the Brazilian state and are commonly known as the Pampas, a biome that is also shared with Argentina and Uruguay.

The title of Veríssimo's first volume – *O Continente* – is illustrative, since it expresses a central theme of the environmental imaginaries of Latin American literature that I will explore in this book: the role of continental topographies in the settler ecologies that emerge in canonical narratives since the nineteenth century. Instead of directly naming the Pampas as the scenario of the historical narrative, Veríssimo writes of the 'Continent' that spans from the coast all the way into the interior of Rio Grande do Sul. The term is a reference to the colonial administration of that region under Portuguese rule after the Treaty of Madrid (1750), when it was established as the 'Capitania do Rio Grande de São Pedro' and commonly known as 'Continente de São Pedro'.[4] It was the military engineer Francisco João Roscio who began naming the interior of Rio Grande do Sul as a 'continent' in his cartography of the region after the new demarcation of borders between Spain and Portugal.[5] In fact, these first cartographic projects were part of a large colonizing effort to control a region that had resisted imperial control due to the alliance of Jesuit missions and the Guaraní communities. It manifests what scholars in island and archipelagic studies have coined as 'continentalism'.[6] Elizabeth McMahon suggests that the eighteenth century saw a shift from insular imaginaries towards continental narratives, a shift closely linked to how 'the temporal coordinate of Modernity worked to obscure islands as topographies outside the modern, as sites against which continental modernity could be defined'.[7] As Atlantic empires became more invested in resources inland, islands and coastlines became less present in narratives.[8] Veríssimo repeats this continentalist discourse already present in the colonial cartography of João Roscio, naming the grasslands of Rio Grande do Sul as 'the Continent', in contrast with coastline or insular geographies. This abstraction renders the land as an empty scenario on which historical conflicts play out between descendants of settlers in the saga of the Terra-Cambará family. In other words, geography gives way to the temporality of human conflicts in the trilogy *O tempo e o vento*.

Yet for all the importance of historical time in Veríssimo's novels, the entire multivolume narrative is encased within the binary between continental and archipelagic geographies as they appear in the titles of the first volume (*O Continente*) and the third and final volume (*O Arquipélago*). The continentalist imaginary repeated by Veríssimo deploys those geographies as abstract categories to frame a history of settlement in Rio Grande do Sul. It portrays the plains as a *terra nullius*, a practice that 'actively creates space for the tangible expansion of the one world by rendering empty the places it occupies and making absent the worlds that make those places'.[9] The land on which the plot unfolds has hardly any specificity, becoming a mere surface for the history of colonization. One overarching narrative is offered, making all the other imaginaries of those lands absent. As readers we should ask ourselves what other stories were told of the Pampas before, during and after the colonizers arrived? Are other knowledges and ontologies of these lands possible? These sorts of questions allow us to reframe the link between how natures are imagined and the dominance of colonial tropes upon those imaginaries. Scholars and anthropologists have been emphasizing the need to move away from a single globalizing discourse towards what they consider is a 'pluriverse' or the 'heterogenous worldlings coming together as a political ecology of practices'.[10] Often these other epistemologies and ontologies are effaced in favour of a single narrative. The Latin American plains have also suffered such a wiping of the plurality of knowledges of the land, 'invisibilized by modernity' in Mario Blaser's words.¹¹ The nineteenth and twentieth centuries saw the emergence of independent nations throughout Latin America, all of them engaging the themes of modernity. Rather than being conducive to the modernizing of these young nation states, the plains were predominantly seen as averse sites to modernity, as backlands that resisted the order of civilization. It was these diverse lands that underwent the imposition of series of tropes, repeated over and over, that guaranteed a single narrative of their being. As Arturo Escobar makes manifest in Designs for the Pluriverse, the 'overriding concern is with difference, and how difference is effaced or normalized'.¹² They are a salient example of how the colonial narrative acts against the pluriverse in favour of a single epistemology that legitimizes the exploitation of resources and the wiping out of Indigenous communities inhabiting these lands.

In his memoirs, Veríssimo writes that the fictional family of the Terra-Cambará's was 'isolated in that green sea of horizons without end'.¹³ The struggles of the family unravel in an abstract space where the land is a 'green sea' whose salient characteristic is having 'horizons without end'. Moreover, the original passage in Portuguese makes the dichotomy between continental and insular geographies all the more explicit, since the family is 'isolated' (*ilhada*) as in stranded on an 'island' in the continent. Following Lawrence Buell's distinction, the land portrayed in O tempo e o vento is conceived as an abstract space, rather than a place.¹⁴ The image of the land as sea is present throughout the Americas in texts depicting grasslands and plains. It is what Robert Thacker argues are the 'prairie/sea parallels' that European settlers exploited in describing the Great Plains of North America, attempting to make sense of a landscape unknown to them.¹⁵ The metaphor of the ocean of land is also central in the continentalist imaginaries, especially as it emerges from pioneers as they travel westward across the Americas, trying to give names to a world they were unfamiliar with. It is important to note that the lack of a language to depict the land does not mean that the land was nameless – Indigenous knowledge of the plains had long been present before the settlers arrived and survives in the dominant images present in canonical writers, if only concealed by European modes of representing the landscape.¹⁶

Veríssimo's choice of words to describe that particular plains geography as 'immense' and part of a 'desert' repeats a continentalist trope with a long tradition in Latin America, one that often depicts such lands throughout the Americas as empty and barren, especially since the 1800s.¹⁷ Regardless of the actual flora and fauna found in grasslands across South and North America, canonical writers – white and privileged men of letters, descendants from European settlers – have imagined the vast plains of the continent as deserts that need the intervention of civilization to allow progress to take hold. This is another central theme that I will explore at length throughout this book, seeking to reveal how the dominant depictions of the plains in Latin American literature repeat settler ecologies that efface the prior history and knowledge of these rich and biodiverse lands. Often the plains are portrayed as 'empty', as if they were a blank slate upon which to cast the settler imaginations of writers.[18] Given that many of the foundational fictions of Latin America since independence use as their setting plains geographies, I am interested in raising the question as to why such a setting is recurrent. Why do canonical fictions in Latin America primarily take place in plains? By exploring the colonial tropes latent in the way writers of the foundational fictions of Latin America imagined the plains, we may begin to understand how the construction of 'nature' is central to the emerging *national* territories in Latin America.[19] I argue that the imaginaries of the plains have played a salient role in that ideological construction of Latin American nation states, acting as an abstract territory to be populated with a view of nature that legitimizes modernizing projects. More importantly, I am invested in exploring the specific modes through which canonical writers have represented plains geographies in an effort to demonstrate how they became the dominant imaginaries of nature in Latin America since the nineteenth century. Just as in Veríssimo's *O tempo e o vento*, many of the novels discussed in this book are committed to establishing a narrative in which the plains form part of the national imaginary. Insofar as the plains become a surface upon which the ideals and desires of nationhood can be projected, the dominant mode of representing them in canonical fictions enacts what Boaventura de Sousa Santos calls 'epistemicide'.[20] on other possible modes of knowing the various grasslands throughout the Americas. That is, the dominant representation of the plains as barren and empty constitutes an epistemology that relegates other knowledges of the Americas to obscurity, especially those of Indigenous communities.

In what follows, I will discuss the ecocritical approach I have adopted in my readings of the Latin American literary canon through the lens of plains geographies throughout the Spanish- and Portuguese-speaking Americas.

Settler ecologies of the Latin American plains

I am particularly committed to reading Latin American literature through a transnational perspective that bridges languages and national borders, so as to better understand how regional writings are entwined in the continental imaginaries of settler ecologies since the nineteenth century. My approach to Latin America incorporates the literary canon of Brazil, along the rest of the Spanish-speaking nations in the Americas. I argue that settler ecologies share similarities across canonical literary texts, whether written in Spanish or Brazilian Portuguese. By addressing the role of the plains in the emergence of a continentalist narrative, my ecocritical reading frames the literatures of Latin America in terms of several important grassland biomes that are so often ignored: Pampas, Altiplanos, Llanos and Pantanal. Although each of these biomes has its own ecological traits, canonical writers have tended to deploy a fixed repertoire of images to portray grasslands across the Americas in the past two hundred years. For example, as I read Domingo Sarmiento's *Facundo: Civilización y Barbarie* (1845) alongside Rómulo Gallegos's *Doña Bárbara* (1929), I was struck by the fact that both texts, written almost a hundred years apart, deployed the same tropes to depict very different grassland biomes. The same could be said about the connections between texts written in different languages. James Fenimore Cooper's *The Prairie* (1827) uses the metaphors of the plains as wasteland and the plains as ocean that are present not only in Sarmiento's *Facundo* but also in Brazilian writer Euclides da Cunha's *Os sertões* (1902). Although differing in historical epoch, national literary tradition and even language, many of the canonical texts throughout the Americas engage with plains and grasslands in strikingly similar ways. Hence, two questions emerge: What are those tropes that are repeated by canonical writers in Latin America in portraying plains geographies and how are those images linked to the shift towards a continental narrative in the eighteenth century?

Throughout this book, I have attempted to answer these two questions. I have already anticipated a partial answer in my initial discussion of Érico Veríssimo: canonical texts in Latin America deploy a settler ecology that represents the plains as barren, ruined and hostile in the interests of a continentalist narrative that is closely linked to capital interests to the interior of the Americas. The Manifest Destiny policy spread throughout North America in the nineteenth century, as did the Argentine Desert Campaign (1833–4) and the Brazilian Canudos Campaign (1896–7) in South America. All of these political projects were not only oriented towards building the emerging nation states in the Americas but also invested in the exploitation of the potential resources to be found in the vast plains inland. Many of these grasslands have gradually become what Macarena Gómez-Barris identifies as 'extractive zones', lands that have been and continue to be intensively exploited for their resources.[21] Often, grasslands are considered as potential farmland to sustain the growing need for food in industrialized nations. The last fifty years have seen transgenic soy production take off in the Argentine Pampas, going from just 38,000 hectares in 1970 to approximately 10 million hectares in 2001.[22] Sarmiento's emphasis in *Facundo* on bringing civilization to the 'desert' of the Pampas manifests the interest in making grasslands productive in terms of agriculture throughout the Americas. I will explore the trope of the plains as 'desert' in Chapter 1, addressing the role that abstraction plays in rendering the land an empty surface that allows progress to literally harvest its ideals in the form of monoculture. Plains have also become mineral and oil extraction sites in Latin America. In the highlands or Altiplanos of Bolivia, for example, we find the mines of Potosí, a historical site of silver and other mineral extraction that continues to this day. Jeffrey Bury and Anthony Bebbington argue that such extractive industries since the colonial period and after Latin American independence 'deeply affected the spatial configuration of most modern Latin American states'.[23] The metaphor of the Altiplanos as a ruined natural landscape, which I discuss at length in Chapter 2, invites extractivist projects that are seen as making a profit of a land that is already damaged and inhospitable. Bolivian writer Alcides Arguedas, for example, begins his book *Raza de bronce* (1919) with the following depiction of the highlands: 'Some sown fields of barley, already yellowish from maturity, gave coloured stains on the sad and opaque tones of this land, almost sterile from the constant cold of the heights.'[24] The land as sterile not only suggests a gendered image of the land – one that requires masculine civilization to harvest its soils – but also a devaluing of its capacity to sustain modern practices of agriculture in the form of 'fields of barley'. Civilization needs to literally reach down into the mineral ground to extract its potential value. Exploitation of plains geographies does not always follow an extractive model, since these grasslands are also segmenting into ranching enterprises. In the Orinoco river basin, where abundant and biodiverse grasslands known as the Llanos are shared between Colombia and Venezuela, the rise in livestock industry came at the cost of placing the native Orinoco crocodile (*Crocodylus intermedius*) as an endangered species. In Chapter 3, I will explore in detail how the trope of the plains as a hostile environment plays an important role in the emphasis of the predatory encounter as part of life in these grasslands in canonical fiction.

My ecocritical reading of the settler imaginaries of the plains seeks to reveal how the depictions of grasslands in canonical fictions of Latin America deploy a fixed set of tropes that legitimize the exploitation of these biomes as part of the continentalist rhetoric of progress, capital and modernity. It addresses the colonial dimension of those dominant images that canonical texts repeat since the nineteenth century by identifying their ideological construction. The depictions of the plains by male writers accepted into the literary canon – not to mention the political corpus in many cases – are not just aesthetic representations but in their repetition establish a mode of knowing the grasslands of the Americas that ignores the local knowledge of the different bioregions.[25] The tropes repeated in canonical fictions of Latin America deploy settler representations of the land, whether it be the plains as desert, wastelands, hostile or potential gardens. As Lee Clark Mitchell argues regarding the continental spaces of America, the land 'had been imagined from the beginning in terms of timeless space as a vacant land awaiting the starter's gun of history'.[26] Neither the North American Great Plains nor any of the other grasslands throughout South America were 'timeless' or 'vacant' when European colonizers arrived. Rather, they brought with them the experiences of landscapes that they had experienced back home and projected them upon arriving. Yet it is striking that in the nineteenth and twentieth centuries, Latin American fiction continued emphasizing those same portrayals of the plains as 'empty' and 'barren', making these images into much more than mere subjective portrayals of the grasslands.

The repertoire of grassland depictions turned the local knowledge of European settlers into global knowledge of these biomes. Walter Mignolo suggests as much when he argues that 'coloniality' of knowledge responds 'to the movement forward of a global design that intended to impose itself and those local histories and knowledges that are forced to accommodate themselves to such new realities'.[27] I argue along those lines, suggesting that what I call the 'dominant' images of the plains in canonical fiction establish a particular representation of the grasslands that effaces other local knowledges of these biomes and responds to capital interests in the exploitation of the land according to modern agriculture and industry. A 'dominant' image of the plains is one that suppresses other alternative depictions. It is not a question of whether that representation is true or not, but rather that it occupies all the epistemological space – it does not allow for other forms of getting to know the grasslands. Elsewhere, Mignolo has argued that 'decolonizing knowledge and being' is to unshackle that which 'coloniality of knowledge and being prevents to know and become'.[28] Or as philosopher Enrique Dussel claims, it is necessary to 'originate from other ontological horizons'.[29] To be able to acknowledge those other possible knowledges and ontologies of the grasslands of the Americas, biomes which have had a salient role in structuring the continentalist narrative of modernity, we must first reconsider the fixed repertoire of representations offered by canonical writers as dominant. They are not just *depicting* the land but also establishing *a way of knowing that land* which hinders local knowledges. My ecocritical engagement with Latin American fictions seeks to reveal the ideological component to the repeated tropes of the plains so as to open up a space for local knowledges.

One specific way in which local knowledges of the land emerge through colonial filters is in the very act of naming. Dufva Quantic, for example, explains that settlers in North America 'had no vocabulary to describe the unfamiliar landscape' of the Great Plains.[30] The names given to places become etched into the land they reference. Settler ecologies often either give new names to places or repurpose Indigenous names. A clear example of this is the word 'Pampas', which is often taken to refer to the grasslands shared between Argentina, Uruguay and Brazil. However, the word is derived from the Quechua language in the Andes region of South America, where it refers specifically to the highlands. Another example of the colonial ecologies present in naming is the numerous scientific journeys throughout South America by European botanists, such as Aimee Bonpland or Carl Friedrich Philipp von Martius, who collected specimens of flora and began giving them Latin names.[31] The repurposing of the word in the settler ecologies of Argentina manifests how local knowledge can be effaced by the act of naming and renaming of places, rivers, plants and animals. I will explore the role of naming in portraying nature in Chapter 4, considering both how naming can both generate a coloniality of knowledge and also serve to leverage local knowledges. Language is a powerful tool by which we come to know the world around us, for it is not only through metaphors that we imagine nature but also through the names we use to refer to specific things in nature.

Often local knowledge of a particular region takes the form of specific words for plants and animals. Take, for example, the large American feline known as the jaguar. Throughout different regions of the Americas – especially in plains geographies near rivers, such as the Pantanal wetlands – the jaguar is known under different names: 'yaguareté' (Guaraní), 'onça' (Brazilian Portuguese), 'ocelotl' (Nahuatl) and 'tigre' (Argentine Spanish) are some of the names that the feline is referred to throughout Latin America. An analysis of the meaning of each of these names reveals the knowledge embedded, such as the Nahuatl voice 'ocelotl', which in Aztec mythology associates the large feline with the night, dark magic and the masculine god Tezcatlipoca.[32] Not only does the Aztec symbolism reveal the warlike and masculine attributes attached to their view of the jaguar but also the seeming nocturnal predatory habits of the feline. When the Spanish arrived in Mexico, they quickly translated the term 'ocelotl' as 'tiger' in an attempt to make sense of the feline indigenous to the Americas.[33] The Argentine name for the jaguar seems to continue this misnomer that reveals a latent Orientalism in the settler ecologies repeated in canonical fictions of Latin America – the tiger being a primarily Asian feline not found in Europe or the Americas.[34] The protagonist of Sarmiento's essay, Facundo Quiroga, is also known by the name 'tigre de los llanos' or 'tiger of the plains', referencing the supposed encounter between the caudillo and a jaguar out in the Pampas.

An important aspect of my ecocritical readings is the centrality of the non-human elements of the narratives. At the very core of ecocriticism is the 'understanding of the intimacy of humans and nonhumans'.[35] Its approach seeks to bring into relief aspects of written texts that are often overlooked as part of the setting of narratives, challenging readers to reconsider how plants, animals, rivers, mountains and other non-human beings interact in how we imagine the stories and poems we read. As Jane Bennett describes the politics of 'vibrant materialism', engaging with the non-human is about establishing 'more channels of communication'.[36] These elements embedded in literature generate a resistance to the traditional way in which we read. Narrative emphasizes temporality, the succession of events as the plot unfolds. To read a text through the non-human is to suspend the story and linger in the details at the interstices of the plot. Rather than dwell on what happens to the human protagonists, an ecocritical reading that addresses the non-human tries to make sense of the role that animals and plants have in the scenarios of the action taking place. By 'non-human', I broadly understand those beings categorized as 'animals, affectivity, bodies, organic and geophysical systems, materiality, or technology'.[37] The non-human is always at the very margins of the human, whether it be the domestic species that coinhabit with us or the technologies that are an extension of our own bodies.

The non-human is crucial in reframing how we understand what it means to be human. The non-human puts into question what it means to be human, hence facilitating a more in-depth discussion of the notion. Donna Haraway has made a compelling case for this entanglement between the human and the non-human in several of her books. In her most recent book titled *Staying with the Trouble* (2016), she writes that our current environmental crisis 'requires making oddkin' in 'unexpected collaborations and combinations'.[38] I find the term 'oddkin' is particularly appropriate to my ecocritical approach concerning the Latin American plains, for, by focusing on the network of non-human elements that constitute the grasslands biomes as they appear in canonical fictions, I offer a reading that will most likely seem 'odd' to readers acquainted with the novels I discuss in this book. This is precisely the point. Foregrounding the plains and their non-human constituents resists the romanticized and national narratives that have repurposed those valuable biomes into scenarios in which to play out human conflicts.

My ecocritical reading is partly a 'disanthropocentric reenvisioning of the complicated biomes and cosmopolities within which we dwell'.[39] It frustrates the overarching narratives of canonical fictions by reading them against the grain, displacing the human characters as they become entangled with the grasslands. Rather than read Sarmiento's *Facundo* as an essay on the caudillo Facundo Quiroga, I challenge my readers to consider the book as it deploys the Pampas grasslands as an empty desert on which to play out the drama of the Argentine nation state. I enquire as to what non-human elements of the grasslands are present in the essay. Does Sarmiento refer to any specific plants that belong to the grasslands? How is the topography of the plains described? These questions make us engage with the text 'oddly', orienting our reading down strange and surprising paths that prioritize the depictions of the non-human over the narrative sequence. They lead us to the strangeness of coexisting, which is at the core of ecological thinking.[40] It is this strangeness that can shift our way of imagining the world around us, especially as we suffer the consequences of climate change in what has been coined as the age of the Anthropocene. Deborah Bird Rose suggests that 'the Anthropocene shows us the need for radically reworked forms of attention to what marks the human species as different'.[41]

However, my ecocritical readings of Latin American fictions[42] attempt not only to read against the grain in bringing the non-human grasslands into focus but also to suggest that the manner in which canonical writers have imagined nature is ideological. I am committed to reading the Latin American plains in a way that manifests how the repertoire of images used in canonical fictions impedes alternative modes of representing these biomes. That is, I not only point to the repeated tropes to portray the plains but also argue that such tropes legitimize a settler ecology that was central to exploitation of these grasslands as part of capitalist expansion. Jason W. Moore's approach to understanding the production of nature as dialectically linked to capitalism is a valuable contribution from which my ecocritical readings draw. Rather than separate 'nature' from 'society', Moore reframes the dichotomy in attempting to understand the current climate crisis in terms 'of what nature does for capitalism, rather than what capitalism *does to* nature'.[43] In its production of a commodified nature, capitalism is a 'world-ecology'.[44] This dialectical relationship between the human and non-human is particularly useful in understanding the relationship between the dominant images of the grasslands in canonical fiction and the exploitation of these biomes under the guise of modernity. The dominant imaginaries of the plains build a common repertoire of metaphors that constitute a knowledge that justifies expansion of capitalism in those regions. In other words, these images accompany capitalism in its production of nature. The establishment of large transgenic soy monoculture in the Argentine Pampas is dialectically bound to the dominant metaphor of these grasslands as a desert. This is why we need to be careful of how we understand the Anthropocene, since 'it does not challenge the naturalized inequalities, alienation, and violence inscribed in modernity's strategic relations of power and production'.[45] Responsibility should not be equally distributed among all peoples in the planet.

Ecocriticism needs to go beyond merely focusing on the non-human and rethink how the oppressed human other is also entangled in the Anthropocene. The violence of colonial and neocolonial projects has long affected both the human and non-human. Rob Nixon argues, 'Postcolonialism can help diversify our thinking beyond the dominant paradigms of wilderness and Jeffersonian agrarianism in ways that render ecocriticism more accommodating of what I call a transnational ethics of place.'[46] The plains are a biome host for humans and nonhumans alike, both of which are often effaced in continentalist narratives. Although most of my readings in this book engage with canonical fictions that espouse continentalist narratives directed at imagining the grasslands of the Americas as barren places that could potentially become sites of modern agriculture and resource extraction, my decolonial gesture is to identify these as *dominant*. The act of delimiting the continentalist repertoire sets up the possibility of a sustained critique and an opening to alternative imaginaries and politics. I take my cue from decolonial philosopher Enrique Dussel in understanding the decolonial as a dialectic process of liberation.

Dussel argues that a politics of liberation entails three moments: (a) the established totality, (b) a messianic rupture and (c) a creation of a new order.[47] The first moment is foundational or architectural insofar as it refers to an awareness of the established order. Any process of liberation requires a delimitation of the structures that enact oppression. It is the necessary first step prior to its critical, decolonial deconstruction.[48] This first moment offers a description of the ontological field, tracing the limits of the established totality. Dussel, however, is aware that ontology leaves very little space for difference: 'in order to construct a new system, it is necessary to de-construct (or simply destroy) the prior established order'.[49] To decolonize is to generate an ontological rupture in the established order so as to allow alterity to structure the new order. It is in that sense that the decolonial turn in Dussel is different from that of pluriverse theorists, for it conceives of the oppressed other as exterior to the established totality. Any given ontology will always generate an exteriority, those left out of its conception of the world. The relationship between totality and exteriority is dialectical, thus generating new orders that create an exteriority that will serve as a new basis for the critique of the established order.

Dussel's philosophy of liberation is built around the exteriority generated by totality, the human other that is always pushed out beyond the margins to a place of vulnerability.[50] The second moment – which sets up the decolonial turn of his philosophy – is a critique of the established order from the exteriority/difference of the oppressed other. My decolonial gesture is located within those two first moments of liberation insofar as it seeks to delimit the dominant repertoire of imaginaries of the Latin American plains, while also offering a critique based on the exteriority that such a repertoire of images generates. Throughout this book, I encourage the reader to consider what other modes of imagining the plains are possible beyond the set of tropes analysed. What knowledges and peoples have been marginalized in the creation of the corpus of depictions of the plains that recur in canonical texts in Latin America? Alongside Latinx ecocritics, I also 'caution against totalizing narratives, the erasure of incommensurabilities'.[51] Any totality will leave something out, an exteriority displaced.

The plains across the Americas offer a transnational scope through which to understand the conflict between the local knowledges of the different grasslands against the repertoire of settler ecologies that recur in canonical fictions. My argument suggests that not all portrayals of the plains are on a level playing field, but rather that some images have become more widespread since the nineteenth century, alongside an increased interest in developing the vast continents of the Americas. An important step to listening to the other voices of the plains that have for centuries espoused a particular knowledge of the grasslands and other biomes is to recognize the presence of dominant images of the plains. My ecocritical reading identifies the ideological and dominant dimensions of depicting the plains of the Americas as barren, inhospitable and threatening lands. My contribution to the postcolonial ecology of the Latin American plains is inevitably incomplete, precisely because it engages directly with those canonical fictions that it denounces as warranting a continentalist narrative that hinges on a settler view of lands that were inhabited long before the colonizers arrived. As Sousa Santos confesses in his *Epistemologies of the South*, 'Although this book was written on this side of the line, it was generated on the other side of the line.'[52] My hope is that this book initiates a wider discussion of the imaginaries of the plains throughout Latin America that includes other local narratives and knowledges, so as to present the many other sides of the continental imaginaries of the Americas.[53]

Literatures of the Latin American plains

Plains geographies figure prominently in Latin American literature, especially since the nineteenth century. The independence movements throughout the colonies of the Americas moved writers to narrate the stories of emerging nations, establishing a sense of community through powerful images of the land and its peoples. Literature and politics became 'inextricable' in 'the history of nation-building'.[54] From the patriotic romances of the nineteenth century to the *novelas de la selva* and the *novelas de la tierra* in the twentieth century, Latin American literature has attempted to write the land on countless occasions. One of the aims of this book is to ecocritically reconsider Latin American literature by insisting on the significance of the literatures of the plains throughout the Americas. Dufva Quantic and Jane Hafen have compellingly argued in favour of a literature of the Great Plains in North America, bringing together the valuable *A Great Plains Reader* (2003) in an effort to offer the rich diversity of voices of Native Americans, settlers, travellers, immigrants and scholars in portraying their experiences of those vast grasslands shared between the United States and Canada. In the words of the editors of the anthology, 'The stories, essays, excerpts, and poems in *A Great Plains Reader* reflect the intricate and complex relationships of land and people in the Great Plains.'[55] Drawing inspiration from the work of Great Plains scholars in North America, this book is an initial tracing of the literatures of the plains in Latin America.

Just as scholars are now reconsidering the *novelas de la selva* under a more specific ecological framework as 'Amazonian perspectivism',[56] so do I suggest rethinking the *novelas de la tierra* under the rubric of 'literatures of the plains'. The *novelas de la tierra* or regional novels are traditionally considered to be those narratives that emerged between the latter nineteenth and early twentieth centuries with a particular interest in depicting 'the uniqueness of individual countries owing to their peculiar natural features, mainly their geography, and how the available resources were exploited'.[57] Alonso has studied in-depth regionalist novels in Latin America, identifying their commitment to writing the autochthonous, a discursive strategy that entails a double-bind between trying to express the unique regional traits and commenting on the very possibility of writing the autochthonous.[58] In other words, Latin American regional novels seem to be self-aware of the performative strategy of trying to imagine the uniqueness of the national territories. They are re-creating and re-producing the lands as if they were tapping into the origins of these territories. For example, when Venezuelan Rómulo Gallegos writes the Llanos of Venezuela in his *Doña Bárbara* (1929), it is as if he was trying to discover these lands for the very first time, as if his writing established an immediacy with these unique grasslands surrounding the Orinoco river basin. The novel is filled with geographical information concerning the rivers, flora and fauna of the Apure plains. Yet the novel also includes passages that seem to critically comment on the possibility of writing the autochthonous of the land. As the protagonist Santos Luzardo travels to the interior of Venezuela, into the vast grasslands known as the Apure plains, he reflects on 'the spectacle of the empty plains' and considers the need to 'fight against Nature [. . .] against the desert that does not allow civilisation to penetrate'.[59] Santos Luzardo repeats the trope of the plains as desert and also comments on the possibility of representing 'nature' (the land) as it resists 'civilization' (writing). To write the autochthonous, one would presumably have direct access to the unique nature of the country, yet the protagonist of *Doña Bárbara* acknowledges the problematic imposition entailed in that discursive strategy. Moreover, the passage reveals the masculine gaze present in settler ecologies that sees the land as virginal, awaiting the 'penetration' of civilization. Alonso's critical assessment of the *novelas de la tierra* sheds light on the ideological construction taking place in these canonical fictions. Regional novels attempt to document national landscapes as if their depictions are the original representations of the land, while also acknowledging that they are artifice – just another representation that became dominant over other possible portrayals. However, the name 'novelas de la tierra' ultimately repeats the discursive gesture that Alonso points out. If these novels attempt to write the *uniqueness* of the land, they are ultimately defined in abstract terms as novels *of the land*. My ecocritical reading of these texts starts out by asking *what* land these novels are portraying.[60]

Many of the regions that are the setting of canonical fictions in Latin America are grasslands. From the Pampas to the Llanos and Altiplanos, these unique biomes have been the primary setting for Latin American literature since the independences of the colonies. This book aims to reframe how we understand Latin American literature beyond national narratives set up to legitimize the emerging nation states. Rather than continue to deploy abstract terms to understand the literary landscape of the Americas, I am invested in anchoring these literatures in the specific biomes that they attempt to portray. Instead of referring to the scenarios of canonical fictions as 'lands', I choose to explore the specificity of those settings whose local knowledges are effaced in favour of abstract cartographies. The grasslands of the Americas are neither 'empty' nor 'deserts'. To initiate a discussion as to how the plains in Latin America have been depicted is to begin a fascinating survey of the mosaic of imaginaries beyond the overarching continentalist narrative that has dominated since the nineteenth century.

The book is structured into chapters in which a selection of settler images of the plains is explored in several canonical texts as they portray a specific grassland biome in Latin America. This way readers can follow the deployment of these dominant tropes to depict the Pampas, Altiplanos, Llanos and Pantanal. Each chapter includes several canonical fictions that depict a specific type of grasslands in Latin America. The aim is to allow the reader to chronologically follow some of canonical works in Latin American literature as they portray the plains, so as to trace the deployment of continentalist images of the plains. The first two chapters (Pampas and Altiplanos) directly address these continentalist images of the plains as deserts and wastelands. It is important to note that although I have made an effort to isolate these concrete tropes, often these texts are not monolithic in their representation of the plains. An ecocritical reading centred on the grasslands depicted in each canonical fiction reveals the embedded local knowledges in the form of references to native flora and fauna. My aim is to demonstrate not only how continentalist tropes are repeated in canonical fictions but also how these imaginaries are fractured if we read them against the grain with an ecocritical apparatus. Hence, each chapter will present the ways in which these texts adhere and at times deviate from the portrayal of the grasslands as barren deserts, ruined lands and predatory environments. The second two chapters (Llanos and Pantanal) are particularly pertinent in showing how some texts at the margins of the canon clearly incorporate alternative modes of portraying the plains, especially through the ambivalent use of predation in narratives and the act of naming plants and animals.

The first chapter discusses the depictions of the Pampas grasslands by two Argentine writers, Domingo Faustino Sarmiento and Ezequiel Martínez Estrada. Both authors clearly engage with the representation of the grasslands as a desert of a vast extension. If in Sarmiento the image of the Pampas as a desert is framed in terms of their potential development, in Martínez Estrada the emphasis on their dimensions turns them into an abstract surface on which the trauma of Argentine identity is projected. Both authors, however, do deviate from the dominant images of the plains in significant ways, especially in the treatment of the *ombú* tree that is native to these grasslands.

The second chapter follows the trope of the grassland as a ruined landscape in the representation of the Altiplanos in Mexico and the Andes, offering the close readings of Ciro Alegría, João Guimarães Rosa and Juan Rulfo. This chapter presents the grasslands of the highlands as a transnational environment that is similarly depicted by three canonical writers from Peru, Brazil and Mexico. As in the first chapter, these authors adhere to dominant images of the plains insofar as these are depicted as barren and lifeless, yet they also offer glimpses of local knowledges in their references to, for example, the chicalote plant. This small flower encapsulates the harshness and survival of life at high elevations.

The third chapter analyses the imagining of the plains as threatening through the predatory encounters that take place in novels by José Eustasio Rivera and Rómulo Gallegos, as they portray the Llanos in the Orinoco river basin that is shared by Colombia and Venezuela. Although both writers exploit the image of the plains as a threat to civilization as it attempts to control the land, they also recover the presence of certain predatory species that are near extinction in the region, as is the Orinoco crocodile. Through an ecocritical reading of the role of predatory encounters, we can shed light on the significance of these inevitable entanglements between humans and non-human animals out in the open fields of the plains and their riverways. Instead of entrenching the separation between both as the continentalist trope initially suggests, predation blurs distinctions in these encounters.

Finally, the fourth chapter explores unique wetlands in South America that were considered a biodiversity sanctuary in the 1960s, the Pantanal wetlands. These wetlands are transformed annually from large grasslands on which cattle ranching takes place to one of the largest wetlands in the world. This chapter strikes a different note from the previous three insofar as it presents a short story by Guimarães Rosa and the poetry of Manoel de Barros as representative of the how local knowledge counters the dominant images of the plains as empty and barren. This chapter explores in-depth how the act of naming can leverage local knowledges in literary works.

This book is meant to help readers begin tracing the multiplicity of imaginaries available in depicting the grasslands that are fundamental to the Americas and the world. Moreover, its organization is also meant to invite readers into critically rethinking Latin American literature from an ecological perspective that leaves behind national boundaries in order to better understand the significance of grasslands biomes throughout the continent. I firmly believe that by ecocritically reading Latin American literature through the bioregions it portrays we not only get a better sense of how dominant images of the plains in canonical works has accompanied the global discourse of the grasslands as a garden of industry and progress, but it also opens up a critical space on which to leverage the local voices and knowledges at the interstices of continentalist narratives since the arrival of European colonizers. Pablo Neruda begins his *Canto General* (1950) by evoking what he poetically names the 'planetary pampas' that occupy the Americas:

> Antes que la peluca y la casaca
> fueron los ríos, ríos arteriales:
> fueron las cordilleras, en cuya onda raída
> el cóndor o la nieve parecían inmóviles:
> fue la humedad y la espesura, el trueno
> sin nombre todavía, las pampas planetarias.[61]

> [Before the wig or frock coat
> were the rivers, arterial rivers:
> were the mountain ranges, on whose ragged waves
> the condor or the snow seem motionless:
> it was the humidity and denseness, the thunder
> nameless still, the planetary pampas.]

The powerful rhetoric of Neruda's poem invites us as readers to linger on those grasslands that have for millennia shaped the contours and cultures of the Americas. As in the poem, we are led to descend from the heights of Machu Picchu and experience alongside the plethora of writers the mosaic of images of the plains. This book traces the initial routes that settler imaginaries have etched unto Latin American literature, but in identifying the path that has been often tread upon, it also leads readers to consider what other paths are available to imagine the plains of Latin America. This book is an invitation to rethink how local ecological knowledges and imaginaries are often effaced by dominant metaphors in canonical works of literature yet are always already present at the interstices of these continentalist narratives.

1

The empty desert of the Pampas

Perhaps one of the most widely referenced environments in Latin American literature, the Pampas are generally considered to be a large plain that extends throughout Argentina, Uruguay and southern Brazil. The word 'pampa' is derived from the Quechua voice *phampa*, a noun that signifies 'plain' or 'flat' in terms of regularity or overall flatness.[1] In Argentina alone, it covers approximately 720,000 square kilometre and includes a variety of grassland vegetation. It is also 'one of the most highly threatened biomes in the world', given its extensive exploitation for agricultural purposes and overall degradation of the land.[2] In Brazil, it is considered by geographers to be a separate biome found in the interior of the state of Rio Grande do Sul.[3] Constituted of mostly grasslands and small shrubs, the Brazilian Pampa is also a vulnerable biome due to the 'natural fragility of the soil, combined with the climatic conditions'.[4]

These unique grasslands have inspired countless writers and musicians, especially in Argentina and Uruguay, where they prompted the emergence of gaucho literature and the *milonga*. The list of established writers who have penned poems, narratives, plays and essays on gauchos – with the Pampas as a setting – is extensive and diverse: Domingo Sarmiento, Esteban Echeverría, José Hernández, José de Alencar, Eduardo Gutiérrez, Ricardo Güiraldes, Ezequiel Martínez Estrada, Roberto Bolaño, Leopoldo Lugones, Jorge Luis Borges, Érico Veríssimo, João Simões Lopes Neto and Eduardo Galeano are some of the most notable authors who have written books with these plains as the setting. The list reveals something very important, for these numerous writers are male canonical authors, many of whom held important political positions in their time. If as David Lowenthal suggests – that 'Landscapes are formed by landscape tastes'[5] – then the Pampas in Latin American literature reflect a male aesthetic of the land. These plains geographies constitute an important part of the male settler ecologies that contribute to the continentalist narrative in Latin America. Similar to the Great Plains settler fiction in North America, the literatures of the Pampas manifest the encounter between European descendants and these lands to the interior of the Argentine, Uruguayan and Brazilian coastlines. Thacker explains that in North America 'Europeans did not foresee and often misunderstood the practical and epistemological problems posed by prairie topography'.[6] This raises the important issue of the connection between a given portrayal of the plains, the political justification of its development and the mode of knowing that particular geography. How these men saw and wrote about the Pampas reveals not only the symbolic role of the plains in establishing a national narrative but also the capitalist ecology latent in the depiction of the plains as barren and vacant.[7]

In this chapter I will ecocritically read two canonical works of literature that are foundational[8] to the way that the Latin American plains are portrayed in terms of the trope of the desert lands: *Facundo* (1945) by Domingo Faustino Sarmiento and *Radiografía de la pampa* (1942) by Ezequiel Martínez Estrada. Both essays have had an influential legacy in Latin America. Sarmiento's *Facundo* inaugurated the binary of civilization and barbarism in Latin American literature, which is still present in contemporary texts such as *Calibán* (1971) by Roberto Fernández Retamar or the short story 'El gaucho insufrible' (2003) by Roberto Bolaño. As I will argue throughout this chapter, the inauguration of the dichotomy between civilization and barbarism is bound to the portrayal of the Pampas as a desert. That is, the scenario on which the polemic between progress and backwardness that many canonical writers engaged with in Latin America is a plains geography. This projection of economic and political ideals unto grasslands also emerged elsewhere in the Americas. In the United States, the Great Plains were doubly conceived as a wasteland and a potential garden on which to sustain the industrial development of the eastern coast.[9] The dichotomy in Facundo also oscillates between the Pampas as a barren space and a territory to be tapped into for its potential resources. Ezequiel Martínez Estrada's essay pushes the portrayal of grasslands to its utmost abstraction, emphasizing the geometrical and metaphysical dimension of the experience of the seemingly endless extension of the plains.[10]

The representations of the plains in both texts are constructions that favour generic concepts such as immensity and extension to portray the grasslands. Each essay presents the land not as a real place but as an abstract surface or geometry. Once emptied of those elements that constitute its ecological elements, the Pampas are then portrayed as a desert that resists the endeavours of civilized man. I am interested in exploring these aspects of the continental narratives present in the two texts, for the depictions of the plains as an abstract space and as a desert exemplify the way literary images can create an ecological knowledge of a biome that does not respond to its biological and climatological context.

Instead of looking to the variety of ecological abundance at the ground level, these canonical writers prioritize the phenomenological experience of the horizon and the strangeness of a land unlike any found in Europe. The grasslands are neither a geometrical plane nor a desert landscape. Yet these images popularized in canonical literary works are now widespread and have contributed to the institutional devaluation of such a unique biome as the Pampas. In Brazil, for example, these plains were not officially recognized by the federal government until 2004 and are currently suffering a loss of biodiversity at an alarming rate.[11]

The choice of the two texts from such a wide range of authors is due to the intimate connection between *Facundo* and *Radiografía*, especially in regard to the role that the Pampas plays in both essays. Carola Hermida argues that *Radiografía* 'is presented as a continuation or actualisation of the *Facundo*'.[12] Martínez Estrada establishes an intellectual dialogue with Sarmiento, both in the themes that organize his book and in the language deployed.[13] Moreover, the essays by Sarmiento and Martínez Estrada attempt to decipher the effect that nature has on Argentines.[14] In their portrayals of the Pampas grasslands, both authors see the plains as a symbolic scenario on which to project the ideals of the Argentine nation. A significant distinction between both texts that I will further explore is that while Sarmiento is confident and optimistic on the role of European progress in turning the bioregion into a garden for civilization in Buenos Aires, Martínez Estrada recognizes the transformation of the grasslands into an abstract value by settlers in their attempt at possessing the land.

The desert of the Pampas in Domingo Sarmiento's *Facundo*

Sarmiento's *Facundo* is considered one of the most important and popular books in Latin American literature. The book is framed as a biography of Facundo Quiroga (1788–1835), one of the notable Federalist caudillos in Argentina in the politically tumultuous years after the country's independence from Spain. However, the book is also an essay on the problems faced by the Argentine nation. Sarmiento narrates the life of Facundo as a means to explain what he considers is the terrible dictatorship of Federalist Juan Manuel de Rosas (1793–1877) that lasted almost twenty years after he became governor of the province of Buenos Aires in 1829. The book sets up some of the recurrent themes of Latin American literature, such as the dichotomy between civilization and barbarism or the significance of regional stereotypes in national imaginaries. In Argentina, *Facundo* initiates the tradition of gaucho literature in Argentina.[15] Sommer argues that the book is one of the foundational narratives in Latin America insofar as it establishes a link between heterosexual love and patriotism in Sarmiento's reading of American writer James Fenimore Cooper.[16]

The link between Sarmiento and Cooper is also worth revisiting in this chapter, since both writers attempted to portray plains geographies from a settler imaginary that saw the grasslands as a barren desert. I will pay close attention to the similar tropes used by both authors to describe the plains as wastelands and through the metaphor of the land as sea. Moreover, both Sarmiento and Cooper read the plains through second-hand accounts of other travellers.[17] Similar to nineteenth-century American writers of the Great Plains, Sarmiento is attempting to create a language borrowed from European experiences to describe the Pampas that he himself had not personally seen. That is, he chooses to 'see' the Pampas through the travel accounts of foreigners unacquainted with the grasslands. Its importance in Latin American literature simply cannot be overstated. Although I am not interested in discussing its place in the literary canon, I would add that *Facundo* is one of the most important texts in the ecological imaginaries of the plains in Latin America. Many of the themes set out in its portrayal of the plains reverberate in the works of other writers of the plains, especially those themes linked to settler ecologies in the Americas encompassed in the Manifest Destiny: 'that the lands stretching beyond the settlements were empty and wasted, used only by roaming native tribes, and that they were destined to be settled and cultivated by civilized (i.e., European) people'.[18]

Critically rereading *Facundo* is a task that is not exempt from difficulties. Much has been written on the intricacies of this ambivalent, and at times contradictory, book. From an ecocritical standpoint, Sarmiento manages to both incorporate and inaugurate a continental narrative of the plains that echoes in the works of other writers of the plains in Latin America. He is well aware of his audience, writing at the crossroads between the Americas and Europe. Aarti Madan explains that Sarmiento presents a 'marketable geography' geared towards European immigrants, drawing from Alexander von Humboldt's geographic discourse.[19] The epigraph of the second chapter in *Facundo* makes explicit the significance of the German geographer in how Sarmiento imagines the plains: 'Ainsi que l'océan, les steppes remplissent l'esprit du sentiment de l'infini'.[20] Sarmiento quotes the French translation of Humboldt's *Views of Nature*, which dedicates an entire chapter to the 'Steppes and Deserts':

> Like the ocean, the steppe fills the mind with the feeling of infinity, and through this feeling, as if pulling free of sensory impression, with intellectual and spiritual

inspiration of a higher order. But while the clear ocean surface in which ripples the graceful, softly foaming wave is a friendly sight, dead and stiff lies the steppe, stretched out like the naked rocky crust of a desolate planet.[21]

The passage is particularly significant, for it deploys the metaphor of the plains as a body of water and as a wasteland, two images that are recurrent in canonical fictions across the Americas. The metaphor of 'sea of grass' is already present in the Spanish conquistador Francisco Coronado in the sixteenth century.[22] Whereas Coronado uses the metaphor to emphasize the lack of landmarks, Humboldt deploys the comparison initially to suggest the sublime experience of a boundless body of land. Sarmiento is ambivalent in his use of the 'infinite' grasslands. At times the vastness of the Pampas produces a sublime aesthetic experience, while at others it is linked to the empty and barren condition of the grasslands. Sarmiento often refers to the grasslands as 'an immensity without limits' that can evoke the 'spectacle of a solemn, grandiose, incommensurable, silent nature'.[23] Yet that vast extension is also the problem of Argentina in that it is a 'desert' that 'oppresses' the civilization of the cities scattered across the Pampas.[24] The image of the plains as a 'desolate planet' that is 'dead and stiff' is present not only in *Facundo* but also in canonical depictions of the Altiplanos, which I will discuss further in the next chapter. To write Argentina, Sarmiento decides to use the grasslands as an 'ocean' and 'wasteland' that paint the image of vast desert grasslands on which the national struggle between Federalists and Unitarists takes place.

Another source closely linked to these metaphors that Sarmiento exploits is that of the American pastoral tradition as it appears in the writer James Fenimore Cooper. *Facundo* appropriates many of the pastoral and wilderness images that Cooper deploys to describe the American Great Plains in *The Prairie* (1824), while at the same time translating them into a tension between civilization and barbarism – a dichotomy of interest to the Spanish American *letrados* invested in constructing national symbols. Sarmiento translates the pastoral mode into a narrative of wilderness that plays into his 'marketable geography' insofar as it legitimizes projects of modernization and immigration in rural Argentina. To do so, he imagines the Pampas to be far different from its ecological context. In *Facundo*, the grasslands become an immense and empty landscape, a desert that awaits the arrival of civilization. This imagined geography is a rhetorical and political device that constructs a powerful continentalist narrative, one which repeats settler ecologies of the plains. Madan reminds us that 'the discourse of emptiness is a metaphor – in other words, a metaphor for land ripe to be populated'.[25]

At the beginning of the second chapter in *Facundo*, Sarmiento makes explicit the influence of Cooper in his conception of the Argentina:

> El único romancista norteamericano que haya logrado hacerse un nombre europeo, es Fenimore Cooper, y eso, porque transportó la escena de sus descripciones fuera del círculo ocupado por los plantadores, al límite entre la vida bárbara y la civilizada, al teatro de la guerra en que las razas indígenas y la raza sajona están combatiendo por la posesión del terreno.[26]

> [The only North American novelist that has managed to make himself a name in Europe is Fenimore Cooper, and that was because he transported the scenes of his descriptions beyond the small circle of plantation owners, at the limit between the barbarous and civilized life, to the theatre of war in which the indigenous races and the Anglo-Saxon race are fighting for the possession of the land.]

Sarmiento is considering the value of Cooper's books in terms of the success they had in Europe. The way the North American writer represents the 'scenes' that are 'at the limit between barbarous and civilized life' is of interest to Europeans. Cooper recreates the bucolic landscapes of plantations and translates them into a 'theatre of war', into a polemics between different peoples. What the pastoral mode is lacking, if it is to be deployed in the American continent, are the struggles to take control of the land from the Indigenous inhabitants. It is tension – rather than pastoral tranquillity – that is attractive. Sarmiento thus learns a valuable lesson from the writings of Cooper that shapes his discourse of the Pampas. If he is to successfully generate a 'marketable geography', he must retell the drama that unfolds in Argentina as rooted in the struggle for the 'possession of the land'. He must transform the portrayal of a serene nature common in European pastorals into depictions of a brute wilderness where 'Indigenous races' and European colonizers engage in battle for the possession of the continent. This rhetorical strategy is not unlike the preconceptions that European travellers and settlers projected unto the Great Plains in North America.

This raises two ecological issues that are present in the environmental images of the Pampas. First, the value of the plains resides in their possible appropriation by those civilized Europeans immigrating to Argentina, as opposed to the rights of the Indigenous peoples to a land that they have inhabited for far longer. How would the Indigenous peoples imagine the Pampas? Second, Sarmiento seems to envision the land as a battlefield motivated by economic interests. Its value is subordinated to its successful exploitation by landowners. Its significance lies in how these lands will help 'write the nation' as modern and industrialized, not so much in their beauty in and of itself. These ecological issues – the marginalization of the Indigenous inhabitants as mere antagonists and the sole economic value of the land – are recurrent in canonical literatures of the plains in Latin America. This is not surprising, for the agricultural practices in the continent have since the Conquest focused on the extraction of resources and the establishment of large plantations and cattle ranches in plains topographies.

So as to persuade readers of the importance of incorporating modern agricultural practices in rural Argentina, *Facundo* inaugurates an alternative to the pastoral mode, one that exploits what Leo Marx argues as the contradiction between ideas of the American landscape:

> If America seemed to promise everything that men always wanted, it also threatened to obliterate much of what they already achieved [. . .] Not that the conflict was in any sense peculiar to American experience. It had always been at the heart of pastoral; but the discovery of the New World invested it with new relevance, with fresh symbols.[27]

The New World presents a different landscape than that of Europe. It is at once attractive, so much so that the impossible journeys to its shores were built on the desires of men in the Iberian Peninsula to discover riches beyond their imagination. Sarmiento, for example, writes that the plains are 'a hilly oasis of fields'.[28] *Facundo* often portrays the land as an exotic Orient.[29] Sarmiento also imagines the American continent as a threatening land, one filled with dangers – a wilderness. Again he writes the following: 'Masses of darkness that cloud day, masses of livid light, trembling, that illuminates for an instant the darkness, and reveals the pampa in the infinite distances.'[30] The 'infinite distances' of the Pampas set an ominous horizon, one that instils fear even in the *gauchos* as they camp out at night. These two conflicting images of the New World constitute the binary between civilization and barbarism that appears time and again in *Facundo*.

Exploiting that tension between an 'oasis' and an ominous land, Sarmiento transforms pastoral images into those of a wilderness. The links between pastoral and wilderness images have not gone unnoticed by scholars. Garrard, for example, explains, 'Wilderness narratives share the motif of escape and return with the typical pastoral narrative, but the construction of nature they propose and reinforce is fundamentally different.'[31] Although scholars continue to debate what defines the pastoral as a genre,[32] the trope of escape and return is pertinent in *Facundo*. The book's retelling of the life of Facundo Quiroga plays out the 'motif of escape and return' and transforms the idealized nature of pastoral into that of a threatening wilderness. By 'wilderness' I mean the image of a nature that is not domesticated. Garrard defines the idea of 'wilderness' as 'nature in a state uncontaminated by civilisation'.[33]

The tension between the idealization of a virgin landscape and the promise of progress through industrialization is at the core of the American pastoral during the eighteenth century. Based on the ambiguous relation between the city and the countryside, North American writers manifest the pressures of technological progress upon the landscape. They represent the countryside while incorporating the 'symbol of the machine'.[34] Withdrawal from the city is but one stage in the pastoral journey to the countryside: 'It begins in a corrupt city, passes through raw wilderness, and then, finally, leads back toward the city.'[35]

Sarmiento quite possibly inherits from Cooper both the idea of wilderness as defining the landscape of the American continent and also the image of the empty plains to be accessed by pioneers and settlers. In the *Leatherstocking Tales* (1823–41), Cooper narrates the life of frontiersman Natty Bumppo in the American wilderness. Composed of several books, the tales tell of Bumppo's experiences living away from cities. In them, the journey to the wilderness of the West is central. The son of Anglo-American parents, Bumppo is raised by Native Americans. His adventures imagine the life of pioneers, struggling to survive and finding in the woods a place to call home. In many ways, these tales manifest the settler culture's 'wish fulfilment inherent in the use of allusive rhetoric to empty and to fill new world environments'.[36]

This is mostly clearly seen in *The Prairie* (1827), a book that forms part of the *Leatherstocking Tales*. In it Cooper begins by writing that American pioneers drew from society 'seeking for the renewal of enjoyments which were rendered worthless in his eyes, when trammelled by the forms of human institutions'.[37] The wilderness offers a place away from 'human institutions', for it is an untamed land that is not yet contaminated with the anxieties and perversions of modern life. It is a place of 'renewal', a place to start anew. This idea of a renewed life is also accompanied with abstract images of the plains as an empty land. The protagonist of the novel is 'Pressed upon by time', for 'The sound of the axe has driven him from his beloved forests to seek a refuge, by a species of desperate resignation, on the denuded plains that stretch to the Rocky Mountains'.[38] He seeks 'refuge' from the encroaching civilization in the form of the 'axe' cutting down 'his beloved forests'. The pastoral trope of retreat is latent in the motivations of Bumppo as he flees to the Great Plains. Unlike the other books in the series, *The Prairie* depicts the plains in abstract terms. The reader is often presented with landscapes that contain 'forests' and 'rivers', yet little else to establish the specificity of the land:

> In the little valleys, which, in the regular formation of the land, occurred at every mile of their progress, the view was bounded on two of the sides by the gradual and low elevations which give name to the description of prairie we have mentioned; while on the others, the meagre prospect ran off in long, narrow, barren perspectives, but slightly relieved by a pitiful show of coarse, though somewhat luxuriant vegetation.[39]

The preceding passage speaks of 'valleys', 'land', 'elevations', 'prairie' and 'vegetation' to describe the natural scene on which the narrative takes place. Aside from the term 'prairie', the language seems geographically abstract, as if the narrator was a surveyor commenting on 'elevations', 'prospect' and 'perspectives'. Instead of describing the types of vegetation or trees that populate the Great Plains, the text evokes a generic landscape. Moreover, the term 'prairie' is also not ecologically specific, for its previous mention in the book refers to its origins in the French language.[40] William Kelly argues that *The Prairie* represents the Great Plains as a 'vacant landscape'.[41] This abstract approach to describing landscape is also present in Sarmiento and Martínez Estrada, both of whom will imagine the Pampas as surveyors little interested in its ecosystem or biodiversity.

Sarmiento incorporates Cooper's abstract depiction of the land, although the wilderness is not so much a place of escape, but rather a place to flee from in search of civilization. He inverts the trope of escape by using the life of Facundo Quiroga as an indictment of the dangers of the wilderness. The character Facundo represents the anarchy of the countryside: 'Facundo Quiroga connects and links all the elements of disorder that until before his appearance were stirring separately in each province.'[42] His biography provides a testimony of the problems of Argentina after its independence, an account of how the immense wilderness is not a place of respite as in European pastorals but rather a geography of disorder that needs to be tamed. Sarmiento represents the grasslands as an obstacle to the influence of civilization. It is in that sense that they are a site of resistance to the values of an industrial society. Whereas Cooper emphasizes the significance of the wilderness as a place free from the anxieties and contradictions of urban life, Sarmiento sees in the Pampas a land that has not been domesticated by European values. The plains are also a site of banditry, a place where gaucho leaders such as Facundo Quiroga or Juan Manuel Rosas roam free, constituting a threat to 'the entire state-formation process in Buenos Aires'.[43] Withdrawal from urban centres is a symptom of anarchy, fatal to the construction of Argentina.

Facundo is the son of a shepherd of the plains, a rural character that begins his military campaigns in the provinces and eventually makes his way into the city.[44] Always threatening, the wilderness is a savage landscape that offers no respite. It is in the cities that Facundo finds safety and repose. In chapter five, Sarmiento begins his narration of Facundo's life with an episode in which the hero finds himself in the plains between the cities of San Luis and San Juan without his horse. As he enters the wilderness, the growls of a 'tiger' can be heard in the distance. Facundo is forced to run for his life, finding a low-lying tree to climb while the plains tiger circles its prey. In a final moment of the encounter, feral cat and gaucho lock eyes: 'The violent posture of the gaucho, and the terrifying fascination that he exerted over him the sanguinary and still gaze of the tiger, from which an invincible force of attraction he could not look away, had begun to weaken his strength.'[45] Recognizing himself as prey, Facundo feels completely vulnerable. The misnomer 'tigre' reveals his lack of knowledge and language to describe the feline species that inhabits the Pampas, for there are no 'tigers' as such in South America. The 'tiger' he most likely is referring to is the puma or cougar. The plains are 'seen' with an orientalist perspective that describes the land using tropes generated by European to depict the Orient – the tiger is after all a native species in India. Faced with this predator, Facundo becomes aware that there is no possible retreat to the plains. Rather, cities are the only 'oasis of civilisation' left to humans.[46] Savage and terrible, the wilderness of the plains is a landscape from which humans are forced to withdraw. No idyllic landscapes of the grasslands are depicted in *Facundo*, for the plains are a hostile environment from which civilized men must find repose in urban centres.

Important to the reversal of the retreat from the city trope is the portrayal of the Pampas as a desert. Civilization and barbarism shape a dialectic antagonism that takes place 'in the pampas of Argentina', as the subtitle of *Facundo* suggests. Indeed the problem of Argentina is to be found in the physical contours of its surrounding land: 'The sickness that the Republic of Argentina suffers is that of extension: the desert surrounds her on all sides.'[47] The plains are seen as a problem that necessitates the influence of civilization. The opposition between civilization and barbarism – between cities and wilderness – is translated into an antagonism of space, a tension between the surrounding plains and the urban centres represented by the city of Buenos Aires. Those plains that surround the capital are a 'desert', a desolate and oppressive wilderness: 'The desert surrounds them at a greater or lesser distance, fences them in, oppresses them; the wilderness reduces them to a narrow oasis of civilisation pinned in an uncivilised plain of hundreds of square miles.'[48] Sarmiento deploys the terms 'desierto', 'naturaleza salvaje' and 'llano' as synonyms in the phrase. All three are interchangeable, which reveals the settler ecology of the Pampas as a 'desert', 'wilderness' and 'plain'. Unlike Cooper, here the wilderness is not a place to escape the violence of urban life. The plains are an inhospitable and abstract space that threatens civilized and industrious society.

Sarmiento's insistence on the 'immensity' of the Pampas engages his readers in a representation of the biome that emphasizes space and scale, a theme present in Humboldt's depiction of the 'steppes and deserts'. The following passage is very illustrative and resonates the ambivalent deployment of the imagery of the grasslands in *Facundo*:

> Allí la inmensidad por todas partes: inmensa la llanura, inmensos los bosques, inmensos los ríos, el horizonte siempre incierto, siempre confundiéndose con la tierra, entre celajes y vapores ténues, que no dejan, en la lejana perspectiva, señalar el punto en que el mundo acaba y principia el cielo. Al sur y al norte acéchanla los salvajes, que aguardan las noches de luna para caer, cual enjambres de hienas, sobre los ganados que pacen en los campos, y sobre las indefensas poblaciones.[49]

> [There the immensity is everywhere: immense the plains, immense the forests, immense the rivers, the horizon always uncertain, always blurring with the land, between faint clouds and vapours that do not allow, from a distant view, to identify the point at which the world ends and the sky begins. To the south and north the savages threaten, awaiting the nights of full moon to fall upon the cattle in the fields and the defenceless villages like a pack of hyenas.]

The size of the plains is repeatedly described as 'immense', deploying anaphora as a means to insist on the sheer scale of the territory. According to Madan, 'Sarmiento appeals to the Humboldtian notion of immensity as he rewrites the Argentine land'.[50] Notice how, for example, no specific description of the grasslands is forthcoming in the passage. The passage cites 'llanura', 'bosques' and 'ríos', all of which are generic terms in referring to landscape. Many places across the planet could fit the description of having 'plains', 'forests' and 'rivers'. None of the flora or fauna of the bioregion is depicted – none of the more than 3,000 different plant species native to the biome.[51] The land is instead presented in geometric and generic terms: immensity, horizon and distance. If the Pampas are a desert, it is not due to the lack of vegetation or an arid climate. They are imagined as a desert because of their immense size that makes them resistant to the development of an urban industry.

The depiction of the plains as a barren desert plays on a mythology of exclusion, where the land and its inhabitants are marginalized as the other so as to bolster the urban lifestyle. Just as in the pastoral tradition, Sarmiento's readers are urbanites. The devaluation of the grasslands as desert serves to generate an asymmetry between the wilderness and the city. This image enacts the interest of nineteenth-century *letrados* 'making a determined effort to integrate and dominate entire national territories, to domesticate Nature'.[52] Dabove further argues that the depiction of the Pampas as a desert deploys a 'politics of landscape' invested in 'the birth of a moral-political community'.[53] Represented as a desert, the grasslands become the outskirts of civilized urban centres. As borders, they become contested sites or resistance. The campaigns against the Indigenous population take place in those desert lands that surround the 'oasis' of civilization. Described as wastelands or deserts, these lands manifest the geopolitical ambitions of *Facundo*.

The plains as geometries of value in Ezequiel Martínez Estrada's *Radiografía de la pampa*

Written only a few years after the Wall Street crash of 1929 and the Argentine coup by José Felix Uriburu, Martínez Estrada's *Radiografía de la pampa* is a continuation of the exploration of the 'problem of extension' that had been set out in *Facundo*. The book traces the history of colonization in South America from a philosophical perspective that attempts to decipher its underlying structures. From the myth of Trapalanda[54] to the development of capitalism in Argentina, Martínez Estrada sets out to explore in-depth the significance of 'extension' in the national imaginaries of South America. The author sees reflections of Sarmiento's times in the economic and political upheavals of Argentina in the twentieth century. Both Sarmiento and Martínez Estrada turn their attention to the plains, so as to attempt to decode the disorganization of Argentina as a nation. The contrasts between the rural lands and the urban centres of each province are explained through the pressing influence of the grasslands. Pollmann suggests this overarching theme in both essays: 'In this country [Argentina] that, geographically, is because of the pampas seen as divided in two countries of which the one, Buenos Aires, can be considered very civilised, "European;" while the other is not valued at all.'[55] In building an image of Argentina as a modern nation, Martínez Estrada also generates a continentalist narrative of the Pampas that strips them of their local knowledges in favour of abstract images. Through a Eurocentric lens, *Radiografía* allows readers to 'see' only an empty land.

Published in 1933, *Radiografía* constitutes a turning point in Martínez Estrada's work as a poet and essayist. It was during the years prior to its publication that he began to recognize that Argentina was facing many of the challenges described in *Facundo*.⁵⁶ At the time he was a relatively unknown post office worker in Buenos Aires, having published only a few books of poetry, of which only *Argentina* (1927) garnered attention from critics. Dinko Cvitanovic suggests that there is an important continuity between Martínez Estrada's poetry and prose, especially in the philosophical pessimism that is present in all of his writings.⁵⁷ In *Radiografía*, Martínez Estrada is particularly preoccupied with what he sees as the 'vastness of the land' and its effects on the psychology of its inhabitants.⁵⁸ This preoccupation is not unlike that of Sarmiento in *Facundo*, so much so that they both examine the 'problem of Argentina' by tracing the geographical contours of the land in tandem with the cultural manifestations of the nation. The grasslands are an empty scenario awaiting the performance of the Argentine political and economic problems.

However, although the Pampas become a metaphysical surface on which to play out the national traumas, Martínez Estrada is far more aware of how the abstract possession of the land since the Conquest is latent in these traumas. At the beginning of the essay, he suggests as much when he writes, 'The extension is not greatness; it is the idea of greatness. It is not wealth; it is the possibility of a mortgage. It is nothing.'⁵⁹ Martínez Estrada suggests that reality and the image what we have of that reality can be two starkly different things. To own a large extension of land is not greatness per se, but rather a manifestation of that which the settler values most – possession. This possession is also not a material wealth, but rather a debt to be paid. Land ownership is thus linked to notions of value. Throughout *Radiografía*, the abstraction of the grasslands as a metaphysical entity is the consequence of this valuing of the land for its false promise of wealth that Latin America inherited from European settlers. Whereas Sarmiento was optimistic in regard to the possibility of civilizing the grasslands, Martínez Estrada is far more philosophically sceptical. Moreover, the transformation of the term 'extension' into 'value' is very pertinent to understanding how the metaphor of the plains as an empty desert invites extractivist and monoculture enterprises in the plains.

The title of Martínez Estrada's book also expresses some of its motifs in regard to the possible imaginaries of the Pampas. By 'Radiografía' he proposes an examination that goes beyond the superficial, beyond the surface of a phenomenon.⁶⁰ It also suggests a philosophical methodology that seeks the elements that lie at the root of a problem.⁶¹ It attempts to reveal the osseous structures of the plains – that is, the core problem of Argentina – much the same way a physician might request an X-ray of a patient. The image of the physician performing a medical examination also points to the assumption that there is something wrong with the patient that is Argentina. It is as if the land is diseased, awaiting diagnosis. The Pampas thus becomes the body of the nation, a body that is fractured beneath the surface. When examining the continent as a whole, Martínez Estrada writes, 'On these lands of the Atlantic and Pacific, it would not be possible to contemplate their cartography without sensing the shivers along the marrow, where the geological ages have left inscribed the vicissitudes of the human form.'[62] The symptoms of the 'human form' reach down into the very 'marrow' of the land. Notice how the author anticipates an important ecological notion, that of the Anthropocene. Human events are carved into the osseous structures of the land. Rather than suggest that the land itself is ruined, needing the intervention of civilization, Martínez Estrada suggests that it is humans that have damaged the grasslands. The radiography of the Pampas displays those cuts and fractures that explain the pains suffered by Argentina.

His examination also incorporates history, tracing the root of the problem from the arrival of Spanish colonizers until contemporary events. Each chapter is a single radiographic image at a given time during the history of the continent. The reader is offered different snapshots of the skeletal organization of the land. It is in that sense that it is similar to a genealogy of sorts, which is not surprising, given his interests in Friedrich Nietzsche's later philosophy present in, for example, *On the Genealogy of Morals*.[63] Each X-ray image of the plains maps the origins of Argentina's ailment. Just as Nietzsche was invested in isolating the origins of Western values by establishing their genealogy, so does Martínez Estrada outline the evolution of a suffering Argentine society by compiling the X-ray images of the land and its transformation into an abstract value.

This brings us to the latter half of the book's title – 'de la pampa' – which seems to indicate the importance of the grasslands in *Radiografía*. This is yet another shared element with *Facundo*. As we have already seen, Sarmiento argues that the problem of Argentina is linked to its 'extension' in the form of deserts that surround the entire nation.[64] The characteristics of the land are important in the disorganization of the country and its constant oscillations between civilization and barbarism. Martínez Estrada also invokes the Pampas, and he does so by using the lowercase and singular form 'pampa'. This indicates that he is using the term broadly to portray plains regions in Argentina, from the Patagonia all the way to the Andean mountain range. His radiography is broadly directed at the plains geographies of South America, not just Argentina. The 'problem of extension' is thus projected to the entire continent. However, physical geography is not as prominent in *Radiografía*, as it is in *Facundo*. A quick survey of the chapters reveals its abstract and philosophical framework: 'Trapalanda', 'Soledad', 'Fuerzas primitivas', 'Buenos Aires', 'Miedo' and 'Seudoestructuras' are the titles of the six chapters included in *Radiografía*. Two of the chapters – 'Trapalanda' and 'Buenos Aires' – refer to cities in Argentina; one is a mythical city in the Patagonia and the other is the capital of the nation. The other chapters have titles that refer to categories in existential philosophy and psychoanalysis. It would seem, then, that geography is not as central as the title suggests.

Pollmann argues that Martínez Estrada is not interested in documenting the geographies of the Pampas, but rather in deploying them as 'a metonymy of Argentina'.[65] Martínez Estrada writes, 'The physical and psychological spaces are, between individuals, changing and empty, because space cannot be considered without thinking about the soul, since the unpopulated extension is as an experiential truth, solitude.'[66] The plains represent the psychological space of Argentina, as a symbol to be populated with the anxieties of an emerging nation. Martínez Estrada is not committed to recovering the local knowledges of the biome, for the plains are a psychological and imaginary landscape of Argentina. He *constructs* an imaginary of the plains on the foundations of Sarmiento's *Facundo*, even if the images he offers are self-aware of how ideologies in the form of abstract values have been imposed upon the land. He repeats the settler trope of the empty land present in the continentalist narrative of the Manifest Destiny, although he does so via a critical awareness of how the way colonizers imagined the grasslands of South America have transformed them into geometries of value.

Radiografía offers an abstract and geometric portrayal of the grasslands where the land is imagined in terms of its extension and size. This creates at times a pessimistic view of the plains, while at other times it presents the Pampas as a site of ecological resistance. Martínez Estrada writes the following passage that expresses this ambivalence towards the land: 'Within and above everyone is nature: those flat, monotonous, and eternal fields. And human beings live an existence of flat geometry on its surface.'[67] He does not separate nature from society, but rather understands both in a dialectical relationship. In the first phrase, 'nature' is considered to envelop everything. This also suggests the important ecocritical concept of nature as 'environment'.[68] It is all around us and inside everyone, just as the Argentine grasslands surround human habitations. Interestingly, nature is also 'above everyone', suggesting that it is superior to human beings. There seems to be a vertical hierarchy. Nature overpowers the human colonizer.[69] After the semicolon, the reader is presented with an image that presents the grasslands as a 'flat, monotonous, and eternal fields'. The description of plains as 'flat' and 'monotonous' is commonplace in the literatures of the plains. It emphasizes the experience of the horizon, which is often the most salient aspect of such topographies to European settlers who see in that landscape a powerfully symbolic space.[70] It is this symbolic space that Martínez Estrada exploits in *Radiografía*, not so much the regional and local knowledges of the Pampas.

The term 'monotonous' points to a negative aesthetic value ascribed to the land, that of not offering perceptual stimulation and becoming repetitive. The last adjective used to describe the plains in the passage is striking. An 'eternal' land evokes a place with divine properties. When linked to the idea of a nature that is 'Within and above everyone', it is difficult not to imagine a metaphysical entity similar to the Christian god or perhaps the Platonic realm of ideas. The plains that Martínez Estrada is imagining are not a physical environment but rather a metaphysical idea that is not far detached from geometric notions of space. His portrayal of the land is literally filtering it from all its specificities, so as to arrive at abstract notions that hardly resemble grasslands as a biome. The plains are merely a 'surface' on which humans 'live an existence of flat geometry'. In other words, the Pampas are not considered a place – a location that is filled with meaning and symbols that populate our imaginations – and instead become an abstract surface upon which to play out the tensions between civilization and barbarism in Argentine national identity.

Radiografía begins with the provocative statement that raises the important question as to the role of images in experiencing the land: 'The new world, recently discovered, was not yet located anywhere on the planet, and did not have any form either. It was a capricious extension of land populated by images.'[71] Aside from the radically colonial and Eurocentric premise of the 'new world' being 'recently discovered', what is particularly pertinent is the fact that the land is abstracted of any autochthonous elements. It is a formless space, a 'capricious extension of land'. Again, the use of the word 'extension' connects Martínez Estrada's essay to Sarmiento's *Facundo*. Martínez Estrada adds the adjective 'capricious', which suggests the fickle features of the American continent. There is a latent feminization of the land in the use of the adjective, for it is subject to the imaginations of the men who arrive at its margins as colonizers. Martínez Estrada writes, 'On an immense land, that was a reality impossible of modifying, would emerge the precarious works of men.'[72] Unstable and capricious, the land is worked on by 'men'. This links to yet another commonplace the continentalist narratives that see the plains as 'virgin' lands ready for their cultivation by European methods. The large extensions of plains thus become the promise of a future garden on which to sustain the needs of an industrialized nation.

The geometric imagining of the plains is linked to the possession of the land, much the same way that Sarmiento expressed in *Facundo*:

> El afán de ocupar en poco tiempo todo el territorio, de recorrerlo, de galoparlo, diseminó un número pequeño de gente en muchas leguas. De esa posición galáctica de los pueblos surgió una necesidad intrínseca que daría su norma a la vida argentina; la extensión, la superficie, la cantidad, el crédito. El latifundio fue la forma de propiedad adecuada al alma del navegante de tierra y mar, y la forma propia del cultivo y del aprovechamiento del suelo.[73]
>
> [The desire to occupy the territory in a short period of time, of roaming through it, of galloping through it, disseminated a small number of people over many leagues. From that galactic position of the peoples emerged an intrinsic need that would create the norm of Argentine life; the extension, the surface, the quantity, the credit. The latifundia was the adequate form of property for the soul of the navigator of land and sea, and the very form of cultivation and exploitation of the land.]

The words used to portray Argentine life are very pertinent: 'extension', 'surface', 'quantity' and 'credit'. These abstract concepts are all anchored in the forms of 'exploitation of the land'. The Spaniards actually gave the name 'Argentina' because of the silver they believed was found in that region. It is significant that the explanation as to why latifundia type of estates emerged in Argentina is based on these abstract concepts. The Pampas grasslands as an abstract surface on which to generate value seems to suggest that capitalism is generating a Cartesian ontology of the land. In the words of Jason W. Moore, 'Capitalism is a co-produced history of human-initiated projects and processes bundled with (and within) specific natures.'[74] That is, the relationship between nature and capitalism is dialectical, rather than dualistic. The passage in *Radiografía* seems to be aware of the role of capitalism in the ideas of nature that the colonizer had in the history of Latin America, even if the text repeats many of the same tropes in continentalist narratives put forth by those same colonizers. Martínez Estrada will go as far as to argue that the land was converted into a 'metaphysical value'.[75] Quite literally, the land is stripped of its materiality and turned into something that can be economically manipulated into 'credit'. It is an 'intrinsic need', one that forces Argentine society to imagine its surrounding lands as a metaphysical space.

Martínez Estrada is repeating an image of the Pampas that revolves around abstract ideas and notions, not on the specificity of the biome. His is a global discourse that exploits common tropes of the plains as empty and barren that made possible the attachment of value to the vast extensions of land. His readers come to know these plains as if they were 'extension' and 'surface', not as a grassland or a particular topography. Much the same way Sarmiento acknowledged Cooper's genius in representing the landscape of the Americas as a battle for possession of territory, so does Martínez Estrada reveal a similar representation of the Pampas. These plains have been imagined since *Facundo* as a scenario on which the drama of the possession for the land plays out, one in which the land is just a 'surface' that can be manipulated and altered for economic returns. Having their physical presence stripped away, the plains lose their local knowledges in favour of Eurocentric values. An abstract surface can be exploited, modified, measured and sold without any real consequences beyond its economic value. Precisely, this emptying of the plains leads to its portrayal as a desert, an image that is far removed from its ecological characteristics. Even if it is a dominant imaginary in Argentine culture, no such 'deserts' ever existed.[76]

When describing the life of 'pioneers', Martínez Estrada explains that their incessant attempts at conquering nature were motivated by the vacant plains.[77] That metaphysical space of extensions, quantities and surfaces can only be 'empty'. The same way geometric planes are 'empty', so are the grasslands. The plains are portrayed as 'harassing' pioneers into action, as threatening colonizers. What little agency these lands ascribed is basically used to harass and force humans into action. It is in this sense that they are undomesticated lands. Untamed yet vacant, the plains are a geometric wilderness. Such emptiness is later linked to being described as a desert. Martínez Estrada writes, 'Unpopulated areas and deserts are correlative of superterritoriality, and vice versa.'[78] As in other passages of *Radiografía*, the language used to describe the region is often scientific, which further accentuates its abstract dimension. Described as a 'desert' and 'unpopulated', the grasslands are then considered 'correlative' to large extensions of land. Just as in *Facundo*, the language deployed makes the depiction of the Pampas a 'marketable geography', one that is built on the rhetoric of an empty land. When encountering pseudoscientific explanations such as the preceding passage, the reader is impressed with the rigorous tone. It does not attempt to be grand and sublime in the Humboldtian tradition of geography, but rather presents itself as a clinical probing of the ailments that can be found beneath the surface of the Pampas. The last phrase of *Radiografía* bears witness to Martínez Estrada's approach as a physician of culture: 'We have to accept it with courage, so that it ceases to perturb us; become conscious of it, so that it will disappear and we might live in good health.'[79]

There is one striking instance in the book that introduces a reference to a specific tree found in the Pampas, the ombú tree or *Phytolacca dioica*. Native to that biome, it is an evergreen tree that grows a large canopy of a diameter of close to fifteen metres. It is widespread throughout subtropical regions in the south of Brazil, Paraguay, Uruguay and Argentina. Interestingly, the term 'ombú' has not been linked to Guaraní or any other Indigenous language. What local knowledge has been effaced from that word that eventually came to be part of the Spanish language in referencing the tree? Martínez Estrada writes the following passage about the relation between the ombú and the Pampas as deserts:

> El árbol de esta llanura, el ombú, tampoco es oriundo de ella. Es un árbol que sólo concuerda con el paisaje por las raíces; esa raíz atormentada y en parte descubierta, dice del viento del llano. Las ramas corresponden al dibujo de la selva. Bien se ve que es de tierra montuosa, quebrada. Ha venido marchando desde el norte, como un viajero solitario; y por eso es soledad en la soledad. Se vino con un pedazo de selva al hombro como un linyera con su ropa. Lo que rodea al ombú se expresa en signos de otro idioma; grande y sin igual, necesita del desierto en torno para adquirir su propia extensión.[80]

> [The tree of these plains, the *ombú*, is not native to these lands. It is a tree that only fits in the landscape through its roots; that tormented root and partially exposed, speaks of the wind in the plains. The branches correspond to the drawing of the jungle. One can see that it is from a hilly and fractured land. It has marched from the north, as a solitary traveller; and that is why it is solitude within solitude. It came with a piece of the jungle on its shoulders, as a vagrant carrying his clothes. What surrounds the ombú is expressed in the signs of another language; large and without equal, it needs the desert around it to acquire its own extension.]

Rather than explain that the tree is native of the plains in Argentina, Martínez Estrada chooses to describe the *ombú* as a 'vagrant' that arrived in the grasslands from the jungles to the north. He is factually wrong, since the tree is native to the region. In its lush foliage and large canopy, it seems not to fit into the deserted landscape of the plains. However, its 'exposed' and 'tormented' roots are representative of the harsh landscape. This comparison sets up the desolate image of the grasslands. The personification of the *ombú* is ambivalent, for it imagines the tree both as a 'solitary traveller' and a 'vagrant'. It is also considered 'large and without equal'. Perhaps the tree is like a colonial settler who has arrived from far away, only to settle in these empty lands. In other words, the *ombú* is depicted as a foreign settler, at once effacing its role as a native species in the biome and justifying the presence of colonizers attempting to survive in that seemingly forlorn land.

Notice, however, that aside from the name of the tree, the reader is not offered much of a description of the tree itself, which is very striking when seen in the plains by travellers. The personification of the tree is dominant throughout the passage. The last phrase also elicits the theme of possession of the land in abstract terms. The *ombú* needs the desert to 'acquire its own extension'. It seems like the tree is playing out the Argentine problem of the vastness of the land and the struggle for its possession. It manifests the correlation between the Pampas as desert, the lack of human population and 'superterritoriality'. And when Martínez Estrada describes in more detail the *ombú*, it is devalued as 'thick', 'tough' and 'worthless'.[81]

The geometric wilderness of the grasslands thus sustains the image of the plains as a desert, a negative portrayal of the biome that is an abstract construction that responds to Martínez Estrada's philosophical interests in sustaining a dialogue with Sarmiento. Both writers repeat and establish a series of images of the plains as empty deserts that contrast with the ecology of the biome. Neither describes the Pampas as a rich grassland, a unique ecosystem that is threatened by its overexploitation by ranching and agricultural enterprises. Instead, they build an image that emphasizes abstract notions of space, such as extension, horizon, surface and immensity. These abstract notions are coupled with the growing economic interests in exploiting the grasslands. *Facundo* begins stripping away the materiality of the grasslands by reversing the pastoral trope of retreat, transforming the landscape into a threatening wilderness similar to a large desert. Drawing from Cooper and Humboldt, Sarmiento imagines the plains in a manner that legitimizes the campaign of civilization in modernizing the rural regions of Argentina. The possession of the land becomes the core struggle of the nation he envisions – an issue that translates into the problem of extension. *Radiografía* takes the abstract representation of the Pampas to its radical consequences, inheriting from Sarmiento the problem of extension and imagining a geometric wilderness on which the most predominant aspects of the land are its super-territorial surfaces. Although both texts have glimpses of other possible ecologies of the grasslands, their focus on repeating the tropes of continentalist narratives is predominant.

The depictions of the plains in these two texts clearly demonstrate the powerful rhetoric behind imagining the grasslands as empty deserts. The Pampas as a desert is an ideological construction that devalues its ecological value, while it legitimizes the possession and exploitation of the land. Moreover, it generates a dominant mode of knowing that biome insofar as readers of *Facundo* and *Radiografía* recreate its landscape as an empty space and desert. Both texts have deeply shaped the way other writers and poets have depicted the plains, many of which continue to describe these biomes as immense deserts. The plains as deserts are perhaps one of the most recurrent images in the literatures of the plains.

2

The ruined lands of the Altiplanos

The Altiplanicies have a significant place in the imaginaries of the plains in Latin America, especially in Mexico, where the Sierra Madre mountain range levels off into the elevated central plains, and in South America, where the Andes open into the *altiplano*. In this chapter, I will specifically address those two bioregions, the Central Mexican plateau and the Andean *Puna*, while focusing on the works of three important writers from Peru, Mexico and Brazil: Ciro Alegría, Juan Rulfo and João Guimarães Rosa. Although physically similar to other grasslands, the depictions of these plains in canonical fictions present the land as inhospitable and ruined. Often the wind and the cold temperatures appear in these narratives as eroding away at life. The protagonists of these fictions suffer from sickness and gasp for air as they encounter a strange landscape that seems devoid of life. As in the dominant images of the Pampas, many of the images deployed in canonical fictions of the Altiplanicies emphasize the metaphor of a wasteland. Unlike other continentalist images of grasslands, the portrayal of these highlands as ruined forgoes the possibility of turning them into a garden. Worthless and ruined, their only value can only be found beneath the ground, in their mineral deposits. This particular imagery is specific to the Altiplanicies, more so than any other grasslands in the Americas that always oscillate between being considered a desert and a potential garden. In the three narratives that I will explore in this chapter, the despondent and haunting portrayals of the highlands exacerbate the barrenness of these biomes. Yet as in the previous chapter, these canonical fictions also offer glimpses of local knowledge that filters through the trope of the plains as wastelands in the form of regional flora that evokes resistance to the settler imaginaries that only see value in digging up the land.[1] I would go as far as to argue that the local knowledge effaced in the continentalist narratives that have legitimized the continued exploitation of the grasslands is often found in the minutiae of the flora referenced. Plants are often a vehicle of local knowledges that resist effacing by the dominant environmental imaginaries of the Americas.

From an ecological perspective, these elevated plains or highlands have a cold climate, given their altitude. I consider the terms 'altiplanicie' and 'altiplano' interchangeably. Both words are geographically rich, for they refer to a variety of regions throughout North and South America. For example, the Central Mexican plateau is commonly named the 'Mexican altiplanicie'. These highlands extend between the Sierra Madre Oriental and Sierra Madre Occidental mountain ranges, varying in elevation from 1,000 to 2,000 metres.[2] The term 'altiplano' also denotes a specific high plateau in the Andes mountain range in Peru and Bolivia. These grasslands in the Andes are also known by their Quechua name 'Puna', a name that indirectly refers to altitude sickness or *soroche*. In Peru, the *Puna* is found at elevations above 3,900 metres, where temperatures are 'below freezing at night and seldom rising above 16°C by day'.[3]

More specifically, I will examine the portrayals of the Altiplanicies through the close readings of Ciro Alegría's *Los perros hambrientos*, Juan Rulfo's 'Luvina' in *El Llano en llamas*[4] and João Guimarães Rosa's short story 'Páramo' which appeared in *Estas estórias*. These three narratives depict the precariousness of life in the highlands. They place humans, animals and plants in inhospitable locations, where the struggle to remain alive is a testimony to the barrenness of the grasslands. They repeat the trope of the plains as an irreversible wasteland. The land is grim and haunting; life is barely clinging to the ridges of the mountain ranges. It is portrayed as an eroded and cold environment, lifeless and ruined. These despairing images, however, also remind readers of the precarious relations between living beings, especially given the weather of the region. It reveals not only the perilous existence of humans in the Altiplanicies but also the recalcitrant anthropocentrism in seeing the land as lacking value when it is not suitable for human habitation. These environmental images seem to sway between the need for respecting the powerful presence of nature and the hubris of devaluing a biome because of its lack of resources for the use of human settlers unacquainted with the highlands.

More so than other canonical literatures of the plains, the depictions of the Altiplanicies are ecologically ambivalent in their repetition of continentalist tropes. On the one hand, *Los perros hambrientos*, 'Luvina' and 'Páramo' raise our ecological awareness by foregrounding the horrifying aspects of the environment that threaten the lives of humans, animals and plants. The haunting aesthetic of these narratives makes humans aware of their precarious place in the environment. It reveals how all living beings are enmeshed in the world, dependent on each other and the climate for survival. It also manifests the inherent anthropocentrism in depicting the highlands as 'ruined'. Eroded as they may be, they are but the product of the climatic conditions of such high elevations. In *Los perros hambrientos*, for example, the awareness that the prolonged drought affects each and every one of the beings found in the high plains generates a despondent atmosphere that ironically binds humans and canines in the same tragic fate. In 'Luvina' and 'Páramo' the narratives have unexpected shifts that create an asphyxiating atmosphere for the human protagonist walking through a landscape of ruins. The pessimistic narration of events opens up a crack through which the reader is obliged to come to terms with what Morton suggests is the task of ecological thought, 'to figure out how to love the inhuman: not just the nonhuman (that's easier) but the radically strange, dangerous'.[5]

Drought in the Andean grasslands in Ciro Alegría's *Los perros hambrientos*

Ciro Alegría's entry into the Latin American canon came about with his ambitious novel *El mundo es ancho y ajeno* (1941), which was the winner of the prestigious contest hosted by the Farrar and Rinehart publishers in conjunction with the Pan-American Union. His award-winning novel is often considered by critics to be his best work, as discussed by literary critic Cornejo Polar in his prologue to *El mundo es ancho y ajeno*.[6] Not much is known, however, about a Bolivian writer who also participated in the Farrar and Rinehart contest that same year, submitting a book set in the Andean highlands and dealing with themes that are very similar to those that appear in Alegría's book. This largely ignored writer is Raúl Botelho Gosálvez, and the novel he submitted is *Altiplano* (1940). Unlike his Peruvian counterpart, Gosálvez did not even merit the mention of the adjudicating committee of the contest.[7] Some critics even went as far as to denounce the novel as plagiarizing Alegría's earlier novel *Los perros hambrientos*.[8] Although both *Altiplano* and *Los perros hambrientos* share similar themes – especially in regard to the issue of Indigenous rights – the main aspect that distinguishes them, from an ecocritical perspective, is the documentary fashion with which Gosálvez portrays the high plains. The first chapter of *Altiplano* is entirely dedicated to describing the region and its Indigenous traditions. It has strong regionalist traits as the narrator describes the northern and southern regions, as well as the different seasons of the Andean *Puna*.[9] The short novel attempts to compile the local knowledges of the grasslands, to the detriment of the narrative structure. Although *Los perros hambrientos* addresses the importance of the natural environment in the lives of Indigenous communities, the book is not documentary in its portrayal of the highlands. Its repetition of the continentalist trope of the plains as wasteland subdues the local imaginaries of the biome. Hence, it is significant that Alegría's book – a novel that repeats some of the dominant images of continentalist narratives in the Americas – would win the important prize of Latin American fiction in 1941. We can only speculate as to how this difference might have affected the results of the contest, sidelining Gosálvez's *Altiplano* in Latin American fiction of the twentieth century. The coincidence of two writers writing the same grasslands in the same years and who nevertheless enjoyed varying degrees of success suggests the presence of other voices whose imaginaries of the plains are relegated to the periphery by canonical fictions. The recovery of Gosálvez's fictions is an important step in bringing together those other voices that also constitute the literatures of the plains in Latin America.

Alegría himself confessed that his *opera prima* is based on a chapter of his previous novel: 'Back in 1938, while residing in Chile, I was writing my novel *Los perros hambrientos*, and I was about to title one of the chapters "Broad and Alien is the World", when I realised that there was a novel to be written from that chapter.'[10] The chapter to which Alegría is referring to is the eleventh one titled 'A Small Place in the World'. Critics have pointed out the similarities in narrative structure between *El mundo es ancho y ajeno* and *Los perros hambrientos*.[11] Another aspect that connects both novels is the portrayal of nature as an imposing and merciless force.[12] More so than his later novel, Alegría's *Los perros hambrientos* acutely addresses the oppressive nature of the Altiplanos and clearly repeats the image of a dismal and ruined land. It is in this novel that nature becomes a powerful agent in the form of an impending drought that affects the grasslands. Moreover, this short book by Alegría has not garnered sufficient attention from ecocritical scholars. Jorge Marcone has written on the ecology of Alegría's novel *Serpiente de oro* (1936), setting up a nuanced discussion of the role of the jungle biome as a place of encounter with nature.[13] Marcone analyses the 'political ecology' of narratives of the Amazon, especially Alegría's first novel that takes place in the Peruvian border with the jungle.[14] He argues that the 'returns to nature' are also projects of exploitation, of extraction of natural resources – an aspect that displays their political dimension.[15] Continuing the discussion opened up by Marcone, we could raise the following question: Do the depictions of the Altiplanicies as a ruined and eroded land result in a 'political ecology' that values a biome for the resources found underground?

Los perros hambrientos narrates the life of Indigenous communities in the Andes as the drama of a prolonged drought unfolds over the land. It is original in its narration of events, offering the perspectives of human characters and of the dogs that accompany them. Although there is an overarching thread to the story that can be traced through each of the chapters, the narrator often embeds stories within stories, seemingly wandering from the central plot, yet at the same time drawing from the oral culture of the Incas in the way the story is told.[16] The narrative takes place somewhere in the Andean *Puna* and recounts the struggles of an Indigenous community as it faces the impending drought. Central to the book are the melancholic depictions of landscape which create a mood of despondency.

The very first passage of the novel sets the sombre tone of nature in the Andes, while provocatively altering a seemingly pastoral landscape: 'The monotonous and long bark, acute to the point of drilling, sad as a lament, beat on the white fleece of sheep and steered the flock. The flock, trotting through the dry grasses, would paint of white the grey bellicosity of the Andean mountain range.'[17] An aural experience prompts the narrative. It is not a pleasant sound, but rather a barking that is 'acute to the point of drilling'. As with the extraction of minerals from the ground, so the sounds repeat the piercing of the Andean silence. By far, the beginning of *Los perros hambrientos* is one of the most original in the literatures of the plains. Rather than begin with a visual cue of landscape, the narration begins with the sounds of the highlands. Instead of attempting to 'see' the land, it recreates the aural atmosphere. This creates an eerie ambience, one in which 'monotonous', 'long' and 'drilling' sounds fill the air. As we saw in the depictions of the Pampas grasslands, the term 'monotonous' is often attached to the visual representation in which the horizon is prominent. The aural portrayal accentuates the silence of the highlands, while also bringing to the forefront the non-human sounds of dogs barking.

The language deployed is erudite, almost baroque in its choice of words, such as 'vellón albo' instead of 'lana blanca' or 'trisca' instead of 'pisar'. The recurrence of 'dr' and 'tr' sounds in the passage accentuates the 'drilling' barks that echo 'ladrido', 'taladrante', 'triste', 'trote' and 'trisca'. The barking 'lashed' the sheep that are grazing in the fields. Almost hidden in the rough sounds and stark contrasts of the passage is a Quechua term that refers to a particular type of flora found in the high plains, the 'ichu'. The *Diccionario Enciclopédico Quechua-Castellano* defines the term as a simple grass of the Andean high plains that is often grazed by South American camelids such as the llama or alpaca.[18] It reveals the embedded presence of Indigenous knowledges of the land in the language deployed in reference to local flora. The passage oscillates between the language of the Spanish colonizers and that of the Quechua communities, a contrast between the continentalist images of empty plains and the local knowledge of specific type of grass. Whereas settler ecologies overlook the variety of grasses in the highlands, the word 'ichu' reveals an Indigenous epistemology often lost in dominant imaginaries of the plains throughout Latin America.

The one visual cue that is offered in the passage derives from the contrast of light tones, from the white of the sheep and the grey of the mountains. The image begins as if about to offer a tranquil landscape, for the sheep 'would paint of white' the Andes. That image, however, is quickly disrupted by the foreboding view of the 'grey bellicosity' (*rijosidad gris*) of the mountains. It is an intense environment. It is not only conflicting but also latently sexualized by the term *rijosidad* that I have translated as 'bellicosity'. Something that is *rijoso* is said to be restless and also lustful. Succinctly, the narrator chooses an ambiguously sexual term that suggests the larger theme of drought in the Andean grasslands in terms of fertility and barrenness. The land is not abundant but ominous and sterile: a wasteland. By establishing a stark contrast between serene pastoral cues and a haunting vision of the Andes, the narrator deconstructs the image of a peaceful and bountiful landscape. What at first might seem like a bucolic painting of nature – with its flock of sheep spattered as with a brush on a canvas – transforms into an uneasy and charged environment where the mountains loom grey in the background.

Even the shepherd Antuca manifests her despondency when the dog stops barking and she suffers an 'immense and heavy silence'.[19] Life in the Andes grasslands is dependent on its climatic circumstances, awaiting for what never seems to arrive. Each day the shepherds watch 'the convulsed Andean crest, the bleating flock, the sky, now blue, now cloudy and menacing'.[20] Just as monotonous as the barking at the beginning, so does daily life drag on between tending the flocks and keeping an eye for the distant sky that changes tonality. Shifting from 'blue' to 'cloudy and menacing', the sky is charged and dynamic. The mention of the 'convulsive Andean crest' suggests a figurative link between the land and a particular bird, one whose crest is a sign of violence. This link will become more pronounced later on in the narrative, when the connection between the Andean condor and the high plains emerges as the representation of the inhospitable environment that preys on the living corpses humans and dogs alike. When the narrator explores the life of the character Antuca, a brief and seemingly cursory commentary is introduced towards the end of the first chapter, one that reminds the reader of the contrast with pastoral idylls: 'Thus are the idylls in the mountain range.'[21] The notion of the idyll is connected to that of the classical pastoral genre, especially since Theocritus's *Idylls*. Along with the term 'bucolic', the idyll has been linked to the pastoral during the Hellenistic period.²² Alegría's phrase suggests that the Andean range is an idyll, altering the traditional context of the pastoral from fields to the mountain ranges of South America.

As the narrative progresses, the oppressive tension foreshadowed in the opening passage looms heavily in the depictions of landscape. It is in the same chapter that inspired *El mundo es ancho y ajeno* – chapter XI titled 'A Small Place in the World' – that the imagery of the high plains emerges with force:

> El cielo, a esas horas, estaba despejado. Demasiado bien sabían los indios de lo que se trataba, especialmente el Mashe, cuya ancianidad había, como es natural, visto mucho. El viento cruzaba dando potentes aletazos y graznando como una ave mala. La puna erguía sus negros y altos picachos en una actitud de acecho hacia el Norte, hacia el Sur, hacia Occidente y Oriente. Por ningún lado cuajaba el mensaje de la vida.²³

> [At that time, the sky was clear. The natives knew all too well what it was about, especially Mashe, whose old age had, as is natural, seen much. The wind crossed, giving off potent wingbeats and cawing like a malignant bird. The *puna* straightened up its black and high peaks in a stalking stance toward the North, toward the South, toward Occident and Orient. Nowhere did life's message congeal.]

The passage begins with a concise depiction of a 'clear' sky. By announcing the lack of clouds, emphasis is placed on the weather; more specifically, it highlights the impending drought. The Indigenous community looks to the sky for clues as to their future coexistence. They are aware of their dependence on the environment. Introduced in the third sentence is the recurrent image of the wind across the *Puna*. The image exudes hostility. The wind is imagined as a bird that may only bring suffering as hinted at by a powerful beating of wings and its foreboding cawing. The use of the suffix '-azos' instead of the regular ending '-eos' in the word 'aletazos' emphasizes the violence with which the wind crosses the land.

Although no specific bird is named, it is most likely a condor, a bird that was considered sacred by the Incas and is a predominant species of the New World vulture in the Andes. The Andean condor or *Vultur gryphus* is one of the largest of the living birds with a wingspan of almost three metres, able to bring down large prey such as deer. In fact, the *Diccionario de la Real Academia Española* explains that the Spanish word 'cóndor' is derived from the Quechua 'cúntur'.²⁴ Its presence in *Los perros hambrientos* is a reminder of Indigenous language and knowledge in the imaginaries of the grasslands of the Americas, even in canonical fictions that so often repeat setter ecologies of the continent. At the beginning of the narrative, the condor is introduced as a bird of ill omen by one of the Indigenous characters named Mateo.[25] Here the menacing metaphor of the wind as a condor is accentuated in the sentence that follows in which the *Puna* is portrayed as a predator 'stalking' its prey everywhere in the region. Transformed into a condor itself, the land 'straightened its black and high peaks' to hunt for its prey. In the original text, there is a play with the words 'erguía' and 'picachos' that fosters the link between the bird of prey and the Altiplanos. The verb 'erguir' may mean to 'straighten up' or 'stand up', although it is often used to describe the 'straightening of the neck'. As a condor that 'straightens up' and opens its wings, so does the *Puna* straighten itself before taking flight. Notice that the 'peaks' are black, just as the plumage and beak of the condor. Moreover, the word 'picachos' is similar in sound to that of 'pico' (beak) and 'penacho' (plumage).

The identification of the Andean plateaus with the preying condor reaches its most violent climax in the scene where Mateo's son Damian dies of hunger, while the dog Mañu defends his corpse from a stalking condor: 'The condor opened its beak and straightened its neck, also filled with rage, but then regained its normal behaviour and remained with the dignity of a being that dominates the air, even in the face of the dog barking.'[26] Here the difficult and tense relation between the predatory bird and domesticated canine is representative of the vexed relationship between the land and the human. The confrontation between condor and dog places in stark relief the threatening presence of the Altiplanicies. To humans, the Andean grasslands are a source of struggle that makes their lives all the more precarious. This is indeed a common trope in continentalist narratives, one in which the plains are seen as predatory to colonizers struggling to survive in a new environment. Predatory encounters abound in the literatures of the plains, from the tiger preying on Facundo Quiroga out in the Pampas grasslands to the crocodile claiming cattle and human victims in the Llanos. In the next chapter, I will specifically address this trope of the plains in the Orinoco Llanos.

The shift from what might have been a pastoral landscape to a nightmarish world of death is found towards the end of the novel, when the narrator describes at length in an intensely poetic passage the effects of the drought upon the Andean grasslands. The arrival of long days without rain are 'inexorable and oppressive', affecting both 'humans and animals'.[27] It is the common suffering that binds all creatures of the Altiplanicies. The prolonged drought foregrounds the large scale of their environmental crisis, making everyone aware of the agency of nature. The narrator explains, 'All of nature voiced the fatal words of thirst and death.'[28] Through this natural catastrophe, the Altiplanos are given a voice through which to manifest its woes and reach all of its constituents that are enmeshed within it. Unlike the other depictions of the Pampas as a desert, here the Andean grasslands become an active site of resistance in their barrenness:

> 'No llueve', gimió un agonizante hilo de agua desde lo más profundo de un cauce. 'No llueve', repitieron los alisos de las orillas, dejando caer sus hojas y contorsionando sus brazos. 'No llueve', corearon las yerbas, desgreñándose, amarilleando y confundiéndose con la tierra. Hasta el caserón de la hacienda llegó la voz. 'No llueve', admitieron los altos y severos eucaliptos que lo rodeaban, haciendo sonar sus hojas con un ruido metálico.[29]

> ['It does not rain', groans an agonizing thread of water from the deepest riverbed. 'It does not rain', repeat the trees of the river banks, letting their leaves fall and contorting their arms. 'It does not rain', chanted the grasses, becoming dishevelled, yellowing and becoming blurred with the ground. Even in the big house of the estate arrived the voice. 'It does not rain', admitted the high and severe eucalyptus trees that circled it, making their leaves resound with a metallic noise.]

The anaphora 'It does not rain' that prompts each of the phrases in the passage is like an echo that reverberates the voice of nature as it extends throughout the region. Not unlike the barking at the beginning of the narrative, the repetition drills into the land. Four times is the simple phrase repeated, and each time it becomes all the more resounding. Although their suffering is voiced through a human language, the repetition of the short phrase only adds to the oppressive atmosphere. The drought has arrived in full force.

The land expresses its suffering as a haunting chorus of streams, grasses and trees. The personification of nature displays human agony. Trees suffer by 'contorting their arms' and grasses become 'dishevelled'. Most haunting of all is the image of the solemn eucalyptus trees – which symbolize death – as they surround the estate and make 'their leaves resound with a metallic noise'. A deathly procession that encroaches upon a human household holds one final ritual. No matter how distanced these wealthy mestizo settlers might be from the rest of the Indigenous communities and the harshness of life in the Altiplanicies, nature slowly closes its grip. There is no escape, only the awareness that the drought binds everyone and everything together in a precarious relation, for 'Dogs and people were bound even in the tragedy'.[30]

And finally, the passage follows with the ironic contrast between what could have been a pastoral landscape yet is actually a deathly cemetery of the Andean grasslands: 'A polished sun shone in the beautiful blue sky. Life continued beneath a crystal ceiling that would have been joyous had it not consisted also of a vision of the land. The latter began painting by ravines and mountain sides, by hills and plains, with dying grass and skeletons of trees, a desolate symphony in grey.'[31] Beginning with a 'polished sun' and 'beautiful blue sky' only serves to contrast with the 'desolate symphony in grey' that ends the passage. The shift from what 'would have been joyous' to a dying landscape expresses the sombre tone of the novel. The Altiplanicies are a horrifying land that preys upon the living. Whereas the pristine sky opens to a sublime vista, the high plains paint a depressing world – nature's canvass is smeared with 'dying grass and skeletons of trees'. The principal drama of *Los perros hambrientos* is the grasslands, 'generous and good when it rains, yet cruel' if it does not rain.[32]

Windy summits in Juan Rulfo's 'Luvina'

The effects of a ruined landscape upon its human and non-human inhabitants are also a theme in Juan Rulfo's short story 'Luvina', which appeared in *El Llano en llamas* in 1953. The story is told through a narrator talking to an absent interlocutor, as the former remembers his arrival and life at the small village of Luvina, located somewhere in the Mexican highlands.[33] As an outsider, the narrator recounts his encounters with the haunting villagers who seemed like ghosts across the cold ruins of town. As in other short stories by Rulfo, the setting creates an oppressive atmosphere that engages with the images of wasteland. Rulfo himself has confessed to the importance of situating his narratives to generate an uncanny ambience. He explains, 'I need to situate myself in a determinate place', adding that the regions in which his stories take place are 'between the *altiplano* and the western *Sierra Madre*'.[34] In the sparse dialogues and haunting portrayal of the highlands surrounding Luvina, Rulfo exploits an imagery of barrenness and desolation through the material ruins of the land and village, but also in the whirlwinds that scratch and erode at the human and non-human. So barren is the land that there is no value to be found above or below ground. Seen through the eyes of an outsider, the story engages with the settler ecology of imagining the plains as ruined when no value can be extracted from the ground, whether it be monoculture or extraction of minerals.

The story captures what Carlos Blanco Aguinaga suggests lies at the core of Rulfo's narratives, '[the] anxious tension between the interior slowness and the external lightning of violence'.[35] The external landscape of the story freezes time in the narrative, isolating the physical tension between telluric forces and humans in the highlands. This is accomplished by framing the different diegetic levels so as to present the narrator as a witness to static scenes. In 'Luvina' the narrator describes events that occurred in the preterit to an absent interlocutor, deploying demonstrative adverbs such as 'there' and 'here' to juxtapose and contrast the extradiegetic space from that in the narrative itself. These shifting juxtapositions draw the reader's attention to Luvina as a place where time is diluted in the telluric and climatic images of landscape presented. The highlands become a no-place, frozen in time and ruined in space. For example, the narrator explains, '*There* the entire horizon is faded; always clouded by a dense stain.'[36] The absence of a horizon adds to the disorientation of the narrator, as if the fading of the line between the land and sky blurs the past with the present. Gradually, the seeming physicality of the highlands is faded into an ethereal existence in which the villagers appear as ghosts. As the editors of *Arts of Living on a Damaged Planet* suggest, 'every landscape is haunted by past ways of life.'[37] 'Luvina' literally explores how the ghosts of past encroach on the damaged highlands. Although we are not given any details as to the history of the town, the beginning paragraph seems to suggest a past of mineral extraction that is no longer taking place.[38] So damaged has the land become that it no longer has any value.

The narrator repeats the use of the demonstrative adverb to try and situate Luvina for the absent interlocutor, prompting a description of the land: '*there* even the earth would grow thorns'.[39] The ground is harmful, cutting into the feet of those who walk on its surface. Notice how the narrator does not see the resilience of thorns in surviving in the extractive zone that the Altiplanos of Luvina appear to be. Rather, the narrator *sees* the land as a martyrdom of sort, an obliged suffering that he himself feels his life was during the period in which he lived in the village. The use of the demonstrative adverb is gradually more present in the story, as a crescendo that haunts the narrator. '*There* I lived. *There* I left my life . . . I went to *that place* with all my illusions and returned old and exhausted.'[40] It is almost as if the narrator is at a loss of words to try and depict this land that is foreign to him, resorting to merely repeating 'there' over and over.

The narrator explains that Luvina 'sounded like a heavenly name. But that place is purgatory. A moribund place where even the dogs are dead and no one is there to bark at the silence.'[41] An in-between place – neither heaven nor hell – the village is suspended in the heights of the highlands that are imagined as not quite alive, not yet dead. It is more than just barren plains, for its damaged environment has turned into a place where the human and non-human coexist by clinging to life. While the story repeats the image of the plains as wasteland, it also repurposes that imagery into a haunting landscape that bears witness to the ruins left behind in this mineral extraction site. The churned stones on the cliffs of the highlands are a purgatory to those barely alive in the village. On the one hand, these elevated plains are portrayed as an environment awaiting the burial of the villages. It is in that sense that they are imagined as a cemetery, a place of death that has no value attached. The plains as a cemetery is a powerful image, one that suggests lifelessness not only above ground but also below.[42] The canonical fictions of the Altiplanicies exploit the subterranean themes that amplify the presence of the non-human as a threat. That is, the subterranean metaphors of the plains as either cemeteries or as hiding value beneath their barren landscape are central to narratives such as 'Luvina'.

In Rulfo's *Pedro Páramo* (1955), for example, the setting of the novel is the city of Comala, which found downhill from where the initial narrator is located.[43] There is a constant shifting between these binaries, so much so that Jean Franco suggests that the 'topography' of Comala 'serves as heaven, as hell, as purgatory, and as the real world' throughout the narrative.[44] Built on spatial juxtapositions and oppositions, the narrative leads the reader to an awareness of how the non-human elements of the story displace characters. In Rulfo's narratives, characters are forced to negotiate different spaces in the narrative, whether it be arriving to the valley where Comala is found or entering the city of Luvina in the highlands. In other words, there is a conscious emphasis on sombre images in Rulfo's narratives. He tends to depict 'dark environments' that are 'blurred realities'.[45] The settings of his stories portray lands where organic life is hardly sustainable. Although what at first might seem like a hellish setting can also become a paradise of sorts.[46] 'Luvina' enacts such spatial juxtapositions, for example, in the opposition between the high plains filled with a wind that 'scratches as if it had nails' and the place where the narrator tells his story, a place where the 'murmur of the air' moves leaves softly.[47] Although the term 'nails' is used to describe the wind, it need not be an anthropomorphic portrayal. Often in Spanish, the term 'uña' can refer to animal claws as well as human nails. I would further argue that the term accentuates the animal aspect of the wind, as a wild creature preying on humans. The wind is the non-human encroaching upon the lives of the villagers, as a predator stalking its prey.

The first passage of 'Luvina' is worth reading closely, for it offers a drawn-out depiction of the Altiplanicies that are central to the story. It is also an exceptional passage in Rulfo's writings in terms of its length and detail.[48] It sets the harsh atmosphere of the entire narrative:

De los cerros altos del sur, el de Luvina es el más alto y más pedregoso. Está plagado de esa piedra gris con la que hacen cal, pero en Luvina no hacen cal con ella ni le sacan ningún provecho. Allí la llaman piedra cruda, y la loma que sube hacia Luvina la nombran Cuesta de la Piedra Cruda. El aire y el sol se han encargado de desmenuzarla, de modo que la tierra de por allí es blanca y brillante como si estuviera rociada siempre por el rocío del amanecer; aunque esto es un puro decir, porque en Luvina los días son tan fríos como las noches y el rocío se cuaja en el cielo antes que llegue a caer sobre la tierra.[49]

[Of the high hills of the south, that of Luvina is the highest and rockiest. It is plagued by that grey stone with which they make lime, but in Luvina they do not make lime from it, nor do they put it to any good use. There they call it crude stone, and the hill that climbs to Luvina is called Crude Stone Hill. The wind and the sun have caused the hill to crumble, so that the ground there is white and shining, as if it was always showered with morning dew; although this is just a way of talking, because in Luvina the days are as cold as the nights, and the dew congeals in the sky before it manages to fall upon the ground.]

The images of 'grey stone', 'lime', 'crude stone' and 'ground' reinforce the harshness of the land. The ground 'crumbles' through the action of the sun and the wind so that it looks grey and white as when limestone is scraped. Particularly powerful is the image of 'crude stone' which elicits both the notion of a rock untouched by humans and also that of a rough-edged stone. It is both primordial and ominous. Notice also that the depiction of landscape is devoid of human components, except the human narrator who holds a much closer relation to the land than the omniscient narrator in *Los perros hambrientos*. It is a cruel environment in which the appearance of 'morning dew' is just a figure of speech to grasp the raw aspect of the ground. The reigning forces of the passage are the 'ground', the 'cold', the 'sun' and the 'wind' – an emphasis on the non-human. Carlos Huamán López, however, suggests that here nature is personified, 'exercising acts exclusive to man'.[50] He argues that the 'destructive cooperation' of the air and sun is indicative of this anthropomorphic aspect in the narrative. Yet claiming that destruction is purely a human act naively renders the natural environment as benign, a perspective more akin to pastoral idylls. In the passage the non-human elements burst, not as personified but rather as 'raw' and unrestrained, almost violent in their depiction as 'crumbling'. It pushes the non-human to the foreground, actively embedding the narrative voice into the land described.

Most important is the suggestion that the highlands could have been the subject of extraction of limestone. In other places, those 'grey stones' would have been taken to produce something of value in the extractivist economy, but in Luvina those stones remain useless. We are not given much in the way of explaining why those same stones as useless in Luvina, other than the fact that the surrounding lands are damaged beyond repair. Could it be that this place was once a mining site? Is that why the land is so damaged? Regardless of whether or not the village was an extraction site for limestone, the passage links the act of digging up the ground for minerals and the ruined landscape that the narrator remembers. The connection between economic value in the way of extracting mineral resources and the ecological value of the highlands is established. In a seemingly eroded land, the subterranean value of its stones has the final say on whether these elevated plains are a wasteland.

Desolate and harsh, the *cerro* becomes the agent of the story. Lucy Bell identifies this dissolving of the storyteller as one of the characteristics of Rulfo's 'short-story form' which 'is erected as a ghastly void that must be fleshed out, both by characters or settings (that gain a life force of their own) and by the reader (who co-operates in their revival)'.[51] Again, the suggestion that the emptiness of Luvina transforms it into a 'void' or 'non-place' upon which to project the narrative. This rhetorical strategy – this turning the plains into abstract surfaces – is constitutive of continentalist narratives. They are described as silent and lifeless, as well as threatening to human inhabitants. Rulfo's short story is repeating many of the continentalist tropes discussed so far. The high plains are completely barren, not even fit for the extraction of stones. As in *Los perros hambrientos*, the narrative is not entirely committed to deploying the dominant images of the plains. At times, there are fractures in the dominant imaginaries of the plains. Continentalist narratives are not completely hermetic, as we have seen.

In 'Luvina', the highlands are not a passive backdrop in the story but instead are an active telluric force that shapes the narrative. The setting of the narrative is dominant, to the point of becoming the protagonist of a story that is lacking a plot with a defined climax or conclusion.[52] This silencing of the narrator and the corresponding emphasis on telluric elements opens up a space for the 'revival' of that ruined world in the imagination. Humans cannot observe nature from a neutral position but are enmeshed in the environment from the very start. The dismal aspects of landscape open up an awareness of how humans are enmeshed in the environments they inhabit.

The *cerro* of Luvina is presented as an eroded land, one in which the stones themselves are useless. Natural elements such as the air and sun are active agents in the geographic ruins of Luvina. Yet in this desolate land, an image stands out against the rocky mountainsides, that of the *chicalote* plant. In a profoundly inorganic landscape of 'crude stone' and 'deep ravines', the presence of flora is singular:

> Un viento que no deja crecer ni a las dulcamaras: esas plantitas tristes que apenas si pueden vivir un poco untadas a la tierra, agarradas con todas sus manos al despeñadero de los montes. Sólo a veces, allí donde hay un poco de sombra, escondido entre las plantas, florece el chicalote con sus amapolas blancas.[53]
>
> [A wind that does not even allow the *dulcamaras* to grow: those sad little plants that hardly survive spread over the ground, holding on with their hands to the cliff of mountains. Only at times, there where there is a bit of shade, hidden between plants, blossoms the chicalote with its white poppies.]

The contrast between the eroded ground and the blooming of the *chicalote* is striking. Even in a ruined geography such as Luvina, there remains a hint of life in those white flowers. The *chicalote* clings to the cliff, struggling to survive in a desolate landscape as humans with hands desperately clinging to the earth. Even if the air and the sun scrape the rocky surface of the mountainside, the *chicalote* is an expression of resistance and survival. Even more compelling is the contrast established between the scientific name *Solanum dulcamara* and the Nahuatl name *chicalote* in the passage. Not only does the thorny *chicalote* represent a resistance to the harsh conditions of the *Altiplanicie*, but it also represents the struggle of language in referencing local flora insofar as it juxtaposed to the scientific term of another type of flower, the *Solanum dulcamara*. The narrator is knowledgeable enough as to distinguish between the Indigenous and scientific names of flora, not just as a neutral witness but also as an observer committed to the land he is describing.

The differences between both types of plants are also significant. Whereas the *dolcamara* is delicate in its appearance, the *chicalote* is a thistle with a poppy. The latter is a persistent plant, almost threatening in its tenacity: 'But the chicalote soon withers. Then one hears it scratching the air with its thorny branches, making a noise like that of a knife on a whetstone.'[54] Its thorns are sharp as a knife, cutting through the wind that scrapes the land. Notice the appearance of death in the passage. The withering of the *chicalote* is the first manifestation of death in the story, one that emphasizes the precarious conditions of life in Luvina, as the eucalyptus trees in *Los perros hambrientos*. Singular in its presence among the rugged terrain, it is an image of resistance against the telluric forces of the highlands and a reminder of how fickle life can be in such a harsh environment. The reader is challenged to consider the patent struggle for life. As Cynthia Deitering comments on the 'postnatural novel', the narrative 'reflects a world in which the air is in fact no longer necessarily life-sustaining'.⁵⁵ Her comments on novels from the 1980s are fitting to the seemingly inhospitable environment of 'Luvina', even if the story is not necessarily a postnatural novel. Even in death, the *chicalote* continues to resist, 'scratching the air' as a knife sharpening.

There is something profoundly disquieting about the sensorial atmosphere in the story, which is brought about by the whirlwinds that sweep through the village and surrounding lands. Wind is a haunting climatic element, since they 'are hard to pin down, and yet material'.⁵⁶ Winds erode the stone cliffs, cracked ground and village houses as an invisible agent that makes its presence known through the scratching noises it makes when in contact with the land. They invite us to think of the environment as an 'atmosphere' or 'an aerial domain' that can accelerate destruction.⁵⁷ The sounds of the gusts of wind perceived by the narrator are grating, like the withered *chicalote* sharpening against the air.⁵⁸ A few paragraphs later, the wind in Luvina is described in full detail:

> Ya mirará usted ese viento que sopla sobre Luvina. Es pardo. Dicen que porque arrastra arena del volcán; pero lo cierto es que es un aire negro. Ya lo verá usted. Se planta en Luvina prendiéndose de las cosas como si las mordiera. Y sobran días en que se lleva el techo de las casas como si se llevara un sombrero de petate, dejando los paredones lisos, descobijados. Luego rasca como si tuviera uñas: uno lo oye a mañana y tarde, hora tras hora, sin descanso, raspando las paredes, arrancando tecatas de tierra, escarbando con su pala picuda por debajo de las puertas, hasta sentirlo bullir dentro de uno como si se pusiera a remover los goznes de nuestros mismos huesos.⁵⁹

> [You'll see that wind blowing over Luvina. It's grey. They say that's because it carries volcanic sand; but the truth is, it's a black air. You'll see. It sets on Luvina, clinging to things as if biting them. And on many days it carries off the roofs of houses as if it were carrying off a straw hat, leaving the walls eroded, unprotected. Then it scratches, as if it had nails: one hears it morning and night, hour after hour, without rest, scraping walls, tearing pieces of the ground, scratching with its pointy spade beneath the doors, until one feels it roiling inside oneself, as if it were trying to rattle the hinges of our own bones.]

The wind scratches, 'as if it had nails', the walls, and an iron shovel strikes against the ground. These sounds reach into 'our own bones'. Their harsh attributes highlight the mineral landscape – the walls, ground and metal – an effect that is all the more distinct when juxtaposed with the sounds of a bubbling stream where the narrator is presently located while recounting his story. Here the wind is personified, as a human undertaker walking through the city in search of the dead. However, it is not so much the fact that the wind has certain human traits that is striking, but rather the metallic noises it makes. Fingernails that need not necessarily be human are heard 'scraping walls' and 'tearing pieces of the ground', creating an eerie atmosphere. The sounds elicit the presence of something feral attempting to enter through the stone walls. It is as if humans are the prey of some unseen predator that they can only hear as it comes closer to their shelters. Humans are cornered by the non-human presence of the elements. It is the non-human noises that jut out of the descriptions of the wind upon the ruinous city of Luvina.

The non-human presence of the highlands reaches its climax when the narrator interrupts his story to ask the children playing outside to keep quiet, before returning to Luvina and the lack of rain in the region which is not unlike that of *Los perros hambrientos* and many other literatures of the plains:

> Sí, llueve poco. Tan poco o casi nada, tanto que la tierra, además de estar reseca y achicada como cuero viejo, se ha llenado de rajaduras y de esa cosa que allí llaman 'pasojos de agua', que no son sino terrones endurecidos como piedras filosas, que se clavan en los pies de uno al caminar, como si allí hasta a la tierra le hubieran crecido espinas.[60]
>
> [Yes, it rains little. So little or almost nothing, to the point that the ground, besides being dried and shrunken like old leather, is also filled with cracks and that thing that there they call 'pasojo of water', which are but hardened pieces of ground that like sharp stones, they stab one's feet while walking, as if there even the ground had grown thorns.]

The recurrence of the word 'tierra' (ground also dirt and soil) in the sentence is significant. It appears on two occasions, each attached to an image of drought and erosion. In the absence of rain, the narrator observes the contours of the ground. It is a dry and cracked earth, 'like old leather'. Moreover, the entire passage plays on the recurrent sound of the double 'r' ('tierra', 'reseca', 'rajaduras' and 'terrones'), which suggests the roughness of the land. Even if there is a seeming mimetic element to the description, there is also a moral element to the way the narrator renders the landscape. The word 'achicada' has several meanings. It means to 'make smaller' or 'reduce in size' but also to 'belittle' or 'humiliate'. As it quite literally shrinks from the drought, the land itself is 'humiliated' by the harsh climate. The same goes for the word 'endurecidos', for it not only suggests the literal 'hardening' of the ground but also its 'callousness' to the conditions of the highlands. The pain of the land is such that the final phrase evokes the suffering of Christ insofar as the path of rocks is like walking on 'thorns'. This suggests the passion of Christ as the necessary agony of the land in search of redemption. As the narrator mentions, the city is a 'purgatory'.⁶¹ Luvina might be a ruined place, yet it is a place where the land itself agonizes, where the *chicalote* struggles to cling to the mineral surfaces, where the wind scrapes the lime off the stones and walls and where the ground itself grows 'thorns' that 'stab' those who walk upon its paths. This is not an aseptic representation of landscape, but one in which the tormented environment is laid bare for the reader.

With the depictions of the *Altiplanicie* on which the city is found, the brooding narrator of 'Luvina' envelops the reader in the struggle that is taking place. It is important to note what Bell suggests in regard to the portrayal of the environment in *El Llano en llamas*, drawing inspiration from Nancy Tuana's concept of 'viscous porosity': 'Similarly, the "environmental" issues relating to land, weather and natural disasters that proliferate in Rulfo's short fiction can neither be assimilated into, nor separated from, human issues.'⁶² Even if the highlands are an oppressive presence that structures the narrative of 'Luvina', the relation between the *cerro* and its inhabitants manifests the meshing of the environmental fate of humans and non-humans. Not entirely separate, not yet completely embedded together, there is a complex entangling of the human and non-human. The wind preys on human inhabitants, at times like an undertaker and at others like an animal howling outside their shelters: 'We kept hearing it passing above us, with its long howls; we kept hearing it coming in and going out through the hollow concavities of the doors.'⁶³ Although thorny, the *chicalote* clings to the earth with 'hands'. The ruinous landscape and its ghastly inhabitants offer a testimony of how the precariousness of life on the *Altiplanicie* – in the form of the *chicalote* clinging to the rocky ravines – contrasts with the apparent safety of the shop where the narrator tells the story.

Suffocating highlands in João Guimarães Rosa's 'Páramo'

I will now turn to the Brazilian writer João Guimarães Rosa, best known for his *Grande sertão: veredas* (1956), a novel that attracted the attention of critics in Brazil when it was first published. Characterized as 'working out of archaic rural settings', Guimarães Rosa's writing establishes 'modern texts with transcendental dimensions'.⁶⁴ Antonio Candido suggests that both Guimarães Rosa and Juan Rulfo inherit a 'super-regionalism' that reaches beyond the mere documentary.⁶⁵ Unlike their regionalist precursors, they are not invested in simply registering local scenarios, but rather in touching on universal themes. This is particularly true of Guimarães Rosa, since many of his narratives deploy the regional dialect and daily life of the interior of Brazil to build a story that resonates beyond the local. His short story titled 'Páramo' is distinct in his literary production because it takes place in a setting that is not in Brazil. It takes place in an unknown Andean landscape that is ruinous, similar to the other two texts we have seen so far. It tells the story of a foreigner describing life in an unspecified city of the Andes. As the story progresses, the ruined landscape of the Andean highlands transforms into the image of the plains as a wasteland. Throughout the story, emphasis is placed on the significance of an eroded and abrasive land.

The similarities between Rulfo's 'Luvina' and Guimarães Rosa's 'Páramo' are significant, especially in the images of the highlands. Both stories have an outsider as the protagonist, an outsider that encounters the inhospitable world on the highlands and gradually realizes that the land is not unlike a cemetery upon which the dead walk. Caroline LeFeber Schneider argues in a similar vein, when comparing Rulfo's *Pedro Páramo* and Guimarães Rosa's *Grande Sertão*, explaining that 'both translate place into prose'.[66] Her exploration of the two novels reveals interesting continuities that strike a chord in the comparison between 'Luvina' and 'Páramo', especially in regard to the notion of space espoused by both authors. She suggests that the novels by Rulfo and Guimarães Rosa construct space 'through non-linear narratives and coercive invitations'.[67] That is, the narrative does not follow a linear sequence of events, but as has been mentioned in the case of 'Luvina', there are constant shifts between the present and the preterit in the telling of the story. The temporal shifts accentuate the differences between the ruinous landscape of Luvina and the serene place from where the narrator recounts his experiences. Also, the narrators in both 'Luvina' and 'Páramo' are uninvited guests in the cities they visit in the high plains. They seem to be obliged to suffer the oppressive atmosphere of those cities in the heights. I argue that much the same way as the juxtaposition of contrasting spaces serves to engage the reader with the encroaching atmosphere of the high plains of 'Luvina', so does the contrast of spaces reinforce the oppressive environment of the Andean *altiplano* in 'Páramo'. However, the recurrent use of demonstrative adverbs and shifts from the preterite to present tense in the latter story serve to blur spatial and temporal distinctions, creating a disorienting sensation not unlike the *soroche* or altitude sickness felt by the narrator. The reader is left with a disquieting awareness of a dying environment, where death and sickness permeate the Altiplanicies.

The scope of Guimarães Rosa's acclaimed novel has had an impact on studies focused on his lesser-known works: 'No one has attempted to explain the reasons for the relative paucity of studies in Guimarães Rosa's other works, but certainly one of the attractions of this lone novel is its suggestive range.'⁶⁸ The posthumous story collection *Estas estórias* has not received much attention, even if it contains several fascinating short stories such as 'Páramo'. An aspect of 'Páramo' that has drawn the attention of critics is, as Jon Vincent suggests, the seeming 'proximity of the *estória* to the *história*',⁶⁹ which is perhaps the 'oddest note of the story', so much so that it stands out from all the other stories in the volume.⁷⁰ In blurring the boundary between the two, the reader is unsure whether the story being told is just that, a story, or whether the events are true. Vincent goes on to explain that 'the story is told with a straight face and the diction complements rather than contrasts with that seriousness', which adds to the effect of a 'heavy atmosphere'.⁷¹

An element that presents a similarity with Rulfo's story is the title. 'Luvina' seems to refer to a place, a city found somewhere in the *cerros*. The fact that no article precedes the title suggests that it is a proper noun. The same could be said for 'Páramo', which does not include an article. Both stories appear to embed themselves in a place right from the title. They seem to refer to a setting 'locatable on maps and history', thus suggesting a 'regional' dimension to the narrative.⁷² Yet Lefeber Schneider is quick to note that neither Guimarães Rosa nor Rulfo write as 'a practice in documentary precision'.⁷³ There are clues in the depictions of the land in both stories – for example, the presence of a *chicalote* in 'Luvina' and the capitalized word 'Cordilheira' in 'Páramo'. However, in Guimarães Rosa's case, the title is purposefully ambiguous. A Spanish reader will quickly recognize two references hidden in the title: on the one hand, a 'páramo' is common word for an 'elevated plain'; and on the other hand, it also is the last name of the character that forms the title of Rulfo's only novel *Pedro Páramo*. It is important to emphasize that even if the word 'páramo' exists in Portuguese, the term 'planalto' is far more common. In Portuguese, according to the *Dicionário Priberam da Língua Portuguesa* (DPLP), the word 'páramo' can also refer specifically to the 'high lands of the Andes', although it is derived from the Spanish term.⁷⁴ Hence it appears that Guimarães Rosa is at the very least playfully challenging readers to consider the geographic and cultural references within the title itself. The linguistic hybridity of his texts is well documented, from the neologisms deployed to the borrowing of words from other languages and the local lexicon of different regions.⁷⁵

'Páramo' begins in the first person, directed at an unknown interlocutor, 'I know, brothers, that we already existed, before, in this or in other places.'⁷⁶ The narrator also seems to address a community of monks, given the appellative 'brothers' in the phrase. That supposed group of interlocutors will not make an appearance throughout the story but are absent as much of the human characters in the Andean landscape depicted throughout. At times a macabre musing and at others a silent meditation on the Andean landscape, the narrator reaches out to his or her readers, appealing to their judgement on what he witnesses as an asphyxiating environment: 'That of hate – an unknown world. A world that you cannot conceive. Everyone punishes themselves. It is terrible to be dead, as I sometimes know that I am – in another way. With this lack of soul. I can barely breathe; the cold undoes me.'[77] The sentences are short, truncated almost, manifesting the lack of air the narrator experiences, the unbearable shortness of breath from altitude sickness. It is as if the land is the cause of the narrator's sickness. The Altiplanicies are not simply a wasteland but also a source of disease, a threat to foreigners unaccustomed to the high elevations.

The narrator speaks of 'hate' and 'an unknown world' that is asphyxiating. The air of the Andean high plains is not life-sustaining but is detrimental to the narrator, causing a different type of being 'dead'. And the reader suffers that sickness alongside the narrator, the anxious inhalations and exhalations as each sentence cuts gradually shorter. Using dashes mid-sentence generates the sensation of gasping for air, which serves to emphasize the oppressive atmosphere of a 'world unknown'. The broad reference to the 'world' elicits the experience of multiple scales by the narrator. In another passage, the narrator exclaims, 'And I suffer, here, dead among the dead, in this cold, in this not-breathing, in this city, in me, oh, in me; it has been months.'[78] Throughout the story, the words 'cold', 'dead' and 'breathe' recur over and over. Just as in 'Luvina' and *Los perros hambrientos*, the aural elements of the highlands accentuate a dismal nature that encroaches upon human characters, so does the lack of air sustain a dreadful landscape that seems incapable of sustaining life. The Andes 'are ashen, irradiate sadness' ('são cinéreos, irradiam tristeza') and are a 'prison' to its inhabitants.[79] The use of the word 'cinéreos' instead of 'cinzentos' (both of which could be roughly translated as 'ashen') is pertinent, for it plays off the word 'etéreo' (ethereal) and 'aéreo' (aerial). The highlands seem almost immaterial, a non-place upon which the shadows of life are fleeting. It generates a disorienting sensation experienced by the narrator. This raises an interesting issue regarding the experiences of settlers in the plains of the Americas, for the scale of these grasslands is always a disorienting factor in their depictions. The portrayal of the highlands in 'Páramo' repeats this trope and binds it to the image of the plains as a wasteland.

As the narrative progresses, the narrator becomes more and more unreliable, an aspect that heightens the experience of place on multiple scales. We first catch a glimpse of the unreliable nature of the narration in the switch from a first-person to third-person perspective, only to return to the first person in the span of three pages. After the initial preamble in which the narrator reflects on the fickle nature of life, he or she begins a story using the third-person perspective in which a 'young man' is forced to travel to a 'foreign city'.[80] Similar to the narrator in 'Luvina' who moves to the remote city, so too this 'young man' is displaced to some unknown location in the Andes. A paragraph later, the narrator seems to slip, and accidentally returns to the first person by saying, 'Ah, entre tudo, porém, e inobstante o hálito glacial com que ali me recebi' ('Ah, in the midst of it all, thus, and notwithstanding the glacial breath with which I was there initiated').[81]

At the end of the paragraph with the shift back to the first person, the text introduces an ellipsis. As if the narrator finally notices the mistake that has been committed, the rambling is cut off. The recounting of events gradually becomes more anxiety-ridden, reaching a point where the narrator questions whether he or she is dead or alive.[82] The use of 'here', 'there' and 'over there' constantly by the narrator exacerbates the sense of disorientation in the Andean highlands. Sometimes the narrator differentiates between 'here' and 'there' to speak of the unknown city in the Andes, as if he or she was present and distant simultaneously. As readers, we are unsure if those demonstrative adverbs really refer to a remote spatial location or if the narrator is confusing where he or she is. Even the narrator confesses his inability to distinguish north from south.[83] In a state of perpetual 'insomnia', the narrator explains the following: 'But I experience, more often than not, that other state of mind, that is not vivid wakefulness, nor sleep, nor a common transition between the two – but it is as if my spirit was aware of itself at a time in diverse worlds, equally running through planes that are very distant from each other.'[84] Experiencing simultaneity and distance at once, the narrator loses all spatial anchoring as the *soroche* sickness takes hold.

The intensifying of soroche sickness in the narrator gradually transforms the portrayal of the highlands as a very oppressive force. The world becomes hostile, filled with hate and cold. Telluric and glacial, the landscape infringes upon the narrator's aggravated mental state. 'Páramo' introduces several passages that emphasize the uncanny aspect of the Altiplanicies:

> Era uma cidade velha, colonial, de vetusta época, e triste, talvez a mais triste de todas, sempre chuvosa e adversa, em hirtas alturas, numa altiplanície da cordilheira, próxima às nuvens, castigada pelo inverno, uma das capitais mais elevadas do mundo. Lá, no hostil espaço, o ar era extenuado e raro, os sinos marcavam as horas no abismático, como falsas paradas do tempo, para abrir lástimas, e os discordiosos rumores humanos apenas realçavam o grande silêncio, um silêncio também morto, como se mesmo feito de matéria desmedida

das montanhas. Por lá, rodeados de difusa névoa sombria, altas cinzas, andava um povo de cimérios.[85]

[It was an old city, colonial, of an ancient time, and sorrowful, perhaps the most sorrowful of all, always rainy and adverse, in rigid heights, on a high plain of the mountain range, next to the clouds, punished by winter, one of the highest capitals of the world. There, in the hostile space, the air was exhausted and scarce, the bells tolled the hours in the abysmal, with false halts of time, so as to open laments, and the discordant human rumours all but emphasized the great silence, a silence also dead, as if made from the colossal material of mountains. Around there, enveloped by a scattered sombre fog, high ashes, there lived a dark people.]

The syntactical construction of sentences is filled with pauses, as if the narrator is running out of breath while describing the landscape. In the first sentence, the city is described as 'old', 'colonial', 'sorrowful', 'rainy', 'adverse', 'in rigid heights', 'on a high plain', 'next to the clouds' and 'punished by winter'. Each descriptive clause stresses the harsh conditions of the *Atliplanicie* where the city is found. The description is through a serial accumulation of details, becoming a gradually heavier burden. Also, the repeated use of 'v' sounds accentuates the sharpness of the landscape described. There is a threatening aspect to the world in the high plains insofar as the climate is 'adverse' and the land is 'punished by winter'.

The element of wind is also present in this narrative. The Andean *páramos* is a windswept land that brings the cold into the city:

E há, sobranceiros e invisíveis, os páramos – que são elevados pontos, os nevados e ventisqueiros da cordilheira, por onde têem de passar os caminhos de transmonte, que para aqui trazem, gelinvérnicos! Os páramos, de onde os ventos atravessam. Lá é um canil de ventos, nos zunimensos e lugubrúivos. De lá o frio desce, umidíssimo, para esta gente, estas ruas, estas casas. De lá, da desolação paramuna, vir-me-ia a morte. Não a morte final – equestre, ceifeira, ossosa, tão atardalhadora. Mas a outra, *aquela*.[86]

[And there is, soaring and invisible, the *páramos* – that are elevated points, the snowed and windy of the mountain range, through which the mountain paths must pass, that bring here, geli-winternals! The *páramos*, from where the winds cross. There, it is a doghouse of winds, in the whistlers and lugubrious howling. From there the cold descends, very wet, for these people, these streets, these houses. From there, of the *paramune* desolation, death would arrive for me. Not the final death – equestrian, reaping, bony, so overdue. But the other, that one.]

Although the Andean city is saturated with a great silence, the *páramos* are a windswept landscape through which the cold descends. Thus even if there are hardly any sounds in the city, there is also a hostile wind, just like in Luvina. The neologism deployed in the passage attests to the constructing of a language to render the hostile environment. The cold winds that arrive from the *páramos* are not just icy but are 'gelinvérnicos', a fusion of 'gelid' and 'winter' that generates a cavernous sound. Those 'gelinvérnicos' aggravate the sensation of the Andes as a cavernous prison. The exclamation mark punctuates the sentence immediately after the neologism. Scarcely used in the entire narrative, the exclamation mark heightens the intensity of the word. As if the construction of the word was not sufficient to attract the reader's attention, the exclamation serves as a warning that indicates the threat posed by the telluric forces of the high plains. The image of the 'doghouse' to depict the winds rolling down to the city is haunting, for we imagine a group of howling dogs in the 'whistlers' and 'lugubrious howling' heights. We can almost hear the winds approach from a distance, as dogs barking in a remote doghouse. It creates an atmosphere of imminent danger, something that is yet to arrive. However, as was mentioned earlier, the narrator is unreliable. When he or she attempts to locate places in space, there is always an element of uncertainty. What is said to be 'there' may actually be 'here'. Perhaps the *páramos* are not so distant from the city. Perhaps the city is already in the *páramos*: 'The city, cold, cold, in wet winds, they say that those airs are very pure, the winds that come from the *páramos*. This entire city is a *páramo*.'[87] Here the reader is left to dwell on whether the narrator is quite literally considering the city as a *páramo* or whether it is a metaphor for the suffering that occurs. The ambiguity remains, for at that point in the story, the narrator has given ample evidence of being unreliable, of confusing time and space, of questioning the boundary between himself and others.

The Altiplanicies are a prison that prepares for that 'other death' that slowly coagulates throughout the narrative in the form of the 'Man' that follows the narrator. This place is a purgatory of sorts, an intersection between heaven and hell where its inhabitants suffer the pangs of existence. The in-between place is suggested at the beginning of the story, when the narrator evokes the images of the river Lethe as a passage towards death.[88] Similar to 'Luvina', the passage or transition that gradually materializes through the landscape is one of Christian suffering. The land becomes a place of 'rampart of thorns' in which the narrator experiences 'the great torture' and is forced to enact some sacrifices (225).[89] Also, the gradual materialization of the 'Man' from having the 'aspect of a corpse' to having 'an air of a corpse' and finally to being 'a corpse' reflects the passage towards death. The non-human in the form of a corpse intrudes on the narrator, obliges him or her to flee through the streets and gain distance from that materializing of death: 'I needed to, first of all, exile into complete oblivion he who at some prior fate had been transformed in my lugubrious and inseparable brother, perhaps a punishment for some dishonoured crime of ours, complicit: I had to forget the "Man with everything of a corpse."'[90] The 'Man' makes present the non-human hostility of the environment, a reminder that the Andean landscape is hell bent on bringing death to the narrator. Its steady corporealization is an asymptotic approach of the non-human, an ominous presence that finally reveals itself as a corpse, a thing no longer alive. The ecology espoused in both 'Luvina' and 'Páramo' makes explicit the continuities that exist between both texts in the manner in which the landscape becomes an oppressive force that impinges upon human inhabitants and reminds them of the suffering of life against the backdrop of the telluric high plains.

In this chapter, I have argued that the Altiplanicies as portrayed in Alegría's *Los perros hambrientos*, Rulfo's 'Luvina' and Guimarães Rosa's 'Páramo' reveal a dark aesthetic of landscape accentuates how life can be a luxury in the environments of the high plains. In Alegría, the central aspect of the narrative is the impending drought as it binds all entities – whether human, animal or plant – to the tragic fate of an inhospitable environment. The ironic awareness that dogs and humans all suffer equally the drought displays an ecology from which neither can escape. In 'Luvina' and 'Páramo', a negative portrayal of the land is offered, one that aggravates the alienation of inhabitants faced with a 'geographic ruin', a world that does not sustain life but instead takes it away. All three narratives use aural cues to construct an oppressive atmosphere in which the human and non-human are enmeshed. Unlike other geographic imaginaries of the plains, the depictions of landscape in *Los perros hambrientos*, 'Luvina' and 'Páramo' are significant insofar as they stray from the traditional aesthetic values ascribed to nature as beautiful or sublime. These narratives challenge readers to come to grips with an environment that is not beautiful, harmonious or brimming with life. The highlands are portrayed as places where the horrific struggle for survival is quickly met with death, as is the case in the image of the withered *chicalote* or in the dying Indigenous child preyed upon by the condor. Where the *chicalote* grows is not a welcoming environment – never a place of respite – but rather a world that violently puts in motion telluric forces that encroach upon humans. By presenting such ominous places, they offer a glimpse into other modes of representing the environment beyond pastoral and benevolent images, an alternative mode that challenges us to imagine the plains not as a virgin landscape to be domesticated but as an horrific land that makes humans conscious of their precarious situation that is phrased at the end of 'Páramo': 'The hostile city, in its glacial rule. The world. I was returning, to what I knew not if it was life or death. To suffering, always.'[91]

3

Predation in the Orinoco Llanos

Considered one of the biggest crocodilians in South America, the Orinoco crocodile or *Crocodylus intermedius* inhabits 'the Orinoco River and its tributaries in Venezuela and Colombia'.[1] On average measuring more than 4 metres, it can easily be identified by its long and narrow snout as it skims the surface of waterways.[2] Although it was a predominant predator in the rivers and streams of the Orinoco Basin a hundred years ago, it is now a critically endangered species, mainly because it was hunted extensively at the beginning of the twentieth century. According to specialists, 'over-exploitation started at the end of the 1920s'.[3] Although the Orinoco crocodile had been hunted by Indigenous peoples in the region, it was not until the rise of cattle ranching in the surrounding grasslands that the species was seen as a threat to human interests. The decrease in the crocodilian's numbers runs parallel to the emergence of intensive ranching the Llanos. Between 1929 and 1963, the *Crocodylus intermedius* was killed for its skin, especially in the region of Apure in Venezuela.[4] Considered a lucrative commodity, its skin was sold in international markets. In a few decades it went from a metaphor for the dangers lurking at the limits of the grasslands and the waterways in the Orinoco to becoming a profitable product to be purchased globally. This transformation reflects the dialectical relationship between capitalism and nature in the 'drive towards endless commodification'.[5]

The plains imagined as a threat via the encounters with predators is a dominant imaginary in Latin America, as is the later commodification of these creatures well into the twentieth century. We have already seen the role of the jaguar in the continentalist narratives of the grasslands in several canonical fictions. In this chapter, I want to explore fully the significance of predation in the dominant images of the plains, while also discussing the importance of how we frame the relations between humans and non-humans through predatory encounters. Whereas the portrayal of predators as a threat to humans often appeals to the antagonistic separation of the human and non-human, predatory relations can also shed light on the precarious yet ubiquitous entanglements between both. Encounters with apex predators can be imagined as a conflict between two completely different worlds, that of the natural savagery found in the land and that of the civilized humans attempting to colonize the region. In Latin American fictions, predation is generally framed in terms of the dichotomy between barbarism and civilization – a binary that often has the plains as its scenario. To be fair, contemporary conservationist appeals also fall into a similar dualism when considering the role of humans as that of caretakers that must preserve species from becoming extinct.[6] However, predation is also a meeting point between species that reveals the dialectical relations not only between non-humans but also between nature and society. As Haraway explains, it is in those meetings that 'The Great Divides of animal/human, nature/culture, organic/technical, and wild/domestic flatten into mundane differences'.[7]

Two well-known regional novels in Latin America that exploit predatory encounters in the plains of the Orinoco are *La vorágine* (1924) by the Colombian José Eustasio Rivera and *Doña Bárbara* (1929) by the Venezuelan Rómulo Gallegos. Both novels use the grasslands surrounding the Orinoco as the scenario for a significant part of their narratives. In the case of *La vorágine*, the book tells of the escape of Arturo Cova from the city into the Amazon rainforest, where he experiences first-hand the 'Green Hell' of the jungle and the rubber industry.[8] The first half of the narrative actually takes place in the Casanare plains, as the protagonist gradually makes his way through the grasslands and into the rainforest. The novel engages not only with the themes of madness and disease[9] but also with the dichotomy between grasslands and rainforests – two salient biomes that have shaped the literary canon through the genres of *novelas de la selva* and *novelas de la tierra*. Particularly pertinent is the fact that *La vorágine* sets up encounters with wild and feral creatures, especially in the grasslands and waterways. Arturo Cova's flight from the city is a sequence of predatory encounters as he literally becomes enveloped in nature as threatening, so much so that novel ends with the 'devouring' of the human characters by the jungle. In *Doña Bárbara*, the entire narrative plays out on the predatory antagonisms between humans and non-humans on different levels. The antagonism between the protagonist Santos Luzardo, who leaves the city to take part in the cattle-ranching business of his family in the plains, and Doña Bárbara plays out in terms of predation. From the initial predatory rape of Bárbara, which is portrayed in her transformation from prey to a predator that terrorizes the Apure plains, to the cattle rancher's hunt of the large one-eyed crocodile in the waterways of the grasslands, Gallegos's novel narrates the dichotomy between civilization and barbarism already present in Sarmiento's *Facundo* as a predatory relation.

Both novels also mention crocodiles as important predators of the Orinoco region, offering a glimpse into the impact of the continentalist narratives in the loss of biodiversity due to agricultural practices invested on turning the plains into a source of economic value. Most of the Orinoco crocodiles 'have been recorded from seasonal rivers (flood plain environments) in savanna ecosystems', although numbers continue to decrease well into 2017.[10] On the verge of extinction, environmental policies have for the past decades steadily increased its population in the Orinoco. The *Crocodylus intermedius* is a significant and emblematic predator of the Llanos, the grasslands that extend from Colombia to Venezuela. More importantly, the presence or absence of the crocodile reminds us of the precarious interdependence of species within an ecosystem, a relation that is often manifested through predation. It is the disruption of predatory relations that can destabilize entire ecosystems, risking species extinction, as is the case of the Orinoco crocodile. How this endangered predatory species has been imagined is significant to how we as humans engage in its conservation. An animal seen as a threat or as a lucrative business is often hunted to extinction. As Ursula K. Heise suggests, 'biodiversity, endangered species, and extinction are primarily cultural issues, questions of what we value and what stories we tell'.[11] A decrease in biodiversity also makes us aware of our own vulnerability as animals within the same twisting predatory ecology: 'Only animals can teach us that in the end, all organisms need a predator.'[12]

I will examine closely the relations between predators and prey in *La vorágine* and *Doña Bárbara*. How we imagine predation can either blur or legitimize the divide between animals and humans. The two novels exploit the trope of the plains as a threatening place where dangerous encounters with non-human animals occur, yet the way we read those predatory sequences reveals entanglement between all creatures in a given biome. I am thus interested in exploring not only how predators in these novels validate the human/animal division but also how predation can also show fractures in that dominant imaginary of the plains. For example, we can choose to read the confrontation between the Pampas tiger and Facundo as representing the antagonistic dualism between savage nature and human civilization, or it can also offer a glimpse into the dialectic relationship between all beings as Facundo recognizes himself in the gaze of the tiger. Representation of predation is significant to understanding how notions of dualism often seep into our imaginaries of nature. Moreover, predation as a dual conflict is a manifestation of modernity and capitalism, one that turns species from a threat to be neutralized to an international commodity. If capitalism established a global discourse that 'prized dualism, separation',[13] then the ways in which canonical fictions have represented predation fall under this same rubric.

I will begin by briefly discussing the significance of what I term 'predatory ecologies', bringing into dialogue the work of ecocritical scholars in the field, so as to gain a more nuanced understanding of how the way we imagine animals preying on humans affects our representations of the nature. From an ecocritical approach to literature, the presence of predators in the narratives challenges readers to reconsider the role of anthropomorphism and zoomorphism. How those rhetorical figures work in the narratives frame the threatening encounters between animals and humans, justifying or blurring the demarcation lines between humans and non-humans. After exploring the nuances of predatory ecologies, I will go on to analyse *La vorágine* and *Doña Bárbara* from different angles to shed light on how predation in these novels both emerges from continentalist images of the plains as threatening and fracture that imaginary by entangling human characters with non-human predators. Specifically, I will first analyse feral encounters in the grasslands. Feral creatures blur the boundaries between domestic and wild creatures, a binary that is also part of the dualisms of modernity. I will then focus on the predatory encounters that take place in both novels. Finally, I will also engage with the gendered portrayal of predation as inherent to the settler ecologies of the plains in the narratives.

Predatory ecologies

From the plants that act as primary producers and consume nutrients from the soil, all the way to the carnivores that hunt other species, predation sustains ecosystems throughout our planet.[14] As cattle graze on the banks of the Orinoco, they themselves are prey to the reptilian carnivores awaiting in the waters. A food web suggests more than a mere connection between organic beings, because it displays the fragile and shifting relations within a given ecosystem. To explore the interrelations between predators and their prey is to consider the ambivalent tensions that abound in the environment. Predation need not entail fixed hierarchies. Rather, it highlights the dynamic relations in a given ecosystem; that is, it manifests the precarious interactions between organisms. Robert Taylor identifies several definitions for predation, none of which is conceptually bound to a vertical representation of the relations between predators and preys in the food web: (a) 'Predation occurs when one organism kills another for food', (b) 'predation occurs when individuals of one species eat living individuals of another', (c) 'predation is a process by which one population benefits at the expense of another', and (d) 'predation is any ecological process in which energy and matter flow from one species to another'.[15] The four definitions of predation entail external interactions between organisms that hinge on life and death encounters. Predation sustains the diversity of an ecosystem insofar as it puts into action the flow of energy from 'one species to another'. Almost 'every organism is perceived as a potential prey by some other organism'.[16] Predation can thus be understood as a web or loop, an interconnection between species that is neither vertical nor horizontal. It can be as ambivalent as the predator that suddenly becomes a prey. This conception of predation also draws from feedback loops in biology, a theory which claims that a biological system is regulated by triggering responses that can either amplify a given disturbance or inhibit it.[17] This framework allows for a reverse engineering of relations within a biological system. Biologists, for example, have recently applied feedback loops to understand the contributions of predation to biological diversity.[18] Morton also deploys feedback loops in his approach to ecological thinking, explaining that they refer to a biological system 'of finitude and fragility' where 'the politics of coexistence are always contingent, brittle, and flawed'.[19] Organisms can at once be predators and prey, in a constant dialectical twisting of the food web. In other words, predation emerges in the shifting relations between living beings. It is both a struggle and meeting between creatures.

Morton further suggests, 'Thinking interdependence involves thinking difference.'[20] Ecological interconnectedness reveals shifting relations that are never entirely fixed, such as when a new species invades an ecosystem and creates a disequilibrium.[21] Dynamic and open, biological systems are 'subject to significant disturbance inputs from their environments'.[22] Morton argues along the same lines when emphasizing the notion of 'difference' or 'negative' in his understanding of the connections between beings. His dark ecology is based on interconnectedness through negative feedback loops, a notion that is derived from biology. Negative feedback loops inhibit – rather than intensify – a given disturbance within a biological system. Whereas we may be tempted to consider nature as static and holistic, Morton's notion of the 'mesh' is built on ambiguity and constant changes.[23] Predatory ecologies suggest these twisting and precarious relations between creatures, an interconnectedness that often emerges in unexpected ways yet entangles all living beings in the web of life. They dissolve what Bruno Latour suggests is the 'Great Divide' that separates nature and society.²⁴ Human exceptionalism attempts to re-establish the division between the human and non-human, while predatory ecologies entangle both and emphasize the web of life.

However, predation is not always imagined as such. Anthropocentric views tend to see predatory encounters as representing the threat of the wilderness. A quick survey of mainstream documentaries, for example, reveals how predators are often portrayed as aggressors, while their preys are seen as innocent victims. One scene that comes to mind is from the documentary *Blackfish* (2013), directed by Gabriela Cowperthwaite. In the scene, the camera is filming the hunt of a lonely seal stranded on a sheet of floating ice as a pod of orcas works together to try and push their prey off the ice and into the water. Behind the camera we hear a woman terrified by the unfolding predatory encounter, seeing the seal as a helpless victim of the cruel attack of the orcas. Instead of seeing the encounter as part of the web of life in which predators and preys find themselves entangled, this portrayal sees preys as suffering the cruelty of nature. Yet the food chain is constitutive of nature, humans included. Just as the seal is a prey in that specific encounter, so are the penguins that are hunted by seals, and so on. To imagine predation in terms of attackers and victims is to fall back on antagonistic dualisms that form part of the 'Great Divides' identified by Latour and other ecocritics.

Representations of animals affect how we imagine predatory encounters and our relation to them. There is, to be certain, an 'extensive "rhetoric of animality"' in human culture.²⁵ For example, whether a wolf is portrayed as a hostile or a social animal reveals how humans perceive themselves in regard to that particular non-human other. Thomas Hobbes, for example, chooses to describe human interactions in terms of wolf predation in his *Leviathan* (1651), whereas primatologist Franz de Waal begins his *Primates and Philosophers* (2006) by emphasizing the social behaviour of wolves. Their differing representations of wolves indirectly display how they imagine interactions with animals. As is the case of Hobbes, the fear of animals is usually evoked through narratives of predation. Moreover, the depictions of animals often project asymmetrical dichotomies on the basis of the 'principal Others to Man'.²⁶ Haraway suggests that the binary between humans and animals is entrenched in the fears of the other. The animal is capable of making humans uneasy. She further explains, 'these "others" have a remarkable capacity to induce panic in the centers of power and self.'²⁷ The human-animal binary is asymmetric. Insofar as the animal is considered inferior, any encounter on equal terms is a questioning of that hierarchy. The animal's gaze is unsettling, for it places humans back in the predatory loop. Meeting their gaze obliges us to reconsider our place in the world.

In his essay 'Why Look at Animals?' John Berger explores the dialectic of the gaze between animals and humans, explaining that there is both a familiarity and something distinct in the look of the animal, which leads to 'a power' being 'ascribed to the animal, comparable with human power but never coinciding with it'.[28] This gaze is particularly significant in the representation of predation in narratives, for it draws from the difference that tenuously holds together prey and its hunter. *La vorágine* and *Doña Bárbara* present scenes in which humans and animals gaze into each other as predators and prey, enacting the ambivalence of the predatory cycle. To explore the predatory ecologies of narratives is to analyse those exchanges that display the familiar and different 'power' that corresponds to animals as predators and prey.

Haraway is particularly relevant because her work explores the blurring boundaries between humans and animals. Her book *When Species Meet* (2008) explores the 'contact zones' between species, analysing the ways in which different organisms become 'entangled'.[29] Her approach emphasizes the external relations between animals and humans, and how such meetings between them are ontologically significant. She asks, 'When species meet, the question of how to inherit histories is pressing, and how to get on together is at stake.'[30] Encounters between species – just as any encounter with the other – raises the problem of how to get along, how to relate with the other. Although Haraway is far more interested in meetings with domestic species, her approach is interesting to understanding the encounters between wild species and humans. Even if domestic species have been coevolving with humans for centuries, such a period of time is very small in the overall scheme of natural selection. Haraway's book is after all titled 'When Species Meet' – the term 'species' being central to her arguments insofar as it avoids human exceptionalism and incorporates all living beings in a weave of entanglements. Whereas in the past encounters with wild animals occurred mostly in zoos, climate change has reduced natural habitats and increased meetings with wild animals near urban centres, as is the case, for example, with bears searching for food in city garbage dumps. Predation is one manner of meeting between animals and humans in the wild. Understanding how we imagine predation in narratives is important to learning 'how to get on together' when large predators cross paths with us near our cities and in the wild.

Wild predators are those that have not been previously domesticated by humans, whereas feral animals are those that become wild after being domesticated. Encounters with both types of animals highlight the fragile links between humans and animals. Similar to the feedback loops of predator and prey communities in a given ecosystem – where the growth and decrease of either community triggers shifts in populations – so do the predatory ecologies manifest the susceptibility of such interconnections between animals and humans. Levi Bryant's 'black ecology' reveals some interesting insights in this respect, describing interdependence as relations that 'can always be broken, often with dire consequences'.[31] Ecological interdependence is not just a mesh of links between constituents but rather a dynamic interconnectedness that can break down. Biological feedback loops demonstrate the mechanisms through which organisms attempt to cope with disruptions in the environment. 'What ecology should teach us, and what a melancholy black ecology foregrounds, is that relations are *precarious*.'[32] Bryant's argument challenges the common notion that interconnectedness is intrinsic to the natural world. Instead of taking ecological relations for granted, he explains that ecological praxis is constantly assessing relations between beings as external: 'Everywhere ecologists draw attention to what happens when entities are separated from relations they previously enjoyed and what happens when new entities are introduced into networks of existing relations.'[33] Ecosystems are constantly adjusting to changes. Describing ecological relations as precarious underscores the fact that these are not invariable, but are rather prone to changing.

La vorágine and *Doña Bárbara* narrate the changes that took place in the Orinoco Llanos and how these affected the relations between humans and animals. The rise in cattle ranching increased the population of possible prey for the *Crocodylus intermedius*, an event that set off the hunting of crocodiles by humans and their eventual exploitation for the commercial use of their skins. Their depictions of predation emerge as part of the dominant continentalist narrative that perceives the wilderness of the plains as threatening, although if we read the initial encounters against the grain, the predatory ecologies of the novels dissolve the divide between humans and animals which is latent in the civilization–barbarism dichotomy present in many canonical fictions of Latin America. Reading for the predatory ecologies of these two regional novels, we gain glimpses into the interconnections between organisms in the Orinoco Llanos, and how these were altered with the expansion of cattle ranching. Gallegos and Rivera explore the complexity of human and non-human relations in the Orinoco Llanos is through the extensive use of anthropomorphism and zoomorphism. Animals are often personified, while humans are also assigned animal characteristics. A closer reading of these instances sheds light on the relations between animals and humans, for the attributes that separate them seem to collapse in their depictions.

The predatory ecologies present in the novels generate these reversals between anthropomorphism and zoomorphism in tandem with ambivalent predatory encounters. Humans are sometimes considered predators, and at other times they feel as if hunted by animals. They are also sometimes described as wild animals. For example, the three Mondragones bandits that work for Doña Bárbara all respond to nicknames that refer to large feline predators: *Jaguar, Tiger and Lion*.[34] They are not given any other names throughout the narrative, outside of their feline nicknames which allude to their animality in contrast to Santos Luzardo's plans to civilize the plains. Humans seem like animals, and vice versa. I consider both the depiction of predatory relations and the anthropomorphism/zoomorphism of entities as the constituents of the predatory ecologies of the novels. How the relations between humans and animals are envisioned and their characterization shape the predatory ecologies of the narrative. These predatory ecologies are the encounters between humans and animals that can result in death by one or the other, revealing not just the fear of animals present in the environmental imaginaries of the plains but also the enmeshed relations between both.

Predation and ferality in the Llanos

La vorágine tells the story of Arturo Cova, a young and educated man living in Bogotá, who decides to flee from the city with his lover Alicia, only to become lost in the Amazonian rainforest where he witnesses the horrors of the rubber industry and suffers bouts of hallucinations. The novel takes place in two distinct landscapes at the beginning of the twentieth century: the plains of Casanare and the Amazonian rainforest. Critics have mostly focused on the rainforest as the central landscape of *La vorágine*, especially given the beginning of the third part which includes the often-cited prayer to the jungle.[35] It is not, however, the only geography that appears in the novel. The first part is entirely devoted to the plains, narrating some significant events that manifest the predatory ecology of the book. Inserted after the prologue is a fragment of a letter by Arturo Cova that opens the narrative referencing the plains: 'the ruthless destiny uprooted me from incipient prosperity and launched me to the pampas'.[36] Rather than dismiss the role of the plains in *La vorágine*, I am interested in the predatory encounters between humans and animals in that specific geography. Although the journey to the dark forests of the Amazon is central to the narrative, it is during the travels through the plains that the predatory ecology is introduced.

Set in the 1920s, *Doña Bárbara* tells the similar story of Santos Luzardo, a young lawyer who lives in the capital of Venezuela, who is returning to the lands he inherited from his family in the plains of Apure. He entertains plans to civilize the plains by establishing order and regaining property rights from his neighbours, Míster Danger and Doña Bárbara. The former is an Alaskan who has found in the plains of Venezuela a place to live as an accomplice to the outlaws in Apure. He is a co-conspirator with Doña Bárbara throughout the narrative, helping steal cattle from the Altamira ranch inherited by the Venezuelan lawyer. Luzardo's arrival triggers a land dispute between ranchers, for the infamous Doña Bárbara is said to have unlawfully taken over control of the Barquereña ranch that belonged to Luzardo's father. As the primary obstacle of Santos Luzardo and his project to establish property claims, Doña Bárbara is a symbol of the 'barbarian plain, devourer of men'.[37] The depiction of the plains is feminine in the cited passage, identifying women with nature as a predatory threat to men.[38] At times the novel will deploy the masculine 'llanos', although when eliciting the predatory elements of the plains, the feminine 'llanura' is preferred. Such identification is central to how gender affects the predatory ecology of both novels.

Both published in the 1920s, *La vorágine* and *Doña Bárbara* are salient examples of *novelas de la tierra*. In his important book titled *The Spanish American Regional Novel: Modernity and Autochthony*, Alonso explains that 'the *novela de la tierra* purports to write a literary text that incorporates the autochthonous essence'.[39] The search for the 'autochthonous' led writers to construct a cultural discourse that emphasized regional elements in narratives. To narrate the nation, writers looked to the local in constructing narratives and poetry, so as to legitimize Latin America in the face of European literatures. Basically, it meant that writers had to adhere to a continentalist narrative that would justify the advances of civilization in the wilderness of the Americas. To document via a specific repertoire of images played into the European settler imaginaries of the continent. To write the autochthonous is to produce an image of nature to be consumed and exported globally. As capitalism makes its way into the potential resources of the continent, so do the dominant representations of nature accompany this endeavour. In *La vorágine*, for example, the regions of Casanare and the Colombian Amazon are important landscapes, much in the same way that the plains of Apure are central to *Doña Bárbara*. Jennifer French explains that *La vorágine* 'verbalizes the spatial configuration of the land';[40] that is, it expresses textually the contours of the land. The narrative sequence of the novel spatially follows the Río Negro meandering into the Amazon rainforest. The cartography of the rivers reflects the capitalist network of rubber exploitation taking place.[41] Alonso also cites the 'mimetic quality' that Gallegos professes of his writing in *Doña Bárbara*.[42] The novel carefully considers the geography of Venezuela in its narrative. At its core, it is a book about landowners struggling to establish limits on their properties, quite literally drawing property lines on maps. Each narrative reflects the capitalist world ecology that is gradually taking place in the Orinoco Llanos.

In his ecocritical reading of *La vorágine*, Germán Bula suggests that the Llanos are a relevant topography that merits scrutiny.[43] Bula primarily concentrates on the category of 'biophilia' in the novel, without considering the significance of predatory encounters in touching on the theme of the plains and rainforest as a dangerous wilderness.[44] The novel does present the non-human as an agent that binds the fates of all the characters, yet nature is not presented as harmonious. The very title of the book evokes the antagonistic presentation of nature as a 'vortex' that swallows human lives. On the one hand, it exploits nature as threatening, while also portraying the precarious relations enacted through predation. A similar theme is present in *Doña Bárbara*. When Santos Luzardo enters the Orinoco plains, sighting the haunting eyes of crocodiles in the river at sundown, he is thrown into a predatory loop that ambiguously situates him in a shifting role between predator and prey: 'Hundreds of black points bristled on the wide surface: the snouts of many caimans and crocodiles that breathed on the water's surface, unmoving, lulled by the lukewarm caress of the dark waves.'[45] Encountering the gaze of numerous crocodiles, he is unsure whether he is the hunter or hunted, quickly deciding to reach out for his rifle. He is at once threatened by the non-human and also entangled in the food chain of Llanos. The fact that Santo Luzardo intends to use the firearm testifies to the threat he perceives from the reptilian predators. He is no longer outside the reach of predators, being himself a predator ready to strike. The dividing line between him and the wild animals is blurred. During this moment of uncertainty – this twisting and reversing of the predatory relations – the precarious relation between animals in nature, one that can too easily break down, is manifested. Similarly, at the beginning of Arturo Cova's flight from the city in *La vorágine*, he is surprised by an aquatic snake that is actually hunting him; he is visibly shaken by the sudden awareness of becoming part of the predatory cycles in Casanare:

> Partiendo una rama, me incliné para barrer con ella las vegetaciones acuátiles, pero don Rafo me detuvo, rápido como el grito de Alicia. Había emergido

bostezando para atraparme una serpiente 'güío', corpulenta como una viga, que a mis tiros de revólver se hundió removiendo el pantano y rebasándolo en las orillas [. . .] Con espanto no menor comprendí lo que le pasaba, y, sin saber cómo, abrazando a la futura madre, lloré todas mis desventuras.[46]

[Breaking off a branch, I leaned over to sweep the vegetation aside, but Don Rafo seized me, quick as the startled cry of Alicia. A gigantic boa, thick as a two-foot beam, had emerged, mouth yawning. It sank as I fired at it with my revolver, stirring the swamp violently, pulsing the water so the waves overflowed the swamp margins [. . .] With anxiety as great as hers I realised what was the matter; and scarcely aware of what I was doing, I embraced the future mother and wept.]

Unaware of the predator lying in wait in the swamp waters, Cova brushes a few branches away before coming face to face with a boa ready to strike. The encounter is so quick that he hardly has time to realize that he was prey to the boa.

In their journeys to the Orinoco plains, both male protagonists (Arturo Cova and Santos Luzardo) find themselves in a predatory cycle that challenges their urban lifestyles by making them aware that human exceptionalism is an illusion quickly dissolved by predators. In other words, predation obliges them to become aware of their precarious interconnectedness with flora and fauna in the Orinoquía region. Relations with other organisms are dynamic and external. Encountering predators that consider humans as prey portrays the shifting relations between beings in a biological system. Whereas Luzardo and Cova come from an urban context in which relations are stable insofar as civility requires it, their travels to the Llanos place them in an environment where the predatory ecology is constantly adjusting to disturbances. Survival depends on it.

La vorágine and *Doña Bárbara* raise important questions as to what can occur when different species meet. Challenging the seeming superiority of humans, predation unravels the discrimination of the animal other. Those moments in which human characters gaze into the eyes of predatory or feral animals, feeling suddenly threatened, reveal the speciesist assumptions in such a dichotomy, a polarity that is recurrent in the literatures of the plains. After Cova witnesses the dismemberment of one of the cattle ranchers by a feral bull, he wants to escape what he perceives as the nightmarish and savage plains, expressing that it was necessary 'to return to civilised lands'.[47] The bull will simply not be subdued by humans and actually kills one of them, to the horror of Cova:

Aunque el asco me fruncía la piel, rendí mis pupilas sobre el despojo. Atravesado en la montura, con el vientre al sol, iba el cuerpo decapitado, entreabriendo las yerbas con los dedos rígidos, como para agarrarlas por última vez. Tintineando en los calcañales desnudos pendían espuelas que nadie se acordó de quitar, y del lado opuesto, entre el paréntesis de los brazos, destilaba aguasangre el muñón del cuello, rico de nerviosos amarillosos, como raicillas recién arrancadas. La bóveda del cráneo y la mandíbula que la sigue faltaban allí, y solamente el maxilar inferior reía ladeado, como burlándose de nosotros. Y esa risa sin rostro y sin alma, sin labios que la corrigieran, sin ojos que la humanizaran, me pareció vengativa, torturadora, y aún al través de los días que corren me repite su mueca desde ultratumba y me estremece de pavor.[48]

[Although disgust made my flesh creep, I could not avert my eyes from the remains. Thrown across the saddle, belly up, was the decapitated body, rigid fingers trailing the tall grass, as if to grasp it for the last time. Tinkling on the naked heels hung the spurs which no one had thought of removing; and on the other side, in the space between hanging arms, the stump of the neck, rich with yellow nerves like roots freshly plucked from the soil, dripped watery blood. The base of the skull and the jaw that projects from it were missing; only the lower jaw was there, twisted to one side, grinning hideously as if in sport of us. And that faceless, soulless smirk, with no lips to alter it, no eyes to humanise it, seemed to me vengeful, torturing; and even after these many days, that grimace comes to me from beyond the tomb and chills my blood with fear.]

The haunting scene dwells on the mauled corpse of the rancher. Cova experiences both disgust and fear as he comes to grips with the fatal violence that the bull exerted on the body. Parts of the body are missing, making the corpse look non-human. Cova confesses looking at the 'remains', but not a human body. The decapitated neck looks like 'roots freshly plucked from the soil', while the hanging lower jaw has 'no eyes to humanise it'. Looking at the torn corpse, Cova experiences first-hand the encounter with the non-human other. Fear overwhelms him as he realizes that death is a moment away in the plains of Casanare. He is not just afraid of the hideous cadaver, but of the capacity for violence that the bull was capable. Although it is not an act of predation, the attack of the feral bull makes manifest the precarious relations between different organisms in the Llanos. Cova's gradual awareness of his vulnerable situation as yet another being in the region, fighting to stay alive among humans and non-humans, is precipitated by encounters with animals throughout the narrative. Although he never completely lets go of his privileged situation, the predatory encounters serve as a challenge to his anthropocentric view of the world. First was the impending strike of the boa and then the death of the rancher by the bull. It is through these events that he becomes conscious of the blurring boundaries between the human and non-human. What at first was a living rancher becomes a hideous corpse that is more akin to 'roots' and 'remains'.

The ferality of the bull complicates the twisting predatory ecology. According to Garrard, ferality is 'the condition of existing in between domestication and wildness'.[49] Feral animals inhabit an ambivalent role insofar they are neither completely wild nor domesticated. Ranchers in *La vorágine* and *Doña Bárbara* are involved in domesticating enterprises, whether it is the branding and herding of cattle or the breaking of horses. Ferality manifests the imposition of human superiority as it subdues animals to human interests. Those encounters with feral animals partly break down the 'troublesome dichotomy' between wild and domestic animals that Barney Nelson identifies in *The Wild and the Domestic*.[50] It is 'troublesome' because the wild-domestic binary reflects the overall nonhuman-human dichotomy. Wild animals are often seen as a threat to be kept at a distance from civilized life.

The encounter with a domestic animal that suddenly becomes 'wild' questions the validity of the wild-domestic binary. As the feral bull tramples the human cadaver in its rage, Cova no longer identifies it as a bull, but rather as a 'creature' and a 'beast' that poses serious threats to himself and his fellow ranchers.[51] As a feral 'creature', it is no longer part of the cattle that they have been herding, but a 'beast' that challenges human dominion over animals in the plains. Similarly, as Santos Luzardo watches the herding of feral cattle in the Apure plains, he envisions the scene as part of a larger scheme in the dichotomy between civilization and barbarism: 'His nerves, which had forgotten this wild emotion, tensed once more with it, vibrating in accord with the thrill of courage with which men and beasts shook the plain, and the plain seemed to him wider, more imposing and beautiful than ever, because within its dilated limits man made progress in dominating the beast.'[52] Domesticating feral animals plays a significant role in the plans for civilizing the plains. To domesticate is to civilize. To domesticate feral animals is to control them, to guide their 'wild' tendencies towards the benefit of society. That is why ferality questions human exceptionalism and the 'Great Divide' between humans and animals. Feral animals have become wild, have escaped the limits of civilization.

Ferality challenges anthropocentrism, for it confuses the evolutionary narrative from a wild state to a civilized state. The 'civilizing' enterprise of ranchers in both *La vorágine* and *Doña Bárbara* is the domesticating of feral cattle, to bring them back in control as the property of landowners. This domestication is part of the settler narrative of the plains throughout the Americas, which is to turn the seeming barren grasslands into a productive garden on which to sustain progress and industry. Ferality is a point of resistance to such an enterprise, signalling the interstices of continentalist narratives. Cova's immediate reaction to the mauling of the rancher is to return to the city, the bastion of civilization. He is filled with dread at the subversion of the logic of civilization that so easily breaks down in the Casanare plains. For many, the emergence of cattle herding in the surrounding areas of the Orinoco basin during the twentieth century was a display of the powers of capitalism under the guise of 'civilization' spreading to the plains. As Luzardo envisions his role in the Apure grasslands, the ranchers' herding seems a testimony to how 'man made progress in dominating beast'. Ferality in both novels challenges the separation between the human and non-human, setting the stage for the predatory ecologies in which the protagonists inevitably find themselves in.

Human and non-human predation in the Llanos

In the final chapters of *Doña Bárbara*, Santos Luzardo also falls prey to the 'beastly law of barbarism'.[53] He resorts to violence immediately after a tragic encounter between the rancher Remigio's grandson and a tiger of the plains.[54] The death of Remigio's grandson at the hands of the jaguar is yet another predatory event that questions the primacy of humans, triggering the violent outburst of Luzardo as he takes off to confront the Mondragones and Doña Bárbara who reside in the ranch named *El Miedo*. The name of her ranch invokes the trope of the plains as dangerous in the face of progress and industry. Luzardo experiences this threat personally, seeing himself as the standard bearer of civilization. The savagery that Doña Bárbara represents is a source of fear, just as the Orinoco crocodile is feared by cattle ranchers throughout the region. As Luzardo leaves for the ranch *El Miedo*, he exclaims to his associate that 'the offence pushes me to violence and [. . .] I accept that path'.[55] His plan to lawfully civilize the plains dissipates as he is willing to hunt down the criminals and kill them with his own hands, if necessary. It is the death of the child at the hands of the jaguar that precipitates Luzardo to become a predator himself. The attack on the child makes him fully aware of the predatory ecology that cannot be avoided in the Apure plains. Up until this point in the novel, he has attempted to resist participating in the predatory ecology, attempting to establish law and order through dialogue. Yet it is an act of predation upon a defenceless child that pushes him to become a predator himself, hunting the Mondragón brothers down. The boundaries between civilization and barbarism, culture and nature, and human and animal are blurred by these predatory events that undermine human domination.

Such predatory and feral encounters enact 'acts of symbiogenesis' that 'do not produce harmonious wholes' but rather put into place the 'ingestion and subsequent indigestion among messmates, when everyone is on the menu'.[56] All species share the same mess hall in the land. No matter how much humans might attempt to single themselves out from nature, they are embedded and enmeshed: the act of predation foregrounds their inevitable place in the world. Predatory ecologies emphasize that those messy and precarious relations are an important part of human and non-human relations. The network of relations within the food web is never fixed but is constantly shifting to adjust to disruptions. When a new species, as is the case with humans in the Orinoco basin, is introduced, there are shifts in the relations between organisms. Predation is central to ecology insofar as it manifests these relations between animals in the food web. In other words, predation affects the energy flow within a biological system. According to Alison N. P. Stevens, predatory interactions are crucial 'to maintaining the diversity of organisms that make up an ecological community'.[57]

La vorágine is in many ways a novel of the 'ingestion and subsequent indigestion' that occurs in nature, as the jungle itself 'devours' them all at the end.[58] Arturo Cova is trapped in a vortex that slowly ingests his sanity as he travels ever deeper into the jungle. A variety of predators make appearances throughout the book, such as the 'caribes' or piranhas that are a threat to swimming in the waters.[59] The piranha is one of the most widely known fish of the Amazon basin, mostly because of its occasional carnivorous diet. Another interesting carnivore of the Orinoco region is the 'mapanare snake' or *Bothrops atrox* that bites its own tail.[60] This pit viper is extremely venomous and is capable of mimicking its environment extremely well. The 'cachirre' caimans or *Caiman sclerops* also populate the waters of the Casanare plains in the novel: 'The lagoon of yellow waters lay almost unseen beneath a mantle of fallen leaves. Between them swam small turtles called "galapagos," peering above water with their reddish heads; and here and there the small caimans named "cachirres" floated through the scum with lidless eyes.'[61] Smaller than the Orinoco crocodile, these caimans feed mostly on fish. And finally, the panther is also cited as a predator in the Llanos: 'And once again we went away through the dark desert, where panthers were beginning to growl.'[62] It is during the night – when humans cannot see clearly – that the panthers growl in the distance. Again, these predators evoke fear in the ranchers, as a threat that they cannot entirely anticipate. Wild predators seem like an ever-present menace, hidden in the shadows of the wilderness. The predatory encounters of the novels display the suddenness of the attacks. Most of these predators occur in waterways, making these liminal sites as the primary scenarios of predation. Thinking through predatory ecologies makes manifest the fact that these challenge dualisms by taking place at the very borders of continental geographies, where the grasslands transform into forests. In contrast, the open plains are the backdrop of feral encounters with animals.

A pertinent aspect in the representation of predators in *La vorágine* is the glossary that Rivera includes at the end of the third edition published in 1926, a glossary that is later extended in the fifth edition of 1928. A careful perusal of the glossary indeed reveals that the definitions are rudimentary and brief. For example, the 'Conga' is defined as 'poisonous ant' and the 'Caribe' is a 'certain voracious fish'.[63] However, it is important to note that much of the vocabulary introduced corresponds to some of the flora and fauna of the plains and jungle in Colombia.[64] The list of regional names for animals and plants has a documentary effect, even if the definitions undermine its appearance as authentic record of the linguistic and zoological abundance of the different geographies of Colombia. That is, there is no sustained effort to collect the local knowledges of flora and fauna. Instead, the pseudo-regionalistic glossary ultimately effaces those regional aspects that it surreptitiously performs. The use of glossaries in canonical regional novels is recurrent and effectively counters the possibility of local knowledge by anticipating its very existence with an artificial vocabulary.

We have seen some of the numerous predators that appear in the first section of *La vorágine* that corresponds to the Casanare plains, yet perhaps the single most significant predatory scene takes place at the very beginning of the novel, when Arturo Cova encounters an enormous snake with its wide mouth about to strike him, an event that foreshadows the gradual ingestion of humans by nature: 'With its mouth yawning, a gigantic boa, thick as a wooden beam, had emerged. It sank as I fired at it with my revolver, stirring the swamp violently, pulsing the water so the waves overflowed the swamp margins.'[65] Arturo Cova disturbs the waters of the swamp, wanting to clear the flora, completely unaware of the precarious situation in which he is placing himself. When he breaks the branch to 'sweep' away plants on the water's surface, Arturo Cova is placing himself separate from the rest of his environment. Considering himself outside the predatory loop, he disturbs the vegetation as if he has nothing to worry about. He is quickly shaken out of the illusion of safety by don Rafa and Alicia's scream. The construction of the second sentence builds on the stark contrast with the preceding one. If Cova was the subject of the previous sentence, the second sentences opens quite literally with the 'yawning' mouth of a boa in the water. The sentence begins with the verb construction 'With its mouth yawning' which is ambiguous as to who is the subject of the sentence, whether a human literally yawning or the ominous snake. The inverted syntax also traces the predatory event whereby Cova becomes first aware of the action, prior to realizing that it is a boa. As an urbanite, he is not acquainted with encountering snakes in the wild. It heightens the surprise of having a predator emerging from the waters. For a brief instant, the predatory ecology irrupts in the scene. Cova is now the prey, violently forced to reconsider his place in that environment. In fact, he is not in control of the situation. Interestingly, he compares the aquatic snake to a wooden beam, an inorganic thing that testifies to Arturo Cova's binary approach to the natural world. The snake is the other to his presence, which forces him to react by using his revolver. The suddenness of the event is all the more striking. In one sentence, the predator appears face to face with the protagonist – who is also a predator – and dips beneath the water leaving behind only a 'stirring' and 'overflowing' of water in the river banks. After the encounter and seeing Alicia visibly shaken, Arturo Cova breaks down and cries over everything that has happened since he left the city.[66] It is this predatory event that makes him aware of his precarious situation in the Llanos.

In his edition of *La vorágine*, Ordóñez suggests the name 'serpiente güío' is used to refer to the common boa, whose scientific name is *Boa constrictor*, yet it is unclear whether Eustasio Rivera was referring to the larger species known as the 'black boa' or anaconda that inhabits the Orinoco alongside the Orinoco crocodile.[67] Whereas the common boa is primarily found on land and tree branches, where it can easily hide from other predators; the glossary that Rivera provides at the end of his novel describes the 'boa' as an 'enormous aquatic snake'.[68] The anaconda seems to better fit that description, since it is found mostly in waterways where it can move silently through the waters. I would argue that the author is actually referring to the anaconda, a fearsome and salient predator of the Orinoco region that makes the scene all the more ominous. Precisely, the appearance of this emblematic carnivore highlights the predatory ecology of the novel. Nature is not subdued or dominated but remains 'dynamic and vulnerable'.[69] The scene leaves the reader with a sensation of vulnerability to what lies beneath the waters. The protagonist is thrown into the vortex of the predatory loop in the novel from this very first encounter.

Before finally entering the Colombian jungle, Arturo Cova witnesses another violent encounter with nature which he identifies as predatory. Before the end of the first section of *La vorágine*, Arturo Cova sees a great fire consume the plains, first identifying it with a 'mapanare snake' and later suggesting that it is quite literally 'devouring' the flora and fauna it finds in its path: 'The devouring vanguard spread, leaving burning fires in the blackened plains with the scorched bodies of animals.'[70] His depiction of the event manifests his awareness of the twisting predatory loops that interconnect humans and non-humans, organic and inorganic constituents of the Llanos. Zoomorphism shapes his understanding of the vortex into which he is gradually being ingested. In broad terms, the entire narrative tells of Cova's gradual loss of reason as he travels ever deeper into the Amazon jungle. This journey in which he becomes mentally and physically lost in the environment is precisely the vortex that titles the book. Zoomorphism is thus one of the manifestations of that gradually blurring of the limits between what distinguishes Cova from the non-human other. The forest fire is a predator, one capable of consuming all organic life, including humans. Arturo Cova's awareness of the predatory ecology in his environment further pushes him to lose his sanity founded on urban rationality, so much so that after the fire of the plains, he cackles like 'Satan'.[71] Feeling himself part of the predatory cycle of the Llanos, he identifies himself with what he sees as the demonizing forces of nature. It is important to note that the negativity he projects over nature is the reversal of his relationship with the non-human. Questioning Arturo Cova's human superiority, the predatory ecology of *La vorágine* challenges the dichotomies between humans and animals, especially given the seeming mental instability of the protagonist that struggles to insert himself in the precarious relations of all flora and fauna in the Llanos.

The Apure plains in Gallegos's book are also shaped by ingestions and indigestions, principally in the form of Doña Bárbara who is described as the 'devourer of men', but also in several other important predators such as the one-eyed crocodile of *Bramador* or the large aquatic snake – most likely an anaconda, given its description – that pulls an entire cow into the river towards the end of the novel. Other predators include the carnivorous piranhas and the electric eel: 'There are many dangers to be avoided, and if the Little Old Father isn't in the boat, no riverman feels safe. The caimans are watching for you without making a ripple, and the electric eel and the ray are waiting, and the flock of buzzards and the school of caribs is there, ready to strip your bones.'[72] All the animals named in the passage are referred to as 'dangers', indicating the perceived threat by the captain. It displays the fear of the wilderness that crystallizes in an exaggerated view of the number of predators surrounding them. Although the electric eel and the ray are predators, they would not prey on humans. As a relatively new species, humans seem overwhelmed by the potential predators, unaware and fearful of their place in the food web.

The *yacabó* or screech owl also plays an important role as a predator whose screech announces the arrival of death: 'Suddenly the song of the screech owl reached their ears, a knell to strike icy fear to the traveller's heart in the desolate silence of the savage twilight.'[73] The suddenness of the screech owl's nocturnal attacks on smaller prey is seen as ominous and foreboding. Predation instils fear in humans because to those unacquainted with a given predatory ecology, the attacks of hunting predators cannot be anticipated. Just as Cova's sudden realization that something is about to strike him from the water – before knowing exactly what it is – so does predation often evoke the non-human other hiding in the foliage before lashing out. In the 'silence of the savage twilight', a wild predator is awaiting to strike a passer-by.

Yet another predator that accompanies Míster Danger is the 'cunaguara' or ocelot (*Leopardus pardalis*):

> Un día, como diese muerte a una cunaguara recién parida, se apoderó de los cachorros y logró criar y domesticar uno, con el cual retozaba, ejercitando su perenne buen humor de niño grande y brutal. Ya el cunaguaro lo había acariciado con algunos zarpazos; pero él se divertía mucho mostrando las cicatrizes y éstas le dieron tanto prestigio como las gacetillas.[74]
>
> [One day, after he had killed a female ocelot which had recently borne cubs, he took the little ones and succeeded in rearing and taming one of them. He played and frolicked with this one, exercising the humour of the great brutal boy that he was. The cub had given him many a scratch already, but he enjoyed showing the scars, and these added to his prestige as much as the clippings.]

This last predator reverses ferality insofar as it is a wild animal that is not quite as domesticated as Míster Danger expects, for he already suffered claw marks from his ocelot. Humans and animals found in the Apure plains are predators, hunting each other in a constant struggle. The narrative is constructed on the predatory tensions that abound, whether it be through animal encounters or in humans savagely preying on each other. Even the central conflict between landowners on the setting of limits to their lands is a manifestation of that same predatory ecology, one in which the land and its inhabitants are preyed upon.

Doña Bárbara is a book shaped by predation in its many forms. Alonso coins an interesting notion, that of a 'zero-degree of nature' in which the land resonates a violence that serves as a means to measure 'human activity' in the narrative.[75] This suggests the role of nature as a baseline from which all other events in the narrative take place. Landscape is the 'protagonist' of the novel.[76] Many of the predatory events are set in a 'zero-degree of nature' insofar as humans and animals encounter each other face to face, obliged to cross gazes without knowing who is the prey and who is the predator. Similar to the way feedback loops function, the introduction of a new organism triggers reactions from the entire system. Humans enter a situation in which other organisms have to respond, whether it be preying on them or resisting them. The crocodile of Bramador is an alpha predator who must react to the presence of cattle and humans in the region, much the same way humans and cattle must respond to the threat of a predator. It is an ambivalent relation, one that could go either way, since the biological system in which humans, cattle and crocodiles are inserted is still adjusting to the new set of circumstances. The predatory ecology of the novel establishes a 'zero-degree of nature' in which both animals and humans react to each other's presence. Similar to the first predatory scene of *La vorágine*, the encounter of Santos Luzardo with 'el tuerto del Bramador' as he begins his journey to the plains is a significant challenge to human exceptionalism:

> Luego comenzó a asomar en el centro del río la cresta de un caimán enorme. Se aboyó por completo, abrió lentamente los párpados escamosos.
> Santos Luzardo empuñó el rifle y se puso de pie, dispuesto a reparar el yerro de su puntería momentos antes, pero el patrón intervino:
> – No lo tire.
> – ¿Por qué, patrón?
> – Porque... Porque otro de ellos nos lo puede cobrar, si usted acierta a pegarle, o él mismo si lo pela. Ése es el tuerto del *Bramador*, al cual no le entran balas.[77]

[Then began to emerge in the centre of the river the crest of an enormous crocodile. He came completely afloat, slowly opening his scaly eyelids.
Santos Luzardo grabbed his rifle and stood up, eager to make up for his prior shot, but the *patrón* intervened:
'Don't shoot him.'
'Why, *patrón*?'
'Because... Because another one of them might make us pay for it, if you do hit him, or he himself might if you miss. That is the one-eyed of *Bramador*, impervious to bullets.']

The opening of the 'scaly eye-lids' triggers Santos Luzardo, who then attempts to fire a rifle shot at the crocodile, only to be told by the ship captain to stop. The reasoning the captain proposes is that to attack the crocodile will only enact the predatory cycle, whether it be the large crocodile itself or others surrounding the boat. It will trigger a feedback loop by which the surrounding predators will be disturbed. However, the captain of the ship also projects human emotions upon the crocodiles, as if Luzardo's shot would rile up the revenge of the other reptiles. By claiming that they 'might make us pay for it', the captain is anthropomorphizing the animals. Yet what is significant in the passage is that the captain – even from an anthropocentric perspective – is aware of the predatory ecology that shapes the Apure plains. Challenging an alpha predator entails a conflict much larger that the protagonist foresees. As a newcomer from the city, Santos Luzardo ignores the dangers of his environment. Interestingly, the captain uses the word 'pay for' in depicting the predatory relations with the crocodiles, using a language closer to that of a landowner negotiating the sale of property. There is an economy at play in the environment, one in which the struggle between organisms is part of the regulatory processes of the biological system. The energy that goes from one organism to the next shapes the food web. Whether the captain is trying to communicate the predatory ecology to the city dweller in terms he will understand or he is projecting a capitalistic image unto nature, the captain is making Santos Luzardo aware of the precarious interconnections that hold them all together, humans and crocodiles. There is always a threat of 'ingestion and subsequent indigestion' in the Apure plains. Moreover, this geography is not harmonious and free from struggle, for it is intersected with those places that enact a 'zero-degree of nature'.

The second encounter is far more threatening, for crocodile and humans face off in the waters of the river. The scene takes place on a Holy Thursday, when the ranchers spend the day fishing on the river banks and partaking in the tradition of 'cleaning' the rivers of crocodiles that often prey on cattle.[78] Culling crocodiles so as to reduce their threat to cattle – which are seen as property by the ranchers – manifests the precarious interconnectedness of humans, crocodiles and cattle in the Orinoco plains. Zoologist Castro Casal explains in his historic review of the hunt for the Orinoco crocodile that the emergence of cattle ranching in Colombia and Venezuela possibly increased human conflicts with the reptilian predator, especially during the twentieth century when its skin was commercially valued.[79] One of the largest predators of the Orinoco, the crocodile is crucial to the stability of the region's ecosystem. The balance between predators and prey is delicate, and whereas the culling of crocodiles need not be negative if the numbers of such a predator risk destabilizing the equilibrium of flora and fauna, their excessive hunting by humans has pushed the Orinoco crocodile almost to extinction. The scene narrates the excesses of human ranchers, and in hindsight serves to remind us of the precarious interconnections of all organisms within a specific region. That one of the largest predators in the Orinoco is almost extinct bears witness to how relations often break down, leading to the instability of life in ecosystems.

As ranchers partake in the culling of crocodiles, the 'tuerto del Bramador' suddenly appears in the waters:

> Era aquel caimán contra el cual Luzardo había intentado disparar en el sesteadero del palodeagua, el día de su llegada. Terror de los pasos del Arauca, de sus víctimas – gentes y reses – se había perdido la cuenta. Se le atribuían siglos de vida, y como siempre saliera ileso de los proyectiles, que rebotaban en su recio dorso, se había formado la leyenda de que no le entraban balas porque era un caimán encantado. Su apostadero habitual era la boca del caño *Bramador*, ahora en términos de *El Miedo*, pero desde allí dominaba el Arauca y sus afluentes, haciendo por ellos largas incursiones, de las cuales regresaba con la panza repleta a hacer su laboriosa digestión, dormitando al sol de las playas del *Bramador*.[80]
>
> [This was the crocodile Luzardo had tried to shoot in the resting grounds of the *palodeagua* tree, the day of his arrival. He was the terror throughout de Arauca fords, and the locals had lost track of his victims – people and cattle. Centuries of life were attributed to the crocodile, and since he was never injured by bullets, which bounced off his thick dorsal scales, legend had it that he was impervious to them because he was cursed. His habitual resting place was at the mouth of Bramador Creek, now at the edge of *El Miedo*, but from there he dominated the Arauca river and its tributaries, performing long raids through them and returning with a gorged belly to complete his digestion, basking in the sun at the banks of the creek.]

The passage describes at length the crocodilian animal, highlighting its predatory habits. Its ominous depiction, it is the 'Terror' of the Arauca river, so much so that countless 'victims' have fallen prey to its hunts. It is being personified as a criminal who 'raids' the riverways and escapes the shots of its enemies unscathed. It represents the law of the Llanos insofar as it is the incarnation of the 'armed ferocity'.[81] Its thick skin does not allow bullets to penetrate as it hunts on men and cattle throughout the region. Moreover, there is a superstitious element, referring to the supposed enchanted nature of the crocodilian. Castro Casal cites the believed 'curative and mystic' properties of the Orinoco crocodile in the region.[82] The scene seems to coincide with some of the common practices of ranchers in the Orinoco plains. For example, the use of the crocodile's teeth during Good Friday was believed to have medicinal values.[83] The mode of hunting the crocodile in the scene also reveals certain hunting practices deployed by ranchers. One mode of hunting was directly confronting the reptile in the water in pairs: while one person would grapple the ventral area of the crocodile with iron hooks, another would lasso the snout so as to pull it out of the water.[84] The dual attack on the one-eyed crocodile by María Nieves and *Pajarote* similarly depicts that hunting practice: they lie in wait in the river, hiding behind the vegetation as the crocodile surfaces.[85] Before the fatal encounter between humans and crocodilian, there is an exchange of gazes that fully enacts the predatory ecology of the novel: 'suddenly the saurian reptile turned its head and looked at that which was floating on the water's surface.'[86] Having exploited the fact that the crocodile only has one eye, they remained in its blind side, hidden from view. Yet the moment the *tuerto* of *Bramador* turns around to look with its good eye, human and animal face each other. In the meeting of gazes, the predatory loop is once again twisted, for the crocodile immediately becomes aware that it is now the prey, rather than the predator. Every organism has a predator, and the *tuerto* of *Bramador* senses the danger that two humans in the water pose.

A reflection of Doña Bárbara as a predator, the one-eyed crocodile ingests its preys and returns to the lands of her ranch. Both Doña Bárbara and the crocodile are alpha predators in the Apure plains. Whereas the *tuerto* is anthropomorphized as a terrorizing bandit, Doña Bárbara is zoomorphized as ferocious animal that hunts throughout the surrounding lands of the Apure plains. Both crocodile and woman prey upon the land, performing 'raids' into the lands of other ranchers. They are both ambivalent animals, always transitioning beyond the limits imposed by civilization. The crocodile lives on the very edges of *El Miedo*, raiding the vicinities only to return full-bellied. Doña Bárbara is also trespassing the limits of her property to steal cattle, returning to her ranch with newly branded cows. This negotiation of limits sets up the ambivalent predatory ecology of the novel insofar as it suggests that relations between beings are external and depend on the contingencies of each event. Animals and humans are connected by the actions they take, generating disturbances and reacting accordingly. The *tuerto* and Doña Bárbara trigger Santos Luzardo's incorporation into predatory cycle of Apure: 'and he took the path of the Llano so as to throw himself into the vortex.'[87] Interestingly, the way Doña Bárbara is zoomorphized throughout the novel reflects the escalating predatory ecology of the novel. As a young girl called 'Barbarita' and about to be raped by bandits, she is identified with the *gaván*.[88] The *gaván* or *Jabiru mycteria* is a large stork with a characteristic black head and a red ring around its neck. The *gaván* is an emblematic bird found throughout South America, but especially in the Pantanal wetlands where it is called the *tuiuiú*. The scene draws an analogy between the hunt for the Jabiru stork and Barbarita's falling in love for the first time. Just as the stork attempts to fly away but is ultimately brought down by its hunters, so is Barbarita's first love 'brutally smothered by the violence of men, hunters of pleasure'.[89] It is an act of rape that reverses Barbarita's life, inserting her in the predatory cycle of the plains. She was once prey to men, only to later become the 'devourer of men'. It is only then that she begins to be identified with a predatory bird – the hawk – through the movement of her eyebrows, marking her reversal in the cycle of predation.[90] Her strategies towards Santos Luzardo are also compared to the movements of a snake hunting its prey.[91] Yet it is her identification with the *tuerto* of Bramador that most clearly displays the constant shifts between anthropomorphism and zoomorphism that are the core of predation in the novel.

Gendered predators in the Llanos

Doña Bárbara's subsequent predatory zoomorphisms raise an important issue regarding the gendered representation of nature. The ambivalence of the predatory loop is closely tied with the negative portrayal of women in *La vorágine* and *Doña Bárbara*. It is important to note that, as Sharon Magnarelli argues, the depictions of nature and women are dependent on the unreliable projections of Cova and Santos Luzardo.[92] Nature is depicted through the eyes of male characters whose perspective is anything but reliable, seeing in the flora and fauna a threatening alterity they identify with the feminine.[93] The ominous reflection of women and nature reminds us of how the 'Great Divides' are rooted in a male-oriented distinction.[94] Breaking down those binaries is a response to patriarchy, for it undermines the asymmetry of those 'Others to Man'.[95] Cova – one of the most cited unreliable narrators in Latin American literature – dreams at one point that Alicia is walking through 'dismal plains' only to become a snake in his hands when he reaches for her (310).[96] Alicia's transformation into a predator in Cova's dream implies the binary between nature and culture, identifying women as predatory. She is not unlike the biblical Eve and the snake, corrupting Adam in the Garden of Eden. Women, animals and land become a dangerous alterity to Cova. In *Doña Bárbara*, Santos Luzardo is openly attempting to impose his plans of civilizing the plains. As a self-interested landowner, the Apure plains are a business venture in which to exercise his male dominance over the land. He struggles to civilize the land, to bring order to the Llanos. He wants to fence the land, expressing his intent in a masculine gesture by imposing 'the straight line of man inside the curved line of Nature'.[97] The portrayal of Santos Luzardo's plans is overtly referencing the rape of nature. Civilization is a masculine 'straight line' that must be 'inside' the 'curved line of

Nature'. His arrival on the plains is accompanied with the shriek of the *yacabó* owl, the same shriek that sounded during the rape of Barbarita at the hands of the bandits.[98] From the very beginning, Santos Luzardo considers his entire enterprise as struggle against nature, and the biggest obstacle to his plans of civilizing the plains is Doña Bárbara, who is 'creature and personification of the times'.[99] She is zoomorphized and personified into a 'creature'. On the one hand, she is a product of her times, created by the context that surrounds her. She cannot help but become what surrounds her. Yet she is a non-human, closer to the predators that abound in the plains. Yet she is also a 'personification of the times', embodying as a human the difficulties of civilization in that region. Her title also manifests her proximity to predators, for the 'ñ' sound of 'doña' mimics the sound of animal growls, claws and can hurt. This textual performance of animality is close to Aaron Moe's understanding of zoopoetics insofar as it 'pantomimes' through an 'attentiveness to animals'.[100] Gallegos, however, is establishing a pejorative zoomorphism of Doña Bárbara, a pantomime that negatively values her predatory savagery as a vestige of the plains. As ambivalent as the predatory loop that Santos Luzardo now finds himself in, so does Doña Bárbara incorporate those sudden reversals between human and animal.

Her portrayal as the 'Sphinx of the plains', a mythological monster – a hybrid of a woman, a lion and a bird – is one of the more striking zoomorphisms in the novel, intensifying her identification with predatory animals and the enigmatic ambivalence that the predatory ecology of the novel sustains. Even if Santos Luzardo 'perceives doña Bárbara as a totally evil being', there are numerous moments in which the narrative 'suggests she is not really as malevolent as she is believed to be'.[101] There is a particular episode in which Santos Luzardo himself is conflicted with Doña Bárbara's ambivalence during the rodeo:

> La voz de doña Bárbara, flauta del demonio andrógino que alentaba en ella, grave rumor de selva y agudo lamento de llanura, tenía un matiz singular, hechizo de los hombres que la oían; pero Santos Luzardo no se había quedado allí para deleitarse con ella. Cierto era que, por un momento, había experimentado la curiosidad, meramente intelectual, de asomarse sobre el abismo de aquella alma, de sondear el enigma de aquella mezcla de lo agradable y lo atroz, interesante, sin duda, como lo son todas las monstruosidades de la naturaleza; pero enseguida lo asaltó un subitáneo sentimiento de repulsión por la compañía de aquella mujer, no porque fuera su enemiga, sino por algo mucho más íntimo y profundo, que por el momento no pudo discernir.[102]
>
> [Doña Bárbara's voice, the instrument of the androgynous demon within her, was like the deep murmur of the jungle and the harsh lament of the plain, and

had a peculiar timbre, which was the enchantment of men that heard it; but Santos Luzardo had not remained there to entertain himself with her. It was true that, for a moment, he had experienced the merely intellectual curiosity of looking into the depths of her soul, of exploring the enigma of that mixture of the pleasing and terrible, interesting, without a doubt, like all monstrosities of nature; but immediately he was overcome by a sentiment of aversion towards the company of that woman, not because she was his enemy, but because of something far more intimate and profound, that in that moment he could not discern.]

Exchanging gazes as the ranchers' herd cattle, both Santos Luzardo and Doña Bárbara sustain a brief exchange of words that is not unlike a predatory event. Doña Bárbara is dressed so as to impress her prey, something Santos Luzardo quickly acknowledges.[103] Santos Luzardo perceives his predator as ambivalent. He describes her as having the voice of an 'androgynous demon', as if her gendered soul were both feminine and masculine. He finds that duality a threat. It does not follow the 'straight line of man'. It is unstable – as unstable as the predatory relations that occur in the Apure plains. Similar to the incursions of the one-eyed crocodile, so does Doña Bárbara 'raid' across genders. The geomorphism of her voice mimics the sounds of the jungle and plains. Moreover, the words used for both geographies are feminine. Whereas the narrative deploys the masculine term 'llanos', the feminine 'llanura' is linked to the predatory values associated with Doña Bárbara. Lorenzo Barquero suggests as much to Santos Luzardo when he exclaims, 'The plain! The cursed plain, devourer of men!'[104]

However much Santos Luzardo might feel an 'aversion' to Doña Bárbara, he also is attracted to her in a manner which he cannot explain. Like all 'monstrosities of nature' she is an interesting hybrid of beauty and terror. Doña Bárbara the monster – like the *tuerto* of *Bramador* – is a terrifying creature, yet one that attracts the attention of ranchers and men. Insofar as she is a non-human other, the attraction men have for her is a testimony of the 'love *of* country' displayed in *La vorágine* and *Doña Bárbara*.[105] As a predator, her gaze hypnotizes prey, pulls them into a role reversal. This 'paradoxical lesson' questions the 'apparently ideal man who controls barbarism'.[106] Predation challenges the patriarchal binary between male humans and non-human others, making male characters susceptible and fearful as they become aware that they are the prey of women and the fauna of the plains. It is Santos Luzardo's masculine 'opinion and the fantasies he weaves which to a greater or lesser extent create the female in this case'.[107] His gaze is based on the 'Great Divide' that makes any non-male human other a predating monster. The predatory ecology of the novel, however, challenges that distance between the male human and the other, for the former is forced to constantly encounter the hunting or feral animals. These encounters place male humans in ambivalent situations. Santos Luzardo refuses to remain with Doña Bárbara because he becomes aware of how vulnerable he is against that ambivalence. He does not know if he is the hunter or the hunted. The 'Sphinx of the plains' forces him to face that impasse. As the predator of the plains, Doña Bárbara instils ecophobia in men. Her gaze is inscrutable, just like the yawning mouth of the aquatic snake or scaly lids of the Orinoco crocodile. Predators in the Orinoquía region that appear in *La vorágine* and *Doña Bárbara* enact that uncanny reversal. The predatory loop irremediably twists the 'straight lines of man'.

In this chapter, I have focused on the underlying predatory ecology that emerges in specific episodes and in the appearance of numerous emblematic predators of the Orinoco plains, such as the Orinoco crocodile and the anaconda. The appearance of those specific animals suggests not only the importance of the role of predation as a trope to express human exceptionalism bound to continentalist narratives but also predatory ecologies that short-circuit the dominant binaries of such narratives in favour of implying the precarious interconnectedness between humans and animals. Rather than establishing harmonious relations between humans and non-humans, predation sets the stage for the possible disruption of the organic mesh that sustains the Casanare and Apure. We become aware of the dangers and excesses of predation. The culling of crocodiles in *Doña Bárbara* reminds us of the reason why the *Crocodylus intermedius* is an endangered species. The ecophobia that Arturo Cova experiences as he encounters the anaconda preying on him evokes a sense of respect for the role of predators in the environment. The gaze of predators *questions* human superiority, although it never entirely dissolves human dominance. Moreover, the identification of women as predators in both novels also points to the masculine basis for the dichotomies between humans and animals. It is the male protagonists that at first see themselves as outside the predatory loop, only to experience the terror of being hunted, of having their roles reversed as women and animals hunt them. The shifting predatory ecologies challenge the 'Great Divides' projected by the masculine gaze unto nature, for the ambivalent impasse that male characters face when confronted by their predators challenges human exceptionalism.

4

Naming the Pantanal wetlands

Perhaps one of the most idiosyncratic plains geographies in Latin America, the Pantanal wetlands is considered by geographers to be 'one of the largest wet and continuous extensions of the planet'.[1] It is found in the Brazilian state of Mato Grosso do Sul, bordering both Paraguay and Bolivia. Spreading over 150,000 square kilometres, its flood plains are fed by the tributaries of the Paraguay River. These wetlands oscillate between periods of heavy rain and drought. This cycle of precipitation fragments the wetlands into various swamps.[2] Although the biome has only a few endemic species, 'the density or abundance of the populations of species, especially in terms of the herpetofauna and bird fauna and mammals, constitutes in and of itself a spectacle that is far more accessible in the Pantanal than in any other Brazilian biome'.[3] Two of the most emblematic animals of Brazil are found in the region: the Pantanal jaguar, the largest feline in the Americas, and the *tuiuiú* or *Jabiru* stork, which displays its characteristic red collar.

Although the Pantanal holds a relatively minor place in the literary imaginaries of the plains in Brazil and Latin America, its significance has increased since the 1970s when it caught the attention of ecologists travelling through South America. Historian Abílio Leite de Barros explains how it was in those years that the Pantanal became an 'ecological sanctuary', although the *Pantaneiro* people had been living in that same region for centuries.[4] The most notable writer to generate an imaginary of the Pantanal wetlands is Manoel de Barros. During the 1970s, Barros's poetry began focusing on that specific region and finally earned national recognition.[5] Not only has the Pantanal become a literary topic, but it has also entered popular culture through the celebrated television series that aired in 1990. The theme song for the television series was composed by the folk songwriter Almir Sater, who went on to gain popularity with his *Pantaneiro* music. Tourists travel far and wide to visit the wetlands of Brazil in the hopes of seeing the rare *tuiuiú* bird, a phenomenon that attests to the significance of this biome in the ways people across the globe imagine the plains of Latin America.

The increasing visibility of the Pantanal wetlands in Brazilian and Latin American culture justifies a closer reading of their environmental significance. In the previous three chapters, I have concentrated on the Pampas, Altiplanos and the Llanos, all of which are salient in the literary canon. In this chapter, I will focus on the Pantanal as a literary geography that has been portrayed under the continentalist imaginaries mentioned and through a poetics of naming its flora that fractures the former. The Pantanal was recognized as a biome in Brazil long before the Pampas in Rio Grande do Sul. This should not come as a surprise, for whereas there is only one canonical text that engages directly with the Pampas in Brazil – Érico Veríssimo in *O tempo e o vento* – the Pantanal has received the attention of such important writers as João Guimarães Rosa and Manoel de Barros. The emergence of certain biomes in the literary images of canonical texts brings them into public focus. The imaginaries of the Pantanal are an important example.

I will focus exclusively on the Pantanal's literary representations in Brazil, exploring its descriptions in three relevant texts that allow a contrasting of the repetition of continentalist tropes to portray this biome against an alternative poetics of naming the non-human: *Terra natal* (1920) by Francisco Aquino Corrêa, 'Entremeio – Com o vaqueiro Mariano' by Guimarães Rosa and *Livro de pré-coisas* (1985) by Manoel de Barros. Although the three authors chosen are canonical, insofar as they form part of the distinguished intellectual elite, Guimarães Rosa is by far more well known than both Corrêa and Barros. The differences and similarities in the ways that each text represents the Pantanal will help map how these wetlands have shifted from seeing these plains as empty lands to a poetics of the minutiae.

The first text is the poetic work by the archbishop of Cuiabá at the beginning of the twentieth century, a long poem influenced by Euclides da Cunha's analysis of the Brazilian *Sertões*.[6] Francisco Aquino Corrêa (1885–1956), popularly known as Dom Aquino, holds a canonical place in the literary tradition of the state of Mato Grosso, for he was inducted to the Brazilian Academy of Letters. Not very well known at the national level, Dom Aquino is one of the first and most important writers in Mato Grosso. The second text is a relatively little-known short story by the celebrated author Guimarães Rosa, published in the newspaper *Correio da Manhã* in three parts between October 1947 and July 1948 and later published as a book in 1952 with publisher Edições Hipocampo. It was also included in the posthumous collection of short stories *Estas estórias* in 1969. Its narrative centres on a fictional meeting between the author and a cattle rancher from the Pantanal. The third text constitutes Barros's poetical account of the wetlands, explicitly stating in its subtitle that it is a 'Guide for a poetic excursion in the Pantanal'. Barros's poems are of particular interest because they are presented as a 'guide' of the region. It is a rare occasion when his poetry deploys the word 'Pantanal'. Such reticence to refer directly to the biome is linked to Barros's focus on the minutiae of landscape rather than on sweeping vistas, an aspect that I will examine at length in this chapter.

Naming, mutualism and ecological knowledge

An important issue present in the texts is the ecological knowledge that is constructed through naming of plants and creatures. This is an issue that is also recurrent in my overarching argument in this book that explores the connection of environmental imaginaries and ecological knowledge. The use of naming is an invaluable device that constructs the ecological knowledge of a given region or biome. So far, I have focused on the way certain texts offer broad depictions of the land that seemingly effaced the specificities of the land, describing the environment as a desert. In this chapter, I will argue that another possible epistemology of the plains is possible through the use of names to refer to places and creatures in the wetlands. The names used to refer to the constituents of the land are never neutral – never just a fact of grammar – but reveal a mode of knowing the world around us. By analysing the evolution of the environmental images of the Pantanal through the use of names, I bring to the foreground that dimension of language that is crucial in shaping our knowledge of the environment.

Whereas Guimarães Rosa and Barros introduce a plethora of bioregional references that ultimately challenge referentiality in language, Dom Aquino's depictions of the Pantanal in *Terra natal* are generic and abstract. We have already seen how such an abstract portrayal of the plains is central to the environmental images of the Pampas, for example. Both Guimarães Rosa and Barros offer an interesting alternative, one that is based on the poetic enumeration of different animals and plants found in the Pantanal. They saturate their texts with bioregional references. By 'bioregional references' I mean the constant mention of specific flora and fauna, as well as of the specific topography of the region, such as rivers or cities. For example, rather than using the generic word 'trees', a reference is made to a particular species of tree, such as the 'hawthorn'. Guimarães Rosa and Barros favour naming specific living species in their descriptions of the biome.

Malcolm McNee argues that Barros's poetry 'often features and names the richly varied plant and animal life of the region in their specificity'.[7] He also explains, however, that Barros's poetry names specific animals, 'Just as often, though, birds are generically identified just as birds, and trees are simply trees'.[8] There is a juxtaposition between the concrete and the abstract – between the local and the universal. This is also true of Guimarães Rosa, who incorporates regionalisms and universal themes in his narratives. One of the ways these two writers achieve such a juxtaposition is through the use of names, both specific and generic. Names can often reveal an abstract knowledge of the land, as well as a local and indigenous appreciation of the region. I am interested in foregrounding how the rhetoric of listing the living minutiae generates a local knowledge that embraces mutualism in the wetlands and challenges our Western notions of referentiality as a means to represent the world around us.

From an epistemological perspective, the language deployed by Guimarães Rosa and Barros also questions the possibility of nature as a closed whole to be accessed through panoramic vistas. They imagine the Pantanal wetlands as a collection of beings dependent on each other. Contrary to Dom Aquino's hermetic perspective of the Pantanal, one in which nature is presented as a sublime whole, Guimarães Rosa and Barros use a language that attempts to describe the wetlands without necessarily recurring to abstraction, precisely through the act of listing living beings. For example, Guimarães Rosa uses a language that captures the local knowledge of the Pantanal, using colloquialisms to name animals: 'With an electric lantern, I spilled over the grass a small path, avoiding the *jararaca-do-rabo-branco,* which they call here the *boca-de-sapo.*'[9] Rather than offer the scientific or common names for many of the animals described, he chooses local names that bring forth a language saturated with regionalisms. The moment the reader encounters such regionalisms, he or she is challenged to imagine a place that seems entirely foreign. The Pantanal becomes opaque, precisely because the language stresses local names over the common ones. It is hard to imagine a place that is filled with creatures whose names are not known and that cannot be found by looking them up in a dictionary or encyclopaedia. The references are so regional that they resist appropriation by the reader's imagination, which in turn leads to both a reflection of the role of language as mediator with the environment and our role as outsiders looking in. The environment described resists appropriation by the unacquainted reader's imagination. The reader becomes conscious of how language can become so localized that in its regional specificity it fails to elicit the geography described. The specificity of the language makes explicit that ambivalence between wanting to describe a thing by naming it in all its specificity and making clear how language can never completely stick to the thing described. It is also a means of establishing an authority in the knowledge of a given place.

Barros also experiments with the act of naming, testing the limits of words and the constraints of grammar, while also pushing the boundaries of figurative devices so as to generate in the reader a metalinguistic awareness. Both his poetry and prose draw attention to the connotative dimension of language, the strange meanings elicited through nouns and adjectivized nouns strung together in unexpected ways: 'That plant-like frog-like stone-like apathy' ('Essa abulia vegetal sapal pedral').[10] Here the reader struggles to make sense of these constructions, conscious of how language can make no sense and yet express something profound. One cannot take meaning for granted in his poetry. Barros obliges us to read and reread, to take a closer look at what at first glance seems nonsensical. Take, for example, the strange adjective 'sapal', which is formed from the noun 'sapo' or frog. Encountering this surprising adjective, the reader has to engage with the word at a metalinguistic level. Can the word 'frog' be used to describe apathy? What does it *really* mean?

In the preface to his poetic anthology, Barros claims that 'my verbal sketches signify nothing. Nothing. Yet if nothingness disappears, poetry ends.'[11] Ludic in its use of metaphors and similes, his poetry avoids panoramic images and stable conceptual descriptions. His language – especially his focus on naming living things – destabilizes meaning and questions the relationship between words and things. Rather than anchor on the large-scale vistas of wetlands, Barros surveys the sediments of the ground and foregrounds the minuscule organisms that crawl in its undergrowth. It is the infinitesimal scale of that which is strewn across the ground that acts as a lever to suspend the referential and denotative relation between language and the physical reality of Pantanal.

Although nature as a whole is not present in the portrayals of the wetlands in Guimarães Rosa and Barros, naming its flora and fauna assigns an ethical value to the constituents of the biome, emphasizing the abundance and mutualism of species. When reading 'Entremeio' or *Livro de pré-coisas*, we are presented with a plethora of names for the creatures and plants that are to be found within those flood plains. By naming organic and inorganic things, the narratives and poetry create an imaginary that very much resembles an ecosystem in its emphasis on the interrelations between living beings. Not only are animals and plants listed in drawn-out passages but also the relations that they share on land. Guimarães Rosa, for example, introduces the following passage to describe the biome:

> Sempre, enfeitando céu e várzea, o belo excesso de aves, como em nenhuma outra parte: se alinhavam as garças, em alvura consistindo; quero-queros subiam e desciam doce rampa curva; das moitas, socós levantavam as cabeças; anhumas avoavam, enfunadas, despetaladas; hieráticos tuiuiús pousavam sobre as pernas pretas; cruzavam-se anhingas, colheireiros, galinholas, biguás e baguaris, garças-morenas; e passavam casais de arara azul – quase encostadas, cracassando – ou da arara-brava, verde, de voo muito dobrado.[12]

> [Always, decorating the sky and the wetland, the beautiful excess of birds, like in no other place: herons would line up, according to height; *quero-queros* would go up and down a sweet curved ramp; from the bushes, *socós* would lift their heads; *anhumas* would fly, swollen, flustered; hieratic *tuiuiús* would land on their black legs; *anhingas, colheireiros, galinholas, biguás* and *baguaris*, and the *garças-morenas* would cross paths; and partners of *arara azul* would pass – almost leaning against each other, squawking – or the *arara-brava*, green, in a folded flight.]

A wide variety of birds are named in the passage – both using the common name and also their regional name, as is the case with the 'garça-morena' (commonly known as the 'little blue heron') or the 'arara-brava' (commonly known as the 'red-and-green macaw') – while the exchanges between fauna are present in the crossing paths of birds. In the passage, the different behaviours of birds are also described. The herons 'line up', while the 'arara azul' (commonly known as the 'hyacinth macaw') fly in pairs. The text is invested in the 'beautiful excess of birds', portraying the Pantanal as a living and breathing ecosystem of avifauna.

Barros also offers passages that accentuate the abundance of flora and fauna, as well as the dependency between the organic and inorganic constituents of the imagined geography:

> Penso num comércio de frisos e de asas, de sucos de sêmen e de pólen, de mudas de escamas, de pus e de sementes. Um comércio de cios e cantos virtuais; de gosma e de lêndeas; de cheiro de íncolas e de cabados orifícios de tênias implumes. Um comércio corcunda de armaus e de traças; de folhas recolhidas por formigas; de orelhas-de-pau ainda em larva. Comércio de hermafroditas de instintos adesivos. As veias rasgadas de um escuro besouro. O sapo rejeitando sua infame cauda. Um comércio de anéis de escorpiões e sementes de peixe.[13] (189)

> [I think of a commerce of edges and wings, of semen juices and of pollen, of shedding of scales, of pus and of seeds. A commerce of mating cycles and virtual songs; of muck and of nits; of a smell of the inhabitants, of dug orifices

of featherless hookworms. A hunchback commerce of *armaus* fish and *traças* insects; of leaves collected by ants; of larval *orelhas-de-pau*. Commerce of hermaphrodites with adhesive instincts. The torn veins of a *besouro* ('beetle'). A toad rejecting its vile tail. A commerce of scorpion rings and fish seeds.]

Here the act of naming is pushed to its limits. Instead of describing the landscape, Barros names the marginal creatures found in the muck of the Pantanal. He does not name flora and fauna as much as he references the anatomy of creatures: 'larvae', 'veins', 'semen', 'orifices' and 'pus' are among some of the words that appear in the passage. The poem challenges the viability of independent organisms in favour of an exchange of organic and inorganic substances that are the basis of the wetlands. Hardly any verbs are utilized, and instead prepositional phrases are deployed to further modify the core noun of the entire passage – the word 'commerce'. The term suggests a constant exchange between living beings. Both Guimarães Rosa and Barros create an environmental imaginary of the wetlands that lists the minutiae of the region, while also valuing the significance of mutualism. We can define ecological mutualism as the 'interactions between two species that benefit both of them'.[14] The environmental imaginaries of the Pantanal wetlands in these two authors are built on the mutualism between living beings. They offer a looking glass through which to see the wetlands not as immense landscapes but as the web of organic beings interacting with each other and their environment. I will now concentrate on tracing how the Pantanal has been imagined by the Dom Aquino, Guimarães Rosa and Barros, so as to present the evolution of the representations of the wetlands from the repetition of a settler imaginary of the plains in the first author to the poetics of mutualism found in the latter two writers. Not only can environmental imaginaries be dominant over other local knowledges, they can also shift over time. This means that those representations of the plains that are firmly set in a Eurocentric perspective can eventually change into other views that are more aware of the Indigenous and local knowledge of the environment, as is the case of the images of the Pantanal. The fact that these imaginaries do change suggests the crucial importance of incorporating other voices to enrich and shift colonial depictions of the land.

Settler ecology of the Pantanal in Dom Aquino

In his description of the Pantanal in *Terra natal*, Dom Aquino offers a wide vista of the wetlands. Born in Mato Grosso, he went on to become archbishop of Cuiabá and member of the Academia Brasileira das Letras, a prestigious position held by many important Brazilian writers such as Machado de Assis. His first book was published in two volumes in 1917 under the title *Odes*. Three years later he published *Terra natal* in which he closely depicts the landscape of Mato Grosso, referencing rivers and cities throughout the state. The structure of the book is similar to Euclides da Cunha's *Os sertões*, for it is divided into two parts: the first dedicated to the nature of the region and the second to the human component. Just as in the work of other regionalist writers, the synecdoche between land, language and inhabitants is also present in Dom Aquino. The text clearly enacts that organicity between the three in its panoramic description of the wetlands:

> Verde mar de gramíneas, mar parado,
> Que os corixos, qual serpe desconforme
> De cristal, vão cruzando, lado a lado,
> O imenso pantanal se estira e dorme.[15]
>
> [Green sea of grasses, unmoving sea,
> That the waterways, as a colossal serpent
> Made of glass, cross, from side to side,
> The immense pantanal stretches and sleeps.]

The wetlands are compared to an 'unmoving sea', a body of aqueous and unmoving grass. Such a comparison between prairies and sea is not uncommon in literatures of the plains, as we have seen in previous chapters. The metaphor of grasslands as a sea dates back to the first accounts by Spanish colonizers arriving at the Americas.[16] Unfamiliar with the singular terrain of the continental plains, colonizers drew from their experiences in their long journeys through the Atlantic to come to grips with what they were seeing. They imposed a specific mode of imagining the plains for lack of a language adequate, initiating a long history of effacing local knowledges in favour of the ocean metaphor, which Dom Aquino chooses to repeat in the quoted stanza. This settler imagery is central to his poetics of the Pantanal. Moreover, the metaphor exploits the horizontal perception of the plains, making them seem an empty surface. The land is 'immense', suggesting the role of scale in measuring the potential of the bioregion.

Given that names can often reveal the epistemology attached to a given representation of the world, it is worth noting that Dom Aquino does not capitalize the word 'pantanal'. He does not consider the place named as a proper noun, which suggests that the wetlands are not necessarily perceived as a unique region. It is a generic word to portray a land that is likened to a large swamp or 'pântano'. Again, the poet sees the bioregion before him as a vague swamp that he compares to an ocean of grasses, offering us an imaginary that is quite vague. The other notable comparison is that of the rivers to a 'serpent' that evokes the presence of aquatic predators as vague threats beneath the water surface. As such, the word avoids attaching any specificity to the landscape.

The title of the poem ('Pantanal', without a preceding article to suggest it is the traditional proper noun of the biome) sustains the lack of specificity that the wetlands have in Dom Aquino, as if they were empty lands upon which to enact the desires of settlers looking for a territory to colonize. Other poems in the book include specific references to cities and rivers in their titles: 'Rio Coxipó', 'Cuiabá', 'Poconé', 'Corumbá', 'Santana do Paranaíba', 'Nioaque' and 'Rio Madeira' are among some of the places named in the titles of his poems. Moreover, the capitalization of those places is maintained in the poems themselves. For example, in the poem titled 'Cuiabá', the capitalization is sustained: 'Oh! Cuiabá of Brazilian legends'.[17] Even more pertinent is the fact that one of the poems in the volume references the specific biome *cerrado* and is titled with the appropriate article, 'O Cerrado'.[18] A brief survey of the instances in which the terms 'pantanal' and 'pantanais' are used in the volume also points to their generic nature to describe a particular topography of the land. In the poem 'Poconé', Dom Aquino portrays the landscape by writing, 'On the grassy pink *canga* ground / Setting boundaries to the width of the green swamps, / The city is sketched in the distance, calm and graceful.'[19] The use of the plural form without capitalization indicates its generic reference to 'swamps'. In another poem titled 'Corumbá', the term appears once again without capitalization and in its singular form: 'Thus you were born, below the serene skies, / To the flower of the pretty and wild swamp'.[20] Hence it seems clear that Dom Aquino does not refer to a specific place when using the word 'pantanal'. The wetlands are not a concrete location in his poetry, for it is not a singular entity, but rather a terrain.

This generic aspect of the term 'pantanal' shapes its epistemology. Dom Aquino imagines the bioregion as a large swamp without any specific characteristics, not unlike the way settler ecologies often represent the plains throughout the Americas. It is not a concrete place or entity, but rather an abstract geography yet to be populated. Basically, the term he uses is a word constructed by incorporating the suffix -al to the noun 'pântano', so as to depict a large area of swamps. Although these considerations of the term are linguistic, they affect the representation of the wetlands. Insofar as this region is not considered a place in and of itself, it remains a given terrain with no agency or presence.

It is a marginal topography, an accident of the land that the poet mentions in passing. This effacing knowledge of the wetlands is further manifested in the images deployed in the poem:

> Pasta, em manadas plácidas, o gado.
> Lá foge um cervo. E, de onde em onde, enorme,
> Como velho navio abandonado,
> Uma árvore braceja a copa informe.[21]
>
> [Grazing, in placid herds, the cattle.
> There a deer flees. And, from time to time, enormous,
> As an old, abandoned vessel,
> A tree moves its arms its shapeless top.]

Here continues the sweeping depiction of the wetlands. Continuing the overall vagueness of the land described, the animals and plants are also non-specific. Dom Aquino sees 'cattle', 'deer' and a 'tree', elements that a settler would be acquainted with when arriving at these unique grasslands. It is almost as if the poem is validating the potential for cattle grazing in the wetlands, an agricultural activity that is quite extended in current-day Pantanal. The wetlands are a place where livestock can calmly graze on the oceans of grasses. Ultimately, we are offered a pastoral image of the wetlands. The comparison of the plains as a body of water is also repeated in this stanza. The tree is an 'abandoned vessel' that is paddling through the grasslands, as a settler arriving by boat. The depiction of a tree as a settler arriving is strikingly similar to the portrayal of the *ombú* tree in Martínez Estrada. Dom Aquino does not see the tree as a literal tree, but rather as a human artefact that crosses the horizontal portrayal of the Pantanal.[22] The horizon becomes the axis of the depiction, accentuating the emptiness of the wetlands as they calmly await colonizers with their domestic animals. Just as other writers of the plains throughout the Americas, Dom Aquino imagines the plains as an empty space that lends itself to its symbolic and literal colonization. This is particularly troubling given the Indigenous presence in the region prior to the arrival of the Spaniards and Portuguese. Dom Aquino's abstract depiction presents a vacant and Edenic landscape, a virgin land yet to be inhabited.

In the preface to *Terra natal*, Dom Aquino uses lofty language to describe nature found in that state: 'Contemplate its nature that still smiles at us, in that outbursts of virginal beauty so enchanting, that not even the most indifferent scientist can study, without letting himself get carried away.'[23] An alluring nature personified as a seductive virgin who coquettishly smiles at her observer. The environment is receptive to the masculine gaze, inciting Brazilians to populate its virgin territories and bask in its irresistible beauty. It is important to keep in mind that Dom Aquino sees himself as continuing in the vein of Euclides da Cunha and Visconde de Taunay. Both of them participated in military campaigns in Brazil, the former in Canudos and the latter in the war with Paraguay. Dom Aquino's exaltation of the 'virginal beauty' of Mato Grosso comes after the campaigns against Paraguay for control of the region between 1864 and 1870.[24] He further exclaims, 'Let us create a literature that nobly professes the beautiful maxim of one of our men of letters [. . .] literature that knows how to build the moral greatness of our homeland.'[25] The patriotic sentiment behind his poems informs the way Dom Aquino envisions nature as a place in which to install the homeland. Notice how nature is feminine and 'virginal'. Literature must express the 'noble' sentiments of 'our men of letters'. There is a clear gender binary in his view of nature, one that portrays the land as an untouched woman awaiting the embrace of the 'men of letters', such as Dom Aquino.

In his study of what he calls the 'new world pastoral', Lawrence Buell argues that 'the experience – by no means uniquely American, as we have seen, but common to other settler cultures – of the "empty" landscape' is 'arrestingly different from any old world counterpart'.[26] In Dom Aquino's poem that 'empty landscape' is idyllic and far detached from the threatening feel of the wilderness. Nothing in the land described is ominous, except for the fleeting mention of the 'serpent' in the first stanza. It is a vacant garden, a place of rest and respite for settlers, a place where masculine desire can find its reception in the feminine embrace of an empty land awaiting the taking. The poem seems far closer to the European pastoral tradition than that of the 'new world pastoral'. No ambivalence is offered. The wetlands invite the masculine gaze of settlers and manifest no threats:

> Não vibra um eco só de voz alguma:
> Ao longe, silencioso e desmedido,
> O bando das pernaltas lá se perde.
>
> Mas, de repente, em amplo vôo, a anhuma
> Enche do seu nostálgico gemido,
> A infinita solidão do plaino verde.[27]
>
> [Not an echo of any voice alone vibrates:
> In the distance, silent and without measure,
> A band of *pernaltas* is there lost from sight.

> But, all of a sudden, in a broad flight, a horned screamer
> Fills with its nostalgic cry,
> The infinite solitude of the green plain.]

Silence pervades; no 'voice' can be heard. The absence of any 'voice' also suggests that no humans inhabit this land. Only birds can be seen and heard. Tranquil yet nostalgic, the depiction of the wetlands resembles that of a European pastoral scene. The emphasis on sonority – on the reigning silence of the place and the sudden break in that silence that the 'horned screamer' creates – evokes a place of worship where the poet embraces his solitude. It is land lost in time, a place in which the sounds of birds are a 'nostalgic cry' that suggests the idylls of a long-forgotten past. As in previous stanzas, not much detail is given regarding the surroundings. It is a 'green plain' of silence and birds. The portrayal follows in the vein of the Edenic myths that shaped the first accounts of Brazil's landscape during colonial times.[28]

Humans and domestic animals in Guimarães Rosa

The next text to represent the Pantanal is written by Guimarães Rosa, an author that I already discussed in Chapter 2. A prolific writer of short stories, he penned a short story titled 'Entremeio – Com o vaqueiro Mariano' in 1947.[29] The story tells of the encounter between the narrator and a cattle herder in Nhecolândia region in the Pantanal.[30] Gradually, the narrator learnt about the day-to-day life in the ranch, especially concerning the handling of cows in the picturesque nature of the wetlands. Similar to other literatures of the plains, the presence of the cattle industry illustrates how the continentalist narratives are entangled in with the capitalist interest in turning the grasslands into agricultural territories. In this particular narrative, however, the view offered of cattle ranching is that of a local cowboy and his concrete knowledge of the land. There is a tension between the continentalist tropes and the local knowledge of the humble cowboy as he shows the ropes of handling cattle. Story frames this meeting between an outsider and a local, contrasting how each of them sees the ranch in Pantanal.

One of the ways in which the contrast between outsider and local knowledges is established is via the emphasis on naming the flora and fauna. This act of naming traces the local knowledge that the cowboy Mariano has of the wetlands, a knowledge that foregrounds the intimate link between humans and domestic animals, which in this case are the numerous cows of the ranch. According to Brazilian ecocritic Maria Esther Maciel, the story 'makes clear the author's fascination with the world of interactions and articulations between humans and animals'.[31] The Pantanal is presented through a myriad of interactions between ranchers, cattle and wild animals in the region. No less important to the mosaic of imaginaries of the plains, the knowledge of Mariano is important in offering a glimpse into how regional voices can and do fracture continentalist tropes of the plains, while also blurring the seeming division between humans and domesticated, non-human animals. We have already seen how ferality challenges such binaries, yet Guimarães Rosa's story challenges us to rethink how humans working closely with domesticated animals can also deconstruct the anthropocentric dualisms.

Perhaps the first question we must ask ourselves is the following: How does Guimarães Rosa differ from Dom Aquino in his depiction of the Pantanal? The answer lies in the oscillating images of the wetlands that Guimarães Rosa deploys. His narrative repeats some of the tropes of continentalist imaginaries, such as panoramic descriptions of a seemingly empty and flat landscape, while also bringing into relief the role of local knowledge in the explanations that the cowboy Mariano shares with the narrator of the story. For example, the cowboy explains why the narrator should not be afraid of puma attacks in the region. The predator simply does not inhabit that specific area, contrary to what the narrator thinks. Also, Mariano is keen on naming the animals that can be found in the surroundings, especially the avifauna. Whereas Dom Aquino's poetry offers abstract and generic references to birds, Guimarães Rosa introduces an extensive catalogue of birds in the third section of his short story, using several different common and local names. His 'Entremeio' manifests a tension with regionalist representations, juxtaposing panoramic descriptions of the Pantanal with specific references to those beings that inhabit the region. There is a conscious effort to construct universal themes not by effacing the particulars of the region, but by presenting the local as unique discourse.

Throughout the story, the narrator has the opportunity to spend time with the locals in order to learn more about the cattle trade first-hand. As an outsider, the narrator experiences the region with the help of Mariano, travelling on horseback through the Pantanal and seeing with his own eyes what the life of the ranchers is like. The narrator will interview the rancher about life in the Pantanal in three parts, discussing herding and the natural environment of the region. A close reading of the narrative reveals how the binary between universal and local is inverted as the narrative progresses. The voice of the urbanite narrator gradually gives way to the various explanations of the local cowboy, who gives his own account of the Pantanal. It is the narrator that often repeats settler tropes to describe the plains of the wetlands, whereas the local rancher is far more interested in naming the collection of animals and birds that populate the world of Nhecolândia.

The very first sentence of the story situates the reader in a very specific region, not just the Pantanal wetlands, but a specific place called Nhecolândia.[32] We are given specific details about the place and time of the interviews with the cowboy Mariano. The story takes place in July, in a region of the Pantanal known as Nhecolândia, a real place well known to locals. Unlike Dom Aquino's idyllic garden, the wetlands are referenced with specific names – that is, with 'Nhecolândia', 'Pantanal' and 'Mato Grosso'. The 'Pantanal' is, moreover, introduced as a region in its own right, maintaining its capitalization throughout the story. The story takes place in the Pantanal of Mato Grosso, not just any other swamp or wetland.

Several levels of narration operate, creating the sensation of an outsider's immersion in the local folklore. The conversation with Mariano gradually shifts from the narrator's interests to the latter's tales and adventures in the Pantanal. The first diegetic level is the narrator's, as he tells of his encounter with the rancher Mariano. The second diegetic level is the Mariano's recounting of his experiences as a herder in the region. As the story progresses, the second diegetic level becomes dominant. That is, Mariano's discourse becomes the axis of the narration, opening up an interstice in the narrator's continentalist discourse through which to introduce colloquialisms and specific knowledge of the region. The manner in which the two narrative levels interact during the conversation slowly blurs the lines between the narrator's reporting of what was said and Mariano's recounting in the present tense. The use of free indirect discourse bolsters the dichotomy between an outsider's knowledge (the narrator's) and a local's knowledge (Mariano). The outsider-insider knowledge binary is a manifestation of the tension between universal and local epistemologies that runs through the environmental images of the Pantanal in 'Entremeio':

> Tinha para crescer respeito, aquela lida jogada em sestre e avesso. Mas paciência, que é de boi, é do vaqueiro. E Mariano reagia, ao meu pasmo por trabalho tanto, com a divisa otimista do Pantanal:
>
> – Aqui, o gado é que cria a gente . . .
>
> E aguardava perguntas, pronto a levar-me à garupa, por campo e curral. Em tempo nenhum se gabava, nem punha acento de engrandecer-se. Eu quis saber suas horas sofridas em afã maior, e ele foi narrando, compassado, umas sobressequentes histórias.[33]

[He commanded respect, all that hard work handling cattle right and left. But patience, which belongs to the cattle, also belongs to the *vaqueiro*. And Mariano reacted, to my astonishment for such work, with the optimist maxim of the Pantanal:

– Here, it's the cattle that raises us . . .

And he waited for my questions, ready to take me on horseback, through field and corral. Never did he boast or make a point of exalting himself. I wanted to know all about his suffering hours, and he went on narrating, with rhythm, subsequent factual stories.]

The narrator's esteem for Mariano grows as he hears of the latter's feats. He seems seduced by the cowboy's directness and sincerity, describing the rancher's manners as commanding respect without the need to 'boast' or 'of exalting himself'. He wants to 'know all about his suffering hours'. In the narrator's speech, regionalisms seem to slip into his retelling. As an outsider listening to Mariano, such phrases as 'handling cattle right and left' and 'Here, it's the cattle that raises us' seem to derive from the local's knowledge of the place. This slippages in the narrator attest to the growing influence of Mariano in the telling of the story.

As Mariano begins recounting the day-to-day life of a *pantaneiro* rancher in the first part of 'Entremeio', horizontal and panoramic descriptions of landscape are introduced in the narrative, especially the herding of cattle. In a similar vein to other writers of the plains, Guimarães Rosa draws similarities between the land and a body of water: 'brought in groups and placed together in a single herd, round, in the middle of a flat country, oscillating and turning like waves from outside to inside and from centre to periphery'.[34] The image of flat fields in which groups of steers appear as waves lapping on the shores of the Pantanal is similar to descriptions of the Pampas by Sarmiento or the Llanos by Rómulo Gallegos. The local topography is blurred with the image of cattle moving as waves of water on land. Notice, however, the dynamic characteristic of the plains in the description. Undulating in concentric circles, the cattle in the open fields generate a hypnotic view of the land. We are not witnessing a tranquil garden, but a landscape of movement. Whereas Dom Aquino presents the metaphor of the sea as a static perspective of a seemingly vacant landscape, Guimarães Rosa's Pantanal is brimming with activity. This place is not one of pastoral respite, but rather of constant labour. This incessant activity foregrounds the mutual interactions between humans and animals in the wetlands. Ranchers and cattle are always on the move. At the end of the first part of 'Entremeio' the rancher Mariano confesses that 'The Pantanal does not sleep'.[35] Every day brings with it the struggle of ranchers as they depend on their cattle. There is a manifest mutualism between cattle and humans, one that is based on ranching as the mode of subsistence of the region.

The following passage reveals how the interconnections between beings affect the entire wetlands, as well as the wide extension of the region:

> O céu estava extenso. Longe, os carandás eram blocos mais pretos, de um só contorno. As estrelas rodeavam: estrelas grandes, próximas, desengastadas. Um cavalo relinchou, rasgado à distância, repetindo. Os grilos, mil, mil, se telegrafavam: que o Pantanal não dorme, que o Pantanal é enorme, que as estrelas vão chover.[36]
>
> [The sky was wide. Far in the distance, the *carandá* trees were blocks more black, of one sole contour. The stars were everywhere: big stars, nearby, worn. A horse whinnied, torn at a distance, repeating. The crickets, thousands, thousands, sent telegraphs to each other: that the Pantanal does not sleep, that the Pantanal is enormous, that the stars will rain.]

The panoramic perspective is characterized by its width: 'The sky was wide.' The wetlands are 'enormous', an attribute very similar to the oft-deployed 'immensity' of the plains in other writers. Focusing on the horizon and the sky, the reader is presented with a horizontal perspective, one that looks over all things in the land. Yet in the second sentence we encounter the name of a specific type of tree, the 'carandá'. Also referenced in the passage are a 'horse' and 'crickets', both of which are generic names. While the *carandá* tree is native to the region, horses and crickets are ubiquitous. The reference to that native species of tree anchors the depiction in the Pantanal wetlands – the *carandá* is a marker of place. The sound of the horse is reminiscent of the nostalgic cry of the *anhuma* in Dom Aquino. It is not Mariano that voices this panoramic description of the region, but rather the narrator, shifting the narrative back to how an outsider views the Pantanal. This accentuates the distinction between the narrator and Mariano, between the outsider's gaze and the local's accounts. The outsider's view is directed towards panoramic vistas, whereas Mariano prefers to describe in detail the comings and goings that take place in the region. Mariano retells of the incidents that occur in the lives of ranchers as they deal with herding cattle. 'Entremeio' constantly plays with these shifts between outsider/insider knowledge of the Pantanal, juxtaposing and embedding diegetic levels.

After the first day's interview with Mariano, the narrator decides to walk on his own to the rancher's cabin early in the morning. The manner in which he begins to describe his surroundings reveals his lack of knowledge of the region, foregrounding the outsider/insider dichotomy that is at play throughout the story:

> No trânsito de uma fantasmagoria de penitente, a ponte ia côncava, como um bico de babucha, ou convexa, qual dorso de foice, e não se acabava, que nem a escada matemática, horizontal, que sai de um mesmo lugar e a ele retorna, passando pelo infinito. E no infinito se acenderam, súbitos, uns pontos globosos, roxo-amarelos, furta-luz, fogo inchando do fundo, subindo bolhas soltas, espantosos. Parei, pensando na onça parda, no puma cor de veado, na suassurana concolor, que nunca mia. Mas os olhos de fósforo, dois a dois, cresciam em número. E distingui: os bezerros.[37]
>
> [In the passage of a penitent's phantasmagoria, the bridge was concave, like a pointy babouche, or convex, as the back of a sickle, and it did not end, like a mathematical horizontal stairway, that comes out of the same place and to that place it returns, passing through the infinite. And in that infinite they lit up, all of a sudden, some globular dots, iridescent, fire rising from the bottom, loose bubbles ascending, awe-inspiring. I stopped, thinking of the *onça parda*, of the *puma cor de veado*, of the concolor *suassurana*, that does not growl. But the phosphorescent eyes, two by two, grew in number. I made them out: the calves.]

As the narrator ventures into the ranch just before dawn, he begins to see the eyes of creatures he cannot identify in the dark, feeling forlorn in a strange landscape. Frightened by the sight of many pairs of eyes lighting up, his imagination conjures the threat of a puma. The tension in the passage relaxes the moment the narrator realizes that he is surrounded by calves – not bulls or steers, but merely young calves. Unacquainted with life in the Nhecolândia ranch, the narrator mistakes the tame eyes of calves for the feared *onça*. The reader is made aware of the gaps in the outsider's knowledge of the region. Confusing calves with a cougar is quite a slip in grasping the environment of the Pantanal.

An important aspect of the passage are the three names used to refer to a single animal, the cougar: 'onça parda' (literally brown panther), 'puma cor de veado' (literally deer-coloured puma) and 'suassurana concolor' (literally puma concolor). The cougar is a feline of the Puma genus that is widespread throughout the Americas. Its scientific name is *Puma concolor*, although these large cats are most often known by such names as puma, panther and mountain lion in North America. In Brazil, the cougar is often named 'onça-parda' or 'suçuarana'. Guimarães Rosa's spelling differs slightly from the now accepted 'suçuarana'. The terms 'parda', 'concolor' and 'cor de veado' that accompany the different names for the feline refer to its colouration. The Latin term 'concolor' suggests an even colouration of its fur, unlike other large felines such as the jaguar or the leopard.

The adjective 'parda' in Portuguese refers to its brown colour. Similarly the term 'cor de veado' also refers to the brown colour that it shares with deer (one of the cougar's primary preys). All three names refer to the same feline, the cougar.

Each of the names, however, refers to the cougar in a slightly different manner that merits scrutiny. The name 'suassurana concolor' is closest to the scientific name *Puma concolor*, whereas 'onça parda' highlights the similarities between the jaguar and the cougar. It is important to note that the jaguar is commonly named 'onça-pintada' in contrast with the 'onça-parda'. The name 'puma cor de veado' seems the most mundane and local portrayal of the physical attributes of the cougar. The repetition of different names that refer to the same feline reveals a keen awareness in the narrative for referentiality. Although they all name the same large cat, each name evokes a different association, whether scientific ('suassurana concolor'), comparative ('onça parda') or regional ('puma cor de veado').

A closer consideration of the narrator's reference to the cougar as his biggest fear is another reminder of his lack of knowledge of the local region. The alpha predator of the Neotropics which include the Pantanal wetlands is the jaguar.[38] Moreover, 'When the ranges of pumas and jaguars overlap, pumas are more abundant in drier areas and jaguars select wetter areas'.[39] The Pantanal subspecies is in fact the largest jaguar, known by its specific scientific name *Panther onca palustris*. This subspecies has suffered a significant loss of its habitat, a situation which has led to its coexistence with humans in large areas that continue to be converted to 'agriculture, cattle ranching and human settlements'.[40] Unlike the narrator, Mariano is well aware of the presence of both the puma and the jaguar in the region.[41] He will later comment on the encounters between jaguars and ranchers in the Pantanal: 'It is possible that we encounter a jaguar. There are many jaguars around here.'[42] His knowledge of the region allows him to assess the possible threats, while also bearing witness the encounters between humans and jaguars given the growth in cattle ranching in the wetlands.

Gradually, the narrative will incorporate a significant number of references to animals in the region, beginning with the nicknames of different steers and ending with an overwhelming catalogue of avifauna. Maciel explains, 'What can be picked up from Mariano's conversation is, in fact, a large knowledge not only of the bovine life in general, but also a knowledge of each and every animal that integrates the herding.'[43] Naming becomes a rhetorical strategy to specify the constituents of the Pantanal in Nhecolândia, offering an intimate view of the interactions between humans and non-humans. In another passage, the narrator also points out another distinction between the common name of an animal –

the 'jararaca-do-rabo-branco' (an endemic species of pit viper in Brazil) – and then goes on to explain the name by which that same animal is locally known – as the 'boca-de-sapo'.[44] Here, once again, the reader is presented with the dichotomy between outside/local epistemology of the region. On the one hand, we have the common name of the pit viper by which most people outside of the region recognize that snake. Most common names for animals in Brazil have a certain literalness to them. 'Jararaca-do-rabo-branco' literally means 'jararaca (which is a forest from where the snake gets its name) of the white tail'. The word 'jararaca' is of Tupi Guarani origin and literally means 'grabs and poisons'. Guimarães Rosa is deploying Indigenous knowledges of fauna by using such words to refer to regional animals. There is an explicit attempt at maintaining the local and Indigenous idioms in the references used to portray the Pantanal. The local name for *jararaca* viper is not as literal: 'frog's mouth' seems to be a metaphor for the way the snake looks to bystanders. An outsider that was not initiated in the local knowledge of the flora and fauna of the Pantanal would likely not know what to make of the regional name for the pit viper. Knowing that regional and Indigenous name is a glimpse to the regional epistemology of the Pantanal. It is a new mode of seeing the world of that biome, one that seems more intimate and obscure to those outside.

As Mariano takes the narrator through the wetlands on horse, the presence of avifauna dominates the text:

> Fomos por este, norte e este, no meio do verde. O céu caía de cor, e fugiam as nuvens, com o vento frio. Voavam também, ou pousavam, que aquí e lá e ali, multidões de aves – sós, em bando, aos pares – tanta e todas: mais floria, movente, o puro algodão das garças; anhumas abriam-se no ar, como perús pomposos; quero-queros gritavam, rasantes, ou se elevavam parabólicos.[45]

> [We went East, North and East, in through the greenery. The sky would change at sunset, and clouds would flee, with the cold wind. Also flying, or landing, here and there, multitudes of birds – alone, in flocks, in pairs – so many: but flowery, moving, the pure cotton of the herons; *anhumas* would open up in the air, as pompous turkeys; *quero-queros* would cry out, sweeping by, or rising up in parabolas.]

From herons to *quero-queros* ('Southern Lapwing'), the landscape of the Pantanal is a flurry of countless birds. We already encountered the *anhuma* in Dom Aquino's poem. Mariano will later explain to the narrator that the *anhuma* is not just any bird but the 'the queen of the Pantanal'.[46] The *anhuma* is commonly known in English as the 'horned screamer' and has a characteristic plumage atop its head that it opens when threatened by bigger animals. Although seemingly small and inoffensive, its high-pitched cry intimidates possible predators. The expression used by Mariano points in that direction. He not only names the birds found in the Pantanal but also characterizes them, placing them in their corresponding context within a larger ecosystem. Birds are named and described, identifying qualities and behaviours in each bird. Take, for example, the *quero-queros*. They are described as birds with 'courage' and 'anxiety', fighting for survival even against much bigger creatures.[47] Other birds are also personified, such as the 'sad' *baguaris* or the timid *emas*.[48] All in all, more than twenty different species of birds are referenced in the last section of Guimarães Rosa's 'Entremeio'.

The sheer number of references to the avifauna of the Pantanal leaves the narrator astonished at the abundance of the wetlands. Mariano explains the characteristics of each type of bird, initiating the narrator and reader in a knowledge of the region in which the constituents become alive in the imagination. It is not a mere catalogue of birds, but naming of the members of a world that is intimately interconnected. Each bird has a specific place in the ecology of the Pantanal wetlands, each one a distinct creature that interacts with others to form a web of interrelations between living beings. The passage makes clear that each bird has its ecological niche. There is an organic structure to the wetlands described by Mariano, as if each animal named holds an intimate relation with the rest of the creatures of the region, including the cattle and the herders. It is the portrayal of the Pantanal as an ecosystem built on mutualisms and other interactions.

When a pair of *quero-queros* defies the herders as they cross paths, Mariano is quick to say that it would be better for them to leave the birds alone, for they are very courageous and 'are not afraid of anything'.[49] A mutual respect is held between both human and bird, one that acknowledges the importance of each.[50] This mutualism is further stressed in Mariano's description of the Pantanal at the very beginning of the last section, when he claims that 'the Pantanal is a world and each ranch a centre'.[51] The Pantanal is a 'world' in and of itself, a place in which each ranch plays a central role in defining the region. It is a multicentred ecosystem in which humans and non-humans are not so different, in which its constituents share a mutual respect for each other. Everything is connected. Humans and animals are all embedded into the wetlands as a biome. This 'world' in which the herder knows each of his cows by name, that knows the difference between a cougar and a jaguar, while also being able to name and characterize many of the birds found in the region, is a specific place, not simply a vacant garden.

Naming the non-human in Manoel de Barros

We can now turn to Barros and his infinitesimal poetics of the Pantanal. Considered by Carlos Drummond de Andrade and Antonio Houaiss to be one of the most important contemporary poets, Barros has been described by the Brazilian press as the poet of the wetlands of Mato Grosso do Sul, even if on several occasions he himself dismissed the title 'poet of the Pantanal'.[52] This is surprising, for much of his work is anchored in bioregional themes. It amasses a large number of references to the wetlands in the form of all sorts of non-human constituents: plants, animals, garbage and rivers. His poetry clearly avoids continentalist tropes of the Pantanal, choosing to describe the biome through a mosaic of the organic and inorganic traces of these plains. Barros, for example, prefers to talk about the 'ground', 'waters' and 'nature' of the wetlands, rather than refer to the Pantanal by its name. In *Livro de pré-coisas*, he uses the proper name 'Pantanal' in a few occasions, alongside other places such as 'Corumbá', 'o rio Paraguai', 'o rio Taquari' and 'Nhecolândia':

> Este é o portão da Nhecolândia, entrada pioneira para o Pantanal.
>   Insetos compostos de paisagem se esfarinham na luz. Os cardeais recomeçam ...
>   Suspensas
> sobre o sabão das lavadeiras, miúdas
>   borboletas amarelas:
>   – Buquê de rosas trêfegas.[53]

> [This is the gate of Nhecolândia, pioneer entry into the Pantanal.
>   Insects composed of landscape are spread like flour in the light. The cardinals begin ...
>   Suspended
> on the soap washing women, small
>   yellow butterflies:
>   – Bouquet of restless flowers.]

The passage names the wetlands with the proper name 'Pantanal' capitalized. It is no longer just a terrain – as was the case in Dom Aquino. Moreover, a reference to Nhecolândia is introduced, clearly setting up the connection to Guimarães Rosa's 'Entremeio'. Through Nhecolândia, the poet presents a gateway to the Pantanal wetlands. The presence of a 'gate' and 'entry' might lead the reader to expect a panoramic vista of the area, yet the images presented immediately after are of small living creatures in quotidian situations: 'insects' floating in the light of day, 'cardinals' beginning their flights or songs, 'butterflies' gathering around women washing with soap and a 'Bouquet of restless flowers'. No grand view of the wetlands is offered, nor a sublime portrayal of the land as it extends into the horizon. The first phrase is particularly relevant in displaying Barros's imagery of the Pantanal: 'Insects composed of landscape are spread like flour in the light.' Rather than describe the 'landscape' as constituted of 'insects' flying, Barros portrays the bugs of the wetlands as 'composed of landscape'. The insects are made of the land; that is, they contain the land in themselves as they fly about. They seem to have a symbiotic parity with the land. Those insects *are* the region as they buzz around. The Pantanal is an entity on the same grounds as are the different cities and rivers in Mato Grosso do Sul, but so are the insects, butterflies, birds and flowers. The living beings found in the region are every bit as important as the land they inhabit.

Barros chooses to name all the non-human beings that can be found strewn across the ground. He offers a poetics that enumerates the living beings of the Pantanal, a rhetorical strategy that triggers a bioregional specificity not unlike Guimarães Rosa's portrayal of the avifauna in the region in 'Entremeio'. *Livro de pré-coisas* is aptly subtitled 'Guide for a poetic route in the Pantanal' and includes references to the Taquari River and flora and fauna found in the region such as the *tuiuiú* bird or the piranha. Not only are the names of plants and animals in the Pantanal recurrent in his poems but also the weather cycles of the region, especially the transition from drought to rainy season. The abundance of images of the Pantanal wetlands is remarkable, so much so that readers unacquainted with the region find the depictions at times opaque. The book challenges readers to see the Pantanal through the eyes of the poet in his intimate knowledge of the wetlands.

Barros himself admits that his poetry is not very accessible because of his ample use of imagery.[54] The use of nouns and their playful transformation into adjectives mimics the direct experience of that which is named. His use of language attempts to figuratively stick to those non-human creatures that he sees. Barros speaks of frogs, stones and plants – and also of the qualities of being 'frog-like', 'stone-like' and 'plant-like'.[55] It is almost as if the names he deploys want to quite literally stick to the things they mention. In order to understand what he means with terms such as 'frog-like' or 'stone-like', the reader must imagine a frog or stone. That is, he or she has had to experience those things in order to grasp their adjectivized forms. The poet simply points at the entities that make up the region and names them, without any further description or explanation. His language strings together 'nodes of images', minuscule impressions of the Pantanal.[56]

Barros's imagery of the biome engages with two aspects: referentiality and scale. His poetry establishes a primacy of the senses. The overwhelming use of specific names to portray the wetlands prioritizes the senses to imagine the landscape represented that generates in the reader an awareness of the significance of referentiality in language. Generic descriptions often aid in framing the landscape, yet the unrestrained use of names that refer to specific living beings requires a greater knowledge in order to fully recreate what the poet imagines. Dom Aquino, for example, deploys broad vistas with generic terms such as 'tree', 'cattle' and 'plain' to frame the landscape of the wetlands, offering a single specific reference in the form of the *anhuma*. Readers unacquainted with the land can easily imagine a 'green plain' with 'deer', 'cattle' and a 'tree' in the distance. The reference to the *anhuma* functions to add a regional flavour to the passages, but it does not detract from grasping the overall meaning of the representation of the wetlands. In contrast, Barros avoids offering broad brushstrokes of landscape, incorporating many specific references to animals and plants in the Pantanal:

> Incrível a alegria do capim. E a bagunça dos periquitos! Há um referver de insetos por baixo da casca úmida das mangueiras.
>
> Alegria é de manhã ter chovido de noite! As chuvas encharcam tudo. Os baguaris e os caramujos tortos. As chuvas encharcaram os cerrados até os pentelhos. Lagartos espaceiam com olhos de paina. Borboletas desovadas melam. Biguás engolem bagres perplexos. Espinheiros emaranhados guardam por baixo filhotes de pato.[57]

> [Incredible the happiness of tall grass. And the mess of *parakeets*! There is a fervour of insects below the humid shell of the *mango trees*.
>
> Happiness of the morning is having rained at night! The rains flood everything. The *cocoi herons* and the lopsided snails. The rains flood the grasslands up to the pubic hairs. Lizards spread with eyes of fibre. Hatched butterflies cling. *Cormorants* swallow perplexed *catfish*. Tangled bramble guard ducklings below.]

This passage depicts the wetlands after the rain, focusing on the mutualism between living beings after the region floods. Several references to specific creatures are the following: parakeets, mango trees, *cocoi* herons, cormorants and catfish. Each of these living beings is portrayed in connection with each other. Insects gather beneath the mango trees, while cormorants eat catfish. The enumeration of different flora and fauna creates a scene of interdependence. Moreover, the names used also reveal a linguistic interdependence that is not surprising, given that the Pantanal wetlands are shared between Paraguay, Bolivia and Brazil. The word 'periquito' actually comes from Spanish, for example. The word 'baguari' is even more complex, since the term derives from the Tupi Guarani word 'mbaé-guari' or 'maguari' that literally means 'tortuous thing'.[58] In Paraguay and Bolivia, the term refers to the *Jabiru* stork, also known as the *tuiuiú* in Brazil. In Mato Grosso do Sul, however, the term 'baguari' is also used to refer to the 'garça-mourena' or *cocoi* heron, which also inhabits the wetlands.[59] The passage presents the Pantanal as a living tissue that manifests not only the interdependence of animals and plants but also the interweaving of Portuguese, Spanish and Tupi Guarani. This intercrossing of references and languages is challenging to readers unacquainted with the region. The use of local terms such as 'baguaris' offers an intimate yet opaque view of the creatures living in the Pantanal. Barros portrays a wetland that is alive and buzzing with activity, if also filled with anthropomorphisms.

Barros takes the notion of mutualism further, framing many close-ups of the fauna and flora that constitute the biome of the region. He is constantly naming animals and things in the region, disrupting panoramic representations of the Pantanal by refocusing on the interactions between the minutiae of the ecosystem. He often includes poems that act as glossaries of creatures in the Pantanal. Barros includes in *Livro* a glossary of creatures of the Pantanal titled 'Small Natural History' that functions as a few encyclopaedic entries of the following animals: 'Urubu', 'Socó-Boca-D'Água', 'Tatu', 'Quero-Quero', 'Cachorros', 'Quati' and 'Garça'.[60] Although some of the animals described in the section are generic, such as the dog or vulture, others such as the bird southern lapwing or the mammal coati are found in that region and are emblematic:

> 6. DE QUATI
> Aparece um quati escoteiro. Decerto perseguido de cachorro. No chão é ente insuficiente o quati. Imita ser baleado. O rabo desinquilibra de tanto rente na terra.
>   Agora, se alcança árvore, quati arma banzé. Arreganha. Monta episódio. E até xinga cachorro.
>   Igual é o tamanduá. Fora do mato, no limpo, tamanduá nega encrenca. Porém se encontra zamboada, vira gente. E desafia cachorro, onça-pintada, tenente.[61]
>
> [6. OF COATI
> A pioneer coati appears. Surely chased by a dog. On ground, the coati is an insufficient being. He imitates being shot. The tail is unstable from being so close to the ground.
>   Now, if he reaches a tree, the coati raises hell. He shows his teeth. Makes a ruckus. And even insults the dog.

The same is the anteater. Beyond the bush, out in the clear, the anteater refuses conflict. But if he finds undergrowth, he becomes as people. And defies dogs, jaguars, lieutenants.]

Note the number in the title of the poem. It imitates an entry into an encyclopaedia or natural treatise. The coati is depicted in its behaviour with a dog chasing it. When on the ground, it is vulnerable and awkward. Yet the moment it reaches a tree, it becomes ferocious and noisy. The anthropomorphization of the mammal is relevant in the poem. The coati 'raises hell', 'makes a scandal' and 'even insults the dog'. The poem then introduces another animal of the Pantanal that is said to be similar, the anteater. Here the anthropomorphism is even more explicit, for when the anteater finds undergrowth of the wetlands, he 'becomes as people' and 'defies dogs, jaguars, lieutenants'. Again, the emphasis is on the relations between the anteater and other living beings, such as jaguars and people.

The naming of animals and the use of pseudo-glossaries are indicative of the significance of enumerating flora and fauna in Barros's poetry. His poetics of naming is linked to the innocence with which his poems portray the world of the Pantanal. When describing the coati, the sentences are short. As a child that imagines the coati actually communicating the dog that chased it up a tree, the coati is described as 'insulting' and harassing its chaser. The anteater is also seen as turning into 'people' the moment it engages in conflict, as the poet was adopting the view of a child that sees two adults argue. Scholars Paulo Eduardo Benites de Moraes and Josemar de Campos Maciel argue that Barros's language tends towards innocence; that is, it attempts to express the world through a language of innocence characteristic of children.[62] Naming things is part of that turn to a more childlike language that begins to describe the immediate surroundings. That innocent gaze allows for a more close-up perspective of the Pantanal in which the names of creatures are more important than abstracts concepts. Of particular force is the list of birds that the Brazilian poet introduces into his text, many of which are specific the region. When describing the 'garças pantaneiras' as nostalgic, he questions whether he is not 'impregnating with human pestilence' those regional birds by describing them in that way.[63] He acknowledges the human dimension of anthropomorphizing the creatures of the Pantanal.

Barros thus constructs an infinitesimal mosaic of the wetlands that avoids broad and sweeping representations of landscape in favour of referring to the relationships between creatures. By 'infinitesimal' I mean those things which are 'ínfimas' insofar as they are small, unimportant and often ignored for much grander visions of the world. As Barros states in *Tratado geral das grandezas do ínfimo*, 'For me powerful is he who discovers / insignificant things (of the world and ourselves).'[64] Here he is engaging with the colonial tradition of 'Tratados', such as Pêro de Magalhães Gândavo's *Tratado da Terra do Brasil* (1576), a book that is a type of catalogue of the fauna and flora of Brazil. Whereas Gândavo enumerates the important creatures of Brazil, Barros ironically lists those considered insignificant. Barros uses a similar lexicon when describing his poetics of trash: 'infinitesimal', 'insignificant', 'unimportant things', 'nothings', 'useless things' and 'rubbish' are some of the words he uses, always referencing that which is valued as marginal and minute. There is indeed a provocation of exalting the humble. It is not necessarily a question of the actual size of the things mentioned, but rather of the insignificant value traditionally attached to them. His poetics of the infinitesimal draw the reader's attention to the minuscule in terms of value. Such focus on the insignificant disrupts panoramic vistas of the wetlands. Unlike Dom Aquino's abstract depiction of the region, Barros presents us with a microscopic lens through which we can take a closer look at all those things ignored and ultimately effaced from landscape in the former's representation of the region.

Impressionistic and immediate, Barros's poetry portrays the wetlands in minute brushstrokes. When describing his *Livro de pré-coisas*, he writes, 'This is not a book about the Pantanal. It is rather an annunciation. Utterances as constatives. Smudges. Nodes of images. Celebrations of language.'[65] The passage also makes clear the philosophical discussion that underlies his prose. The phrase 'Utterances as constatives' refers to the speech acts theory which distinguishes between those utterances that assert things about the world and those that are performative, that make things happen in the world. Barros is not going to offer an abstract representation of the wetlands. Rather, he is going to assert the Pantanal through the extensive use of names, as if they were nodes of images. He is not invested in totalizing descriptions, reducing the scale of his depictions to the insignificant parts. In fact, the proper noun 'Pantanal' only appears sparsely throughout the book, compared to the overwhelming number of words that refer to the flora and fauna of the wetlands. Indeed, the proliferation of nouns sustains the claim that *Livro de pré-coisas* is invested in enunciating the wetlands. Barros uses specific words for plants and animals found in the Pantanal: more than thirty types of plants and trees (some examples are 'curimba', 'cambará' and 'antúrio'); more than twenty types of birds (some examples are 'amassa-barro', 'bemtevi-cartola' and 'tuiuiú'); more than fifteen types of fish (some examples are 'tordo', 'pacu' and 'cascudo'); more than twenty types of insects (some examples are 'borboleta', 'besouro' and 'aranha-caranguejeira'); and many other animals (some examples are 'quati', 'capivara' and 'anta'). It is similar to an aesthetic of the catalogue, insofar as there is an overwhelming presence of references to flora and fauna. This catalogue of living beings and their interrelations generates an environmental mosaic, one in which mutualism is the cohesive element.

The impact of naming the flora and fauna of the Pantanal in such detail produces in the reader an awareness of referentiality and the importance of the links between living beings. Not only do the nouns for plants and animals make obvious the Indigenous origins of the words and reinforce the sense of autochthony, but they also overwhelm the reader, forcing him or her to struggle in imagining the mosaic of creatures found in the wetlands. Unless directly acquainted with the flora and fauna referenced in the text, it is difficult to picture the wetlands. Barros writes that when he thinks of the Pantanal, he thinks of the 'exchange of favours that is established; the mutualism; the shelter that is there completed between drafts of life of minuscule beings'.[66] His environmental imaginary of the wetlands is not just an enumeration of beings but the portraying of life in that ecosystem as a mosaic of infinitesimal creatures that interact with each other:

> Penso nos embriões dos atos. Uma boca disforme de rapa-canoa que começa a querer se grudar nas coisas. Rudimentos rombudos de um olho de árvore. Os indícios de ínfimas sociedades. Os liames primordiais entre paredes e lesmas. Também os germes das primeiras ideias de uma convivência entre lagartos e pedras. O embrião de um muçum sem estames, que renega ter asas. Antepassados de antúrios e borboletas que procuram uma nesga de sol.[67]
>
> [I think of the embryos of acts. A misshapen mouth of *rapa-canoa* that begins to want to stick to things. Brute rudiments of a tree knot. Indices of infinitesimal societies. Primordial vines between walls and slugs. Also the germs of the first ideas of a coexistence between lizards and stones. The embryo of eel without stamen, that refuses to have wings. Ancestors of anthuriums and butterflies that search for a sliver of sun.]

The passage portrays the 'infinitesimal societies' that thrive at the humid surface of the Pantanal. These communities of living beings are linked in the present and the past. The poet imagines 'primordial vines' in the walls. He considers the 'eel' as the ancestor of anthuriums and butterflies. Every living creature is connected in this web of mutualism, no matter how strange the link. Hence the embryo of an eel that has no 'stamen' and 'refuses to have wings' is part of the lineage that binds a species of flower and a species of insect together. Mutualism reaches farther than living beings. The possibility of a 'coexistence between lizards and stones' is also present in these 'infinitesimal' communities of the wetlands. A common origin is also emphasized in the passage – all things commune in their origins. The references to flora and fauna in the short passage are also representative of the poetic enumeration in *Livro de pré-coisas*. Moreover, the instances of the term 'embryo' – which appears several times – stress the sexual and reproductive aspect of the ecosystem. Life in the Pantanal is not aseptic, but rather a mess of fluids and creatures in embryonic states, awaiting to burst forth into the waters. It is as if the wetlands are a living tissue of organic transfusions.

The constant references to water, rain and marshland are linked to sexualized and embryonic images. In the previous passage, the river Taquari is portrayed as 'pregnant'. The 'Argoval' poem also includes several mentions of 'infinitesimal societies' as embryonic. Barros's depictions of the Pantanal constantly refer to images of birth and death, of exchanges of fluids, seeds and blood. Perhaps one of the most powerful pieces in the book evokes the minute transfusions of life that occur just beneath the surface as the rain finally descends upon the wetlands:

> E ao cabo de três meses de trocas e infusões – a chuva começa a descer. E a arraia vai levantar-se. Seu corpo deu sangue e bebeu. Na carne ainda está embutido o fedor de um carrapato. De novo ela caminha para os brejos refertos. Girinos pretos de rabinhos e olhos de feto fugiram do grande útero, e agora já fervem nas águas das chuvas.
>
> É a pura inauguração de um outro universo. Que vai corromper, irromper, irrigar e recompor a natureza.[68]
>
> [And at the end of three months of exchanges and infusions – the rains begin to fall. And the mantis ray will awaken. Her body gave blood and drank. In her flesh is still present the stench of a *carrapato*. Once again she walks to the full marshes. Black tadpoles with fetal tails and eyes escape the great uterus, and now are bubbling in the waters of the rains.
>
> It is the pure inauguration of another universe. That will corrupt, irrupt, irrigate and recompose nature.]

There is nothing sublime about the imagery presented. In the humid and subterranean placenta of the Pantanal, small creatures are gradually evolving and maturing. There are transfusions of blood and flesh and the stink of putrid matter. The small and negligible creatures – such as the stingray and tick – just beneath the ground emerge with the first rains. Yet these poetics of the sedimented ground, where the minutiae of the wetlands exchange fluids, blood and seeds lead the reader to a different knowledge of the region, one in which the mutualism shapes its understanding. Instead of offering a broad and aseptic view of the land, Barros chooses to enumerate the creatures that populate the wetlands and describe their organic interactions. It is the minuscule events that take place at ground level which manifest the origins of the wetlands. These small creatures that seem hidden from view 'corrupt, penetrate, irrigate, and recompose nature'. No grand and elevated vistas. No immense scale. Just the mutualism of the small and insignificant. Accentuating the infinitesimal scale of the wetlands in Brazil through a poetics of naming the insignificant, Barros offers a depiction of the region that dismisses grand metaphors of landscape in favour of those beings unnoticed yet whose role in sustaining the mosaic of life in the Pantanal manifests the origins of the region. One need look no further than the small animals and vegetation hidden in the wetlands to gain an invaluable image of the world found in that specific region. Barros's poetics in *Livro de pré-coisas* is an attempt to lead the reader to 'unseeing the world' or rather to see it with the innocence of a child, the gaze of she who is naming the world for the very first time.

As I have argued throughout this chapter, the modes of representation of the Pantanal shifted from a continentalist imagery of the region in Dom Aquino to a depiction of the land that avoids panoramic sweeps in favour of portraying the interactions between plants and animals through a poetics of enumeration and an exploration of the insider/outsider knowledge dichotomy in Guimarães Rosa and Barros. The latter two imagine the wetlands as a living web of mutualism. The local and specific become central to their imagined geography of the Pantanal. To that end, naming disrupts the broad and sweeping representation of the wetlands as a garden or vacant space awaiting appropriation. Whereas Guimarães Rosa deploys naming as a way to distinguish between outsider/insider knowledge of the region, Barros takes it a step further and uses it to exploit the gaps of referentiality. In his poetry the Pantanal is not *as* central as are the different creatures that populate the sedimented ground of the wetlands, evoking a sense of mutualism and dependency that does not rely on sublimely beautiful vistas to emphasize its importance and value. Much the same way as Guimarães Rosa elevates the role of local knowledge of the region in the figure of Mariano, so does Barros accentuate the place of the insignificant and negligible creatures to be found inside of the Pantanal. Theirs is a poetics of the Pantanal that, while regional in all its specificity, breaks the mould of regionalist writers of the plains insofar as they disrupt the panoramic gaze of the land through the naming of things inside it, not over and above it as is exemplified by Dom Aquino's poem of the region.

Conclusion

Two decades ago the World Research Initiative published a series of reports on bioregions across the planet under the rubric *Pilot Analysis of Global Ecosystems* (PAGE), addressing the need to 'assess the health of ecosystems' on earth.[1] At the time, it was one of the first sustained attempts at collecting and analysing all available data on various ecosystems with the support of the International Food Policy Research Institute and research institutions worldwide: agroecosystems, coastal, forest, freshwater and grasslands. The last of the PAGE reports is titled *Grasslands Ecosystems* and addresses the specific characteristics and challenges of grasslands biomes, setting a benchmark for future global surveys invested in their potential biological and economic sustainability.[2] The PAGE report on grasslands begins by clearly stating 'why they matter' in the first paragraph, a long passage that is well worth quoting in its entirety:

> Grasslands – as highly dynamic ecosystems – provide goods and services to support flora, fauna, and human populations worldwide. Grasslands have been goldmines of plants used for food. Many of our food grains – wheat, corn, rice, rye, millet, and sorghum – have originated in grasslands. Many grasslands remain the primary source of genetic resources for improving our crops and for increasing the number of pharmaceuticals. Grasslands produce forage for domestic livestock, which in turn support human livelihoods with meat, milk, wool, and leather products. Grasslands provide habitat for breeding, migrating, and wintering birds; ideal conditions for many soil fauna; and rangelands for wild herbivores. These ecosystems cycle water and nutrients, and build and maintain stabilization mechanisms for soil. Grassland vegetation, above and below ground, as well as the soil itself, serve as large storehouses for carbon, helping to limit global warming. Grasslands also supply energy from fuelwood and wind generated from windfarms. These largely open-air landscapes support recreational activities such as hunting, wildlife-watching, and tourism more generally, and offer aesthetic and spiritual gratification.[3]

The opening of the report illustrates how the continentalist narrative is repeated even in scientific discourse about the grasslands in the twenty-first century. Predominant in the cited passage are the 'goods and services' that the grasslands provide to the rest of the world. They are the garden of the world, on which to grow the cash crops consumed globally. The passage repeats the rhetoric of the subterranean value of the plains, citing the important role of the soil in producing economic value. The grasslands act as carbon sinks and water filtering systems, as pharmaceutical laboratories and energy sources. Yet for all the rhetoric on the value of the grasslands, very little is said of the actual flora of the biome, especially since it is the very vegetation that characterizes these biomes. Are the variety of grasses of any value beyond being a source of food for grazing livestock or as weeds extracted from monoculture fields? And just as important, there is no mention of the Indigenous human populations that have been displaced from grasslands in order to transform these biodiverse regions into feeding grounds. Which human populations are fed through the cash crops produced in the grasslands?

As we have seen in the preceding chapters, the grasslands of the Americas have been imagined under an array of tropes that in many ways anticipate and run parallel to the growing economic interests in turning these biomes into productive extensions on which to raise livestock and cash crops. From the initial depictions of the North American Great Plains to the South American Pampas, these diverse grasslands have been imagined as barren deserts that have the potential to become gardens for settlers committed to cultivating the land. As Martínez Estrada suggests in his *Radiografía de la pampa*, colonizers of South America attached a novel set of values to the plains they encountered: 'Through possession were the new values built on the basis of having a price.'[4] Ownership of land in the Pampas grasslands was considered a way to accumulate capital in a region considered barren. Quantic also explains that in North America the 'political and economic theories' of the nineteenth century were based on settler imaginaries that 'the prairies and plains provided limitless arable land for population expansion.'[5] Although other biomes have also been portrayed in ways that invited exploitation of resources, the grasslands have for centuries been described as primarily having agricultural potential for settlers. That is why they are central to continentalist narratives since the eighteenth century, for they are often seen as holding the key to industry and progress – so long as we can harvest and tap into their potential. A global discourse of the need to develop the grasslands into the granaries of the world lies at the heart of such narratives.

At stake in how we imagine and portray the grasslands is the effacing rhetoric of a global narrative that sees continental biomes as providing 'goods and services' at the expense of local knowledges of Indigenous communities inhabiting these lands. Taking a closer look at the foreword of the PAGE reports, it becomes clear that the continentalist narrative is very much a part of the document, which looks to take 'stock of their extent, their condition, and their capacity to provide the goods and services we will need in years to come'.[6] I have so far focused on indicating the array of tropes that the continentalist narrative has imposed as a global discourse on the value of grasslands in Latin America. Often these tropes efface the possibility of other local knowledges of the plains throughout the Americas, whether it be the Indigenous or alternative regional knowledges. For the last two centuries, the dominant imaginaries of continental lands have established a 'cognitive empire' over other ways of seeing the plains in Latin America.[7] My hope is that by pointing out the ideological function of such tropes, we may begin to see the contours of other alternative knowledges that have been there long before the continentalist imaginaries akin to the Manifest Destiny emerged in the nineteenth century and continue to survive embedded in settler ecologies.

Throughout the book I have suggested several moments in which local knowledges resurface to fracture the monolithic imposition of continentalist imaginaries. One of these moments is through the presence of predatory encounters that subvert the initial framing of the grasslands as a wild threat to civilization. What begins as a trope that seeks to exploit the 'Great Divide' between humans and non-human animals actually ends up manifesting the surprising and inevitable entanglement between both. Not only do predatory ecologies dissolve the inherent binaries of continentalist narratives (nature versus society, barbarism versus civilisation and wild versus domesticated), but they also suggest the concrete biological interrelations that take place in that specific biome. Whether it be the Andean condor in Ciro Alegría's *Los perros hambrientos* or the Orinoco crocodile in Rómulo Gallegos's *Doña Bárbara*, the acts of predation in narratives anchor the portrayal of nature in the bioregional web of life. Although ecocritics and scholars in similar fields do not tire of insisting on the importance of relations between humans and non-humans, to my knowledge not much has been written on predation in literature. This venue of research could certainly shed light on several issues in continentalist narratives, while also opening up an epistemological space for Indigenous cultures that have long engaged with the non-human. What roles do predators have in Indigenous narratives and myths? Andean cultures see the condor in a diversity of ways, not just as a threat but also as sacred.[8] Sacrality of predators in narratives opens a philosophical discussion into animal ethics via Indigenous beliefs. Does predation invoke a blurring of the human and non-human? Maya deities are portrayed as wearing jaguar skins, a symbol of power.[9] In fact, 'In Pre-Columbian art, jaguars are rarely portrayed as hunters of man, but jaguars, jaguar impersonators, or mythical jaguars appear – sometimes actively – in sacrificial contexts'.[10] Instead of highlighting the separation between gods, humans and animals, these imaginaries of predators offer a radically different way of understanding predation, one that is prior to settler imaginaries in the Americas. Another issue that is raised by predatory ecologies is how the names used to refer to specific predators reveal the ideology sustaining a given narrative. For example, the use of the misnomer 'tiger' by Sarmiento in *Facundo* suggests an exoticism and orientalism lodged in his discourse to try and sway his European readers, while also revealing his lack of knowledge of the feline predators in the Pampas grasslands. Ultimately, a focus on predators and predation sheds light on how different cultures have imagined the relations between humans and non-human animals in the twisting web of life.[11]

Another moment at the interstices of continentalist narratives is the significance of plants in leveraging local knowledges, especially through the act of naming. Although Western cultures tend to be zoocentric in their portrayal of the natural world, a bias that can be appreciated in the salient role of animals in scientific literature and philosophy,[12] plants have a singular role in the imaginaries of nature in Latin America, especially since the eighteenth century when scientist journeymen such as Alexander von Humboldt, Aime Bonpland and Carl Friedrich Philipp von Martius travelled the continent collecting and drawing flora specimens. The scientific taxonomy of the natural world was propelled by the need to name and catalogue plants, more so than animals. Such an epistemological project plays a crucial role in both effacing local knowledges in Western science (through the imposition of scientific nomenclature) and in the repurposing of such local knowledges in the production of plants as commodities to be consumed in global markets. For example, the native tree known to the Guaraní as *ka'a, later renamed* by the botanist Bonpland as *Ilex Paraguariensis*, became widely known under the Quechua name of the recipient on which the piping hot drink is consumed in South America – yerba mate.[13] The different names attached to the native tree only found at a specific latitude in South America trace their appropriation by Spanish colonizers and later their incorporation into Western taxonomies, before becoming a transnational commodity known as mate. However, the work of those early botanists travelling through the Americas also helped preserve local knowledges through the collection of uses of native plants, as well as the detailed drawings of specimens they encountered.

In the preceding chapters, I have singled out several plants in Latin American canonical fictions of the plains that stood out as resisting dominant images of the grasslands as deserts and wastelands. The *ombú* tree in the Pampas grasslands disengages the metaphor of the plains as a geometric surface upon which to project the desires of colonizers, for it anchors Martínez Estrada's essay in the specificity of that biome. Where did the name *ombú* come from? What local knowledge was effaced in its linguistic repurposing? I also discussed the Quechua name 'ichu' for a type of coarse grass in the Andean Altiplanos, as well as the *chicalote* flower in the Mexican highlands. Although often deployed in regional novels as an element of autochthonous exoticism, plants are central to the differing epistemologies of local communities through the Americas. Traces of these local knowledges are present in their names, as is the case with the Nahuatl roots of the word 'chicalote'. This is intimately linked to the role that glossaries have played in canonical fictions, especially regionalist narratives that attempt to capture the uniqueness of the lands contained within the nation. How do these glossaries recover or efface local knowledges? We saw how Eustasio Rivera uses a glossary in *La vorágine* to substantiate his cartography of Colombian plains and rainforest, as well as Barros's ludic pseudo-glossaries that poetically fabricate entries. Recently, Mexican poet José Emilio Pacheco published a book titled *Nuevo Álbum de Zoología* (1993), which also plays with the theme of poetic taxonomies of creatures in Latin America.

Finally, I have also suggested on several occasions throughout this book the troubling relation between the dominant images of the grasslands and monoculture. As the PAGE report implies, these biomes are primarily considered important for their potential to produce important cash crops, from cereals to transgenic soy. The South American grasslands have been particularly affected by the emergence of soy monoculture. Director Lucas van Esso has filmed the monoculture exploitation taking place in the northern plains of Argentina, in the province of Chaco. His documentary *Gran Chaco* (2014) frames the expansion of large corporations of monoculture alongside the voices of Indigenous communities that are gradually being displaced from their lands. His work is part of a new wave of documentaries in Latin America that is denouncing the degradation of different bioregions in the continent by bringing to the fore the voices of local communities. I have already mentioned the documentary film by Ernesto Cabellos, *Hija de la Laguna* (2015); but we could also cite *La guerra del fracking* (2013) by Fernando Solanas as part of a group of documentaries that narrate the extractivism occurring in South America. All of these recent documentaries bear witness to how the mineral and plant resources of the grasslands of Latin America continue to be a contested site between local knowledges and the continentalist 'cognitive empire'. Nature as commodity is the central theme of continentalist images of the grasslands, more so than any other type of biome. How can an ecocriticism anchored in bioregions address these challenges?

I believe that by engaging with the links between literature, epistemology, ecology and capitalism we can begin to formulate responses to these challenges. During my travels through Brazil, I remember very clearly that many of the people I met describe the plains of the north-east of the country – spread across the Cerrado and Caatinga biomes – as barren deserts that suffered constant droughts. Although the grasslands of the north-east of Brazil do suffer from periodic droughts, as do many other grasslands throughout the Americas, they are far from being barren deserts. On the contrary, the grasslands of the north-east of Brazil host some of the most unique varieties of flora. The Cerrado savannah is a singular bioregion that has been neglected in favour of the agribusinesses that have for decades depleted its soils and grasslands to harvest soy beans. The documentary by André D'Elia *Ser Tão Velho Cerrado* (2018) opens a valuable discussion as to how the monoculture corporations are damaging the biome, without respecting the livelihoods of its inhabitants, especially in the Chapada dos Veadeiros.[14] The recovery of the other voices of the Cerrado, those of the local communities as they struggle to resist the pressure of massive harvesting of soy, is of prime importance. Photographer Melissa Maurer has also used her project 'Caminho do Cerrado' to raise awareness as to the devastation that these savannah grasslands are suffering. Her photographs deploy female nudes in which the subject wears a gas mask as she poses in front of soy monoculture fields in the Cerrado plains. The provocative tension between monoculture harvest and the female nude brings out the theme of toxicity, a theme that challenges the dominant imagery of the plains as inherent wastelands by emphasizing how a specific type of human activity has contaminated the waters and soil of the biome.

The Caatinga biome has recently gained the attention of specialists in reports that 'concluded that the biome has a higher species richness and a greater number of endemic species than previously thought', at a time in which 'the area is already exposed to a high level of conversion of natural land by agriculture'.[15] The authors of the article suggest that the 'perception' of the Caatinga as lacking biodiversity might be due to 'being poorly sampled'.[16] Most likely, that lack of interest in researching the biodiversity of the bioregion, as well as the lack of government policies to regulate the encroaching agricultural practices, is closely tied to how these plains have been imagined under continentalist narratives that repeat again and again the metaphors of the land as a desert and wasteland that can only be of value if transformed into farmland or grazing land. How we imagine a given bioregion ultimately affects our indirect knowledge of the land, which also affects the ways in which we choose to engage with the said biome. Consider the environmental priority placed on the Amazon rainforest in the past few decades. It is often depicted as a place of exotic abundance and mystery in mainstream documentaries. We are told that the rainforest plays an essential role in oxygenating the planet's atmosphere, as the lungs of the earth. It captivates viewers' imaginations as a place worth preserving. Grasslands biomes, however, are often not imagined in the same way. They are the primordial feeding grounds for the world, and as such are relegated to their agricultural value – at the expense of local Indigenous communities and other non-human constituents of the land. If capitalism is a world ecology, then the grasslands are one of the salient manifestations of how capitalism works through nature in commodifying the non-human and oppressing the human other. The dominant continental narratives of Latin America are intimately tied to how capitalism is channelled through nature, and one way we can challenge and resist is by acknowledging this troubling connection and attempting to *see* the plains differently.

Notes

Introduction

1 Érico Veríssimo, *Solo de Clarineta: Memorias*, vol. 1 (Porto Alegre: Editora Globo, 1974), 245.
2 Luiz Ruffato, 'Prefácio: O arquipélago Erico Veríssimo', in *O Arquipélago*, by Érico Veríssimo (São Paulo: Companhia das Letras, 2018), 11.
3 Érico Veríssimo, *O Continente*, vol. 1 (São Paulo: Companhia das Letras, [1949] 2004), 37.
4 Mário Maestri, *Breve história do Rio Grande do Sul: da Pré-História aos dias atuais* (São Paulo: Editora Universidade de Passo Fundo, 2010), 31.
5 See Francisco João Roscio, *Compendio noticiozo do Continente do Rio Grande de S. Pedro até o destricto da Ilha de St. Caterina: extraido dos meus diarios, observações, e noticias, que alcancey nas jornadas, que fez ao ditto continente nos annos 1774, e 1775* (Rio de Janeiro: Biblioteca Nacional do Brasil, 1781).
6 See Elizabeth McMahon, *Islands, Identity and the Literary Imagination* (London: Anthem Press, 2016), 5; John R. Gillis, 'Not Continents in Miniature: Islands as Ecotones', *Island Studies Journal* 9 (2014): 157; Brian Russell Roberts and Michelle Ann Stephens, 'Archipelagic American Studies: Decontinentalizing the Study of American Culture', in *Archipelagic American Studies* (Durham, NC: Duke University Press, 2017), 11.
7 McMahon, *Islands, Identity and the Literary Imagination*, 5.
8 Alfred W. Crosby suggests that island archipelagos, such as the Azores and the Canary Islands, were initially laboratories for the 'biological expansion' of the Spanish and Portuguese empires as they reached out across the Atlantic. This explains the large volumes of fiction produced in the sixteenth and seventeenth centuries that establish island geographies as the setting. See Alfred W. Crosby, *Ecological Imperialism: The Biological Expansion of Europe, 900-1900* (Cambridge: Cambridge University Press, 1986). Warren Dean also sheds light on the role of coastline resources during the colonization of Brazil, especially the gradual depletion of the Atlantic Rainforest in successive waves of human settlement. See Warren Dean, *With Broadax and Firebrand: The Destruction of the Brazilian Atlantic Forest* (Berkeley: University of California Press, 1995). A tracing of the different literary and geographic imaginaries of empires as they launch into the Atlantic,

arrive at the coastlines of their colonies and begin expansion inland would bear witness to the shift from archipelagic to littoral and then continental imaginaries.

9 Mario Blaser and Marisol de la Cadena, 'Introduction: Pluriverse, Proposals for a World of Many Worlds', in *A World of Many Worlds*, eds. Marisol de la Cadena and Mario Blaser (Durham, NC: Duke University Press, 2018), 3.

10 Blaser and Cadena, 'Introduction: Pluriverse, Proposals for a World of Many Worlds', 4. See also Arturo Escobar, *Designs for the Pluriverse: Radical Interdependence, Autonomy, and the Making of Worlds* (Durham, NC: Duke University Press, 2017) and Bernd Reiter (ed.), *Constructing the Pluriverse: The Geopolitics of Knowledge* (Durham, NC: Duke University Press, 2018). Perhaps the most poetic expression of the idea of a pluriverse is to be found in Ernesto Cardenal, *Versos del Pluriverso* (Madrid: Trotta, 2005): 'por qué decir universo, como si fuera uno y no pluriverso' ('why say universe, as if it was one, and not pluriverse').

11 Mario Blaser, *Storytelling Globalization from the Chaco and Beyond* (Durham, NC: Duke University Press, 2010), 102.

12 Arturo Escobar, *Designs for the Pluriverse*, xvi. However, I find it hard to reconcile an emphasis on difference and plurality from a decidedly ontological stance. How can defining the being of a world allow for difference? Is ontology not anchored on essential criteria for Being? How can ontology acknowledge alterity? One of the earliest phenomenologists who broke away from Heidegger's philosophy was Emmanuel Levinas – a philosopher who deeply influenced Derrida and other French theorists. His phenomenological approach engages directly with the significance of difference and alterity: 'But already, in the very heart of the relationship with the other that characterizes our social life, alterity appears as a nonreciprocal relationship – that is, as contrasting strongly with contemporaneousness. The Other as Other is not only an alter ego: the Other is what I myself am not. The Other is this, not because of the Other's character, or physiognomy, or psychology, but because of the Other's very alterity. The Other is, for example, the weak, the poor, "the widow and the orphan", whereas I am the rich or the powerful. It can be said that intersubjective space is not symmetrical. The exteriority of the other is not simply due to the space that separates what remains identical through the concept, nor is it due to any difference the concept would manifest through spatial exteriority. The relationship with alterity is neither spatial nor conceptual' (*The Levinas Reader*, 48). The 'nonreciprocal relationship' with the other makes it conceptually impossible to incorporate into Being. The other becomes transcendent, always exterior to the totality of Being. Although Levinas was not considering the potential of his phenomenological approach to the decolonial cause, Enrique Dussel has in recent decades articulated an entire philosophy of liberation based on the irreducible character of alterity and the other.

See Enrique Dussel, *Ética de la liberación en la edad de la globalización y de la exclusión* (Madrid: Trotta, 1998).
13 Veríssimo, *Solo de Clarineta*, 251.
14 Lawrence Buell, *The Future of Environmental Criticism: Environmental Crisis and Literary Imagination* (London: Blackwell Publishing, 2005), 62.
15 Robert Thacker, *The Great Prairie and Literary Fact* (Albuquerque: University of New Mexico Press, 1989), 108.
16 Diane Dufva Quantic discusses what she terms the myths that European settlers brought with them to the Americas and deployed to attempt to translate the lands they witnessed into landscapes they understood. Although she is mainly discussing the role of settlers and immigrants in the Great Plains of North America, I argue that the very same epistemology is applied elsewhere in Latin America – especially in the fictions of the Pampas in South America. See Diane Dufva Quantic, *The Nature of the Place: A Study of Great Plains Fiction* (Lincoln: University of Nebraska Press, 1995).
17 See Thacker, *The Great Prairie and Literary Fact*, 103–44; Quantic, *The Nature of the Place,* 29–47.
18 Susan Naramore Maher, 'Literature of the Great Plains: Nature, Culture, and Community', in *A History of Western American Literature*, ed. Susan Kollin (Cambridge: Cambridge University Press, 2015), 131.
19 Carlos Alonso analyses the discourse of autochthony in the regional novel of Spanish America in the twentieth century, arguing that the projects of cultural identity since the independence of the Spanish colonies in Latin America are attempts at generating national myths that present themselves as essential to a specific nation. Although Alonso is more invested in the discursive dimension of the regional novel or *novelas de la tierra*, his discussion of autochthony as central to this genre is valuable in understanding the role that the 'land' plays in ideas of autochthony through literature. My reading of several regional novels further emphasizes the fact that it was not just any 'land' that served as a scenario for the autochthonous discourse, but rather the various plains geographies in South America. From an ecocritical perspective, this opens up a discussion as to how 'nature' is ideologically constructed in regional novels as part of the foundational myth of Latin American nations. Jennifer L. French argues in that same line, addressing the neocolonial rhetoric present in a small canon of regional writers. I expand on her approach to the 'invisible empire' in Latin American fiction by establishing a transnational connection through the repeated use of plains geographies as a scenario on which neocolonialism plays out. See Carlos Alonso, *The Spanish American Regional Novel: Modernity and Autochthony* (Cambridge: Cambridge University Press, 1990); and Jennifer L. French, *Nature, Neo-Colonialism, and the Spanish American Regional Writers* (Hanover: Dartmouth College Press, 2005).

20 Boaventura de Sousa Santos, *Epistemologies of the South: Justice against Epistemicide* (London: Routledge, 2014), 92.
21 Macarena Gómez-Barris, *The Extractive Zone: Social Ecologies and Decolonial Perspectives* (Durham, NC: Duke University Press, 2017), 2.
22 Walter Pengue, 'The Impact of Soybean Expansion in Argentina', *Seedling* 18, no. 3 (September 2001): 1.
23 Jerffrey Bury and Anthony Bebbington, 'New Geographies of Extractive Industries in Latin America', in *Subterranean Struggles: New Dynamics of Mining, Oil, and Gas in Latin America*, eds. Anthony Bebbington and Jeffrey Bury (Austin: University of Texas Press, 2013), 36. Their chapter traces the evolution of extractive industries throughout Latin America, offering some valuable insights into the extractivist network built not only since the arrival of the Spanish, but also in the last decades which have seen an accelerated cycle of extraction throughout Latin America. In *Slow Violence and Environmentalism of the Poor*, Rob Nixon points out the connection between 'turbocapitalism' and the 'slow violence' that is exerted over former colonies. His book is very valuable to understanding the need to develop environmental approaches that frame the colonial and neocolonial exploitation that takes place in the Global South. See Rob Nixon, *Slow Violence and Environmentalism of the Poor* (Cambridge, MA: Harvard University Press, 2011).
24 Alcides Arguedas, *Raza de bronce* (Caracas: Biblioteca Ayacucho, [1919] 2006), 8.
25 According to Robert L. Thayer in *Lifeplace: Bioregional Thought and Practice*, 'A bioregion is literally and etymologically a "life-place" – a unique region defined by natural (rather than political) boundaries with a geographic, climatic, hydrological, and ecological character capable of supporting unique human communities' (3). For a collection of ecocritical essays addressing bioregionalism in literature, see also Tom Lynch, Cheryll Glotfelty and Karla Armbruster (eds.), *The Bioregional Imagination: Literature, Ecology and Place* (Athens, GA: University of Georgia Press, 2012).
26 Lee Clark Mitchell, *Witnesses to a Vanishing America* (Princeton: Princeton University Press, 1981), 6.
27 Walter Mignolo, *Local Histories/Global Designs: Coloniality, Subaltern Knowledges, and Border Thinking* (Princeton: Princeton University Press, 2000), 17.
28 Walter Mignolo and Catherine E. Walsh, *On Decoloniality: Concepts, Analytics, Praxis* (Durham, NC: Duke University Press, 2018), 136.
29 Enrique Dussel, *Siete ensayos de filosofía de la liberación: Hacia una fundamentación del giro decolonial* (Madrid: Trotta, 2020), 26.
30 Quantic, *The Nature of Place*, 5.
31 Aime Bonpland (1773–1858) was a French botanist who accompanied the famed geographer Alexander von Humboldt (1769–1859) throughout his travels to South America from 1799 to 1804, which are documented in the *Personal Narrative of*

a Journey to the Equinoctial Regions of America (1808). Bonpland is particularly known for giving the scientific name of *Ilex Paraguariensis* to the yerba mate plant, a plant that was known to the Guaraní Indigenous communities for centuries prior as 'ka'a'. Carl Friedrich Philipp von Martius (1794–1868) was a German botanist who amassed a large collection of plant specimens in South America – the Herbarium Martii. He initiated the multivolume *Flora Brasiliensis*, a work dedicated to the rigorous categorization of Brazilian flora. He is especially well-known for his *Historia naturalis palmarium* (1853), which is an encyclopaedic compilation of different palm trees in South America, alongside detailed sketches of the trees.

32 See Elizabeth P. Benson, 'The Lord, the Ruler: Jaguar Symbolism in the Americas', in *Icons of Power: Feline Symbolism in the Americas*, ed. Nicholas J. Saunders (London: Routledge, 1998), 66; Miguel León-Portilla, *Aztec Thought and Culture* (Norman: University of Oklahoma Press, 1963), 41.

33 See Fernando Horcasitas, 'La Danza de los Tecuanes', *Estudios de Cultura Náhuatl* 14 (1980): 253.

34 Alexander von Humboldt makes note of this misnomer in his *Views of Nature*: 'spotted jaguars (usually called tigers), which are capable of dragging a young steer they have killed to a hilltop – these and many other creatures wander the treeless plain'. See Alexander von Humboldt, *Views of Nature*, trans. Mark W. Person (Chicago: Chicago University Press, [1808] 2014), 36. Humboldt is an excellent observer and compiler of local knowledge throughout South America, not only identifying flora and fauna in the continent during his travels but also including the Indigenous and local names.

35 Jeffrey Jerome Cohen and Lowell Duckert, 'Introduction: Welcome to the Whirled', in *Veer Ecology: A Companion for Environmental Thinking*, eds. Jeffrey Jerome Cohen and Lowell Duckert (Minneapolis: University of Minnesota Press, 2017), 3.

36 Jane Bennett, *Vibrant Matter: A Political Ecology of Things* (Durham, NC: Duke University Press, 2010), 104.

37 Richard Grusin, 'Introduction', in *The Nonhuman Turn*, ed. Richard Grusin (Minneapolis: University of Minnesota Press, 2015), vii.

38 Donna Haraway, *Staying with the Trouble: Making Kin in the Chthulucene* (Durham, NC: Duke University Press, 2016), 4.

39 Jeffrey Jerome Cohen and Lowell Duckert, 'Introduction: Eleven Principles of the Elements', in *Elemental Ecocriticism: Thinking with Earth, Air, Water, and Fire*, eds. Jeffrey Jerome Cohen and Lowell Duckert (Minneapolis: University of Minnesota Press, 2015), 5.

40 See Timothy Morton, *Dark Ecology: For a Logic of Future Coexistence* (New York: Columbia University Press, 2016). His book offers an interesting approach to the entanglement between the human and the non-human, arguing that the relation between both is similar to a twisting loop in which we find ourselves entangled.

As other ecological thinkers attempting to go beyond Cartesian dualism in its dichotomy between *res extensa* and *res cogitans*, Morton offers a logic that I daresay seems quite dialectical. Although Morton seems more invested in the Freudian category of the uncanny in the experience of the loop of coexistence, Donna Haraway also dwells on a very similar image in *Staying with the Trouble*, that of string figures. In her approach, emphasis lies on the strange yet surprising connections that emerge between the companionship between humans and non-humans.

41 Deborah Bird Rose, 'Shimmer: When All You Love Is Being Trashed', in *Arts of Living on a Damaged Planet*, eds. Anna Lowenhaupt Tsing, Heather Anne Swanson, Elaine Gan and Nills Bubandt (Minneapolis: University of Minnesota Press, 2017), 55. Her chapter is particularly fascinating for its exploration of the unexpected symbiosis between Aboriginal peoples, angiosperms and flying foxes in Australia. Her approach not only brings out the presence of the non-human in nature but also amplifies the voices of the Aboriginal people. If ecocriticism wants to steer away from a colonial discourse that values nature as distinct from local inhabitants – both of which suffer the consequences of global empires in their many forms – it needs to incorporate the voices of the human other that is also central to coexistence.

42 Ecocriticism in Latin American studies has gradually gained traction in the past decades. The seminal works of Jennifer L. French, Beatriz Rivera-Barnes, Laura Barbas-Rhoden and Scott DeVries have shaped scholarship in this emerging field. See French, *Nature, Neo-Colonialism, and the Spanish American Regional Writers*; Beatriz Rivera-Barnes, *Reading and Writing the Latin American Landscape* (New York: Palgrave Macmillan, 2009); Laura Barbas-Rhoden, *Ecological Imaginations in Latin American Fiction* (Gainesville: University Press of Florida, 2012); Scott DeVries, *A History of Ecology and Environmentalism in Spanish American Literature* (Lewisburg, PA: Bucknell University Press, 2013).

43 Jason W. Moore, *Capitalism in the Web of Life: Ecology and the Accumulation of Capital* (New York: Vintage, 2015), 27.

44 Ibid., 3.

45 Jason W. Moore, 'The Rise of Cheap Nature', in *Anthropocene or Capitalocene? Nature, History, and the Crisis of Capitalism*, ed. Jason W. Moore (Oakland: PM Press, 2016), 82.

46 Nixon, *Slow Violence and Environmentalism of the Poor*, 243.

47 Enrique Dussel, *Siete ensayos de filosofía de la liberación*, 14. These three moments are present in Dussel's most recent and important work *Política de la liberación*, tentatively set to be three volumes (two of which have already been published as *Política de la liberación I: Historia mundial y crítica* and *Política de la liberación II: Arquitectónica*).

48 Enrique Dussel, *Política de la liberación II: Arquitectónica* (Madrid: Trotta, 2009), 11.

49 Dussel, *Siete ensayos de filosofía de la liberación*, 16.

50 Ibid., 44. The fact that Dussel emphasizes that he is thinking of the 'human other' is hard to combine with an environmental and non-human perspective. His philosophy of liberation is primarily concerned with the human victims of oppression. Yet Dussel also formulates this material commitment of his ethics and politics as the 'suffering corporeality' (see the opening chapters of his *Ethics of Liberation*), which opens up a possible dialogue with decolonial approaches to ecocriticism.
51 Sarah D. Wald, David J. Vázquez, Priscilla Solís Ybarra and Sarah Jaquette Ray, 'Introduction: Why Latinx Environmentalisms?', in *Latinx Environmentalisms: Place, Justice, and the Decolonial*, eds. Sarah D. Wald, David J. Vázquez, Priscilla Solís Ybarra and Sarah Jaquette Ray (Philadelphia, PA: Temple University Press, 2019), 7.
52 Santos, *Epistemologies of the South*, 17.
53 For an example of a postcolonial ecology of the other side of the line see Priscilla Solís Ybarra, *Writing the Goodlife: Mexican American Literature and the Environment* (Tucson: University of Arizona Press, 2016). Her book is a fascinating exploration of the Mexican American ecologies that have shaped Chicanos's view and interaction with the plains shared between the United States and Mexico beyond the settler ecology of possession. Moreover, she draws from the local and Indigenous knowledge of 'buen vivir' or 'goodlife'. Another salient example of ecocriticism that has addressed the other voices of Indigenous communities in the Americas is Joni Adamson, *American Indian Literature, Environmental Justice, and Ecocriticism: The Middle Place* (Tucson: University of Arizona Press, 2001). A book by Brazilian Indigenous leader Ailton Krenak is also recent contribution. See Ailton Krenak, *Ideias para adiar o fim do mundo* (São Paulo: Companhia das letras, 2019).
54 Doris Sommer, *Foundational Fictions: The National Romances of Latin America* (Berkeley: University of California Press, 1993), 6.
55 Diane D. Quantic and P. Jane Hafen, 'Foreword: What Is in This Reader', in *A Great Plains Reader,* eds. Diane D. Quantic and P. Jane Hafen (Lincoln, NE: University of Nebraska Press, 2003), xvi.
56 Lúcia Sá discusses Native Amazonian narrative forms as a mosaic of perspectives that enriches our understanding of other imaginaries of the rainforest, beyond the settler ecologies that have dominated the literary portrayals of this vast biome and its large network of rivers. See Lúcia Sá, 'Endless Stories: Perspectivism and Narrative Form in Native Amazonian Literature', in *Intimate Frontiers: A Literary Geography of the Amazon*, eds. Felipe Martínez-Pinzón and Javier Uriarte (Liverpool: University of Liverpool Press, 2019); Lúcia Sá, *Rain Forest Literatures: Amazonian Texts and Latin American Culture* (Minneapolis: University of Minnesota Press, 2004). The introduction to her book *Literaturas da Floresta* suggests an important approach to the novelas de la selva by leveraging the narratives of the Indigenous communities found throughout the Amazon: 'After Independence in the nineteenth century, South American authors writing in Portuguese, Spanish, and other imported languages became increasingly drawn to the idea of a rain forest literature, to songs,

speeches and narratives original to their part of the world [. . .] Yet literary historians and critics have seldom noticed these developments, largely ignoring the indigenous source texts, both as an antecedent indispensable for later writers and certainly as a literary corpus in its own right' (xiv).

57 Roberto González Echevarría, *Modern Latin American Literature: A Very Short Introduction* (Oxford: Oxford University Press, 2013), 85.
58 Alonso, *The Spanish American Regional Novel*, 66.
59 Rómulo Gallegos, *Doña Bárbara* (Caracas: Biblioteca Ayacucho, [1929] 1977), 25.
60 Although invested in identifying the link between literature and economic underdevelopment, Brazilian critic Antonio Candido indirectly characterizes the lands portrayed in regionalist fictions throughout Latin America as taking place in the plains: 'It is not necessary to enumerate all the other literary areas that correspond to the panorama of backwardness or underdevelopment – such as the Andean altiplanos or the Brazilian *sertão* [. . .] Or even the man of the plains – *llano*, pampa, caatinga – object of a tenacious and compensating idealisation that is derived from romantic writers, such as José de Alencar in the decade of 1870; that also occurs in the *rioplatense* writers, such as the Uruguayans Eduardo Acevedo Díaz, Carlos Reyles or Javier de Viana; and in the Argentine writers, from the telluric José Hernández to the stylised Ricardo Güiraldes; that shifts to the allegoric in Gallegos, in Venezuela, to return to Brasil in the phase of pre-awareness of underdevelopment where it finds its expression in *Vidas secas*, by Graciliano Ramos.' See Antonio Candido, *A educação pela noite e outros ensaios* (São Paulo: Editora Ática, 1989) 158. In framing Latin American literature in terms of areas of underdevelopment, Candido also raises a similar question to the one I raise. What lands and people are portrayed in regionalist fictions? His response suggests the link between continentalist narratives and capitalism insofar as it is in those grasslands that the land and people suffer from economic underdevelopment. Suffering the consequences of becoming extractive zones, the grasslands of the Americas have long been considered backward in comparison to the industrialized urban centres, usually found near the coasts.
61 Pablo Neruda, *Canto General* (Buenos Aires: Editorial Losada, [1950] 1955), 9.

Chapter 1

1 Adalberto A. Rosat Pontalti, *Diccionario Enciclopédico Quechua-Castellano del Mundo Andino* (Lima: Grupo Editorial Verbo Divino, 2009).
2 Lorena Herrera, Malena Sabatino, Aitor Gastón and Santiago Saura, 'Grassland Connectivity Explains Entomophilous Plant Species Assemblages in an Agricultural Landscape of the Pampa Region, Argentina', *Austral Ecology* 42 (2017): 486.

3   According to the Instituto Brasileiro de Geografia e Estatística (IBGE).
4   Luiz Fernando Wurdig Roesch, Frederico Costa Beber Vieira, Vilmar Alves Pereira, Adriano Luis Schünemann, Italo Filippi Teixeira, Ana Julia Teixeira Senna, and Valdir Marcos Stefenon, 'The Brazilian Pampa: A Fragile Biome', *Diversity* 1, no. 2 (2009): 182.
5   David Lowenthal, 'The American Scene', *Geographical Review* 58 (1968): 61.
6   Thacker, *The Great Plains Fact and Literary Imagination*, 2.
7   The introduction by Diane Dufva Quantic and P. Jane Hafen to *A Great Plains Reader* is illustrative in explaining how the way one 'looks' at the plains affects what one 'sees': 'Most residents of the Great Plains learn to appreciate the immensity of a far horizon under a great sky dome. They see groves of trees, the grain elevators, and the water towers as pinpoints that signal human presence between the sharp grids of roads and section lines. Those who have patience and a sharp eye learn to look around their feet for the bravura color of the prairie flowers and the carefully hidden eggs of grassland birds' (xvii). Continentalist narratives tend to 'see' the geometries of the horizon, missing the 'hidden' biodiversity of the grasslands at ground level. See Diane Dufva and P. Jane Hafe (eds.), *A Great Plains Reader* (Lincoln: University of Nebraska Press, 2003).
8   See Gregorio Weinberg, 'Liminar', in *Radiografía de la Pampa*, by Ezequiel Martínez Estrada (Madrid: ALLCA XX, 1996), xv.
9   Quantic, *The Nature of Place*, xvi; Thacker, *The Great Prairie Fact and Literary Imagination*, 107.
10 The plains as a metaphysical entity is a trope that appears in Ezequiel Martínez Estrada's *Radiografía de la pampa* and also in the Brazilian writer João Guimarães Rosa's masterpiece *Grande Sertão: Veredas* (1956), a novel that narrates the life of backlands bandit Riobaldo as he tells of his adventures in the plains of the Brazilian interior. Although the novel takes place somewhere in the state of Minas Gerais, the grasslands portrayed take on a metaphysical and universal dimension throughout the narrative. A comparative analysis of both texts would trace the shift towards the philosophical and phenomenological engagement with plains geographies in the latter half of the twentieth century. Writers such as Mexican Juan Rulfo or Brazilian Manoel de Barros continue in this vein, making Ezequiel Martínez Estrada's essay foundational in the manner in which the portrayal of the plains takes on a more phenomenological exploration of these geographies.
11 Hellen Santos and Cristina Vieira, 'Pecuária ajuda e é ajudada pelo meio ambiente na região do Pampa, RS', *Globo Rural* (August 13, 2017).
12 Carola Hermida, 'Ver el esqueleto de la tierra: *Radiografía de la pampa* de Ezequiel Martínez Estrada', *CELEHIS – Revista del Centro de Letras Hispanoamericanas* 12 (2000): 110.
13 Martínez Estrada wrote several pieces on Sarmiento. See Ezequiel Martínez Estrada, *Sarmiento* (Buenos Aires: Argos, 1946); Ezequiel Martínez Estrada, *Los variantes históricos en el Facundo* (Buenos Aires: Casa de Pardo, [1947] 1974).

14 Joseph Feustle, 'Sarmiento and Martínez Estrada: A Concept of Argentine History', *Hispania* 55, no. 3 (1972): 447.
15 Josefina Ludmer, *The Gaucho Genre* (Durham, NC: Duke University Press, 2002), 10.
16 Sommer, *Foundational Fictions: The National Romances of Latin America*, 55.
17 Although the exact material that Sarmiento used is still discussed by scholars, both James Fenimore Cooper and Alexander Von Humboldt influenced the portrayal of the land in *Facundo*. Doris Sommer discusses how Sarmiento read Cooper in *Foundational Fictions*. An excellent exploration of the role of Humboldt in *Facundo* and other canonical writers can be found in Aarti Madan, *Lines of Geography in Latin American Narrative: National Territory, National Literature* (New York: Palgrave Macmillan, 2017). For an excellent discussion on the possible travel accounts – and their problematic identification – deployed by Sarmiento in *Facundo*, see David T. Haberly, 'Francis Bond Head and Domingo Sarmiento: A Note on the Sources of *Facundo*', *MLN* 120, no. 2 (2005): 287–93.
18 Quantic, *The Nature of Place*, 31.
19 Aarti Madan, 'Sarmiento the Geographer: Unearthing the Literary in *Facundo*', *MLN* 126, no. 2 (2011): 261.
20 Sarmiento, *Facundo*, 75.
21 Humboldt, *Views of Nature,* 29.
22 Thacker, *The Great Prairie Fact and Literary Imagination*, 14.
23 Sarmiento, *Facundo*, 76.
24 Ibid., 66.
25 Madan, 'Sarmiento the Geographer: Unearthing the Literary in *Facundo*', 270.
26 Doming Faustino Sarmiento, *Facundo* (Madrid: Cátedra, [1845] 2008), 76.
27 Leo Marx, *The Machine in the Garden: Technology and the Pastoral Ideal in America* (Oxford: Oxford University Press, 2000), 46.
28 Sarmiento, *Facundo*, 148.
29 Ericka Beckman, 'Troubadours and Bedouins on the Pampas: Medievalism and Orientalism in Sarmiento's *Facundo*', *Chasqui: Revista de literatura latinoamericana* 38, no. 2 (2009): 37.
30 Sarmiento, *Facundo*, 79.
31 Greg Garrard, *Ecocriticism* (London: Routledge, 2004), 59.
32 Paul Alpers's definition of the pastoral mode is enlightening. He suggests that 'we will have a far truer idea of pastoral if we take its representative anecdote to be herdsmen and their lives, rather than landscape or idealised nature' (22). Terry Gifford also indicates the importance of herdsmen in defining the pastoral genre (1). This points to a subtle ecological problem in pastoral narratives and poems, for whereas critics such as Jonathan Bate in *Romantic Ecology* (1991) have read into its depictions of landscape a defence of nature, others such as Lawrence Buell in *The*

Environmental Imagination (1996) have questioned its ideological ambivalence in legitimizing the colonizing projects of the New World.
33　Garrard, *Ecocriticism*, 59.
34　Marx, *The Machine in the Garden: Technology and the Pastoral Ideal in America*, 193.
35　Ibid., 71.
36　Lawrence Buell, *The Environmental Imagination: Thoreau, Nature Writing, and the Formation of American Culture* (Cambridge, MA: Belknap Press, 1995), 73.
37　James Fenimore Cooper, *The Works of J. Fenimore Cooper,* vol. 8 (New York: George P. Putnam, 1851), 11.
38　Ibid., viii.
39　Ibid., 14.
40　Ibid., vi.
41　William Kelly, *Plotting America's Past: Fenimore Cooper and The Leatherstocking Tales* (Carbondale: Southern Illinois University Press, 1983), 88.
42　Sarmiento, *Facundo*, 47.
43　Juan Pablo Dabove, *Nightmares of the Lettered City: Banditry and Literature in Latin America 1816-1929* (Pittsburgh: University of Pittsburgh Press, 2007), 63.
44　Sarmiento, *Facundo*, 132.
45　Ibid., 129.
46　Ibid., 66.
47　Ibid., 56.
48　Ibid., 66.
49　Ibid., 56.
50　Madan, 'Sarmiento the Geographer: Unearthing the Literary in *Facundo*', 264.
51　An article on the abundant biodiversity of the Pampas grasslands is Juliana Medianeira Machado, Marta Gomes da Rocha, Fernando Luiz Ferreira de Quadros, Anna Carolina Cerato Confortin, Aline Bosak dos Santos, Maria José de Oliveira Sichonany, Laila Arruda Ribeiro and Aline Tatiane Nunes da Rosa, 'Morphogenesis of Native Grasses of Pampa Biome Under Nitrogen Fertilization', *Revista Brasileira de Zootecnia* 42, no. 1 (2013): 22–9.
52　Angel Rama, *The Lettered City* (Durham, NC: Duke University Press, 1996), 60.
53　Dabove, *Nightmares of the Lettered City*, 64.
54　Similar to the myth of El Dorado, Trapalanda is a legendary city in the Argentine Patagonia that was filled with riches.
55　Leo Pollmann, 'Introducción del Coordenador', in *Radiografía de la pampa,* by Ezequiel Martínez Estrada (Madrid: ALLCA XX, 1991), xix.
56　Joseph Feustle, 'Sarmiento and Martínez Estrada: A Concept of Argentine History', *Hispania* 55, no. 3 (1972): 446.
57　Dinko Cvitanovic, 'Radiografía de la pampa en la historia personal de Martínez Estrada', in *Radiografía de la pampa,* by Ezequiel Martínez Estrada (Madrid: ALLCA XX, 1991), 331.

58 Estrada, *Radiografía de la pampa*, 64.
59 Ibid., 10.
60 Leo Pollmann, 'Génesis e intención de Radiografía de la pampa', in *Radiografía de la pampa,* by Ezequiel Martínez Estrada (Madrid: ALLCA XX, 1991), 451.
61 This is part of the Latin American genre of 'ensayo de interpretación'. This genre is popular among many Latin American writers, including José Enrique Rodó, José Carlos Mariátegui and Octavio Paz. These essayists delve into issues of national and cultural identities in the Americas.
62 Estrada, *Radiografía de la pampa*, 89.
63 Cvitanovi, 'Radiografía de la pampa en la historia personal de Martínez Estrada', 347.
64 Sarmiento, *Facundo*, 56.
65 Pollmann, 'Génesis e intención de Radiografía de la pampa', 451.
66 Estrada, *Radiografía de la pampa*, 65.
67 Ibid., 74.
68 According to Lawrence Buell in *The Future of Ecocriticism*, 'The verb environ ('to surround') is of medieval provenance. Environment as noun was introduced during the first third of the nineteenth century [. . .] initially to denote cultural milieu but then often with primary reference to physical surroundings specifically. Environment can denote the surroundings of an individual person, a species, a society, or of life forms generally' (140).
69 See Estrada, *Radiografía de la pampa*, 15.
70 Thacker, *The Prairie Fact and Literary Imagination*, 105.
71 Ibid., 5.
72 Ibid., 6.
73 Estrada, *Radiografía de la pampa*, 42.
74 Moore, *Capitalism in the Web of Life,* 18.
75 Estrada, *Radiografía de la pampa*, 14.
76 Fermín Rodríguez, 'Martínez Estrada, Macedonio Fernández: Una ficción para el desierto argentino', *Hispamérica* 95 (2003): 85.
77 Estrada, *Radiografía de la pampa*, 41.
78 Ibid., 65.
79 Ibid., 256.
80 Ibid., 71.
81 Ibid.

Chapter 2

1 A recent documentary by filmmaker Ernesto Cabellos titled *Daughter of the Lake* (2015) bears witness to the devaluing of the Altiplanos as an important bioregion

that sustains the local Indigenous communities. An Indigenous woman tells of an extraction site that is polluting the water sources of her community, as well as of a Dutch jeweller who travels to the place where the precious metals she uses are dug up. The imagery of the documentary portrays the churning of the land in search of minerals, at the cost of the lives of humans and non-humans inhabiting the grasslands of the Andes highlands.

2   Tim Merrill and Ramón Miró, *Mexico: A Country Study* (Washington, DC: Library of Congress, 1997), 83.
3   Rex Hudson, *Peru: A Country Study* (Washington, DC: Library of Congress, 1993), 68.
4   The first translation of the book *El Llano en llamas* in Brazil by Eliane Zagury was titled *O Planalto em Chamas* (1977). Theresa Katarina Bachmann argues that while such a translation sustains the 'reference' of the original, it also loses the alliteration of the title (400). I would moreover argue that the translation offers an interesting insight as to the geographic imaginary of the plains in Rulfo's collection of short stories, one that supports interpreting the flatlands in *El Llano en llamas* as 'high plains'. In Brazil the term 'planalto central' also refers to the region where the capital, Brasília, is found. In fact, most of the plains regions in Brazil are considered 'planaltos' or 'high plains'. Except for the Pantanal, the Amazon river basin and the coastal plains in Rio Grande do Sul, the plains found in Brazil are elevated, although not nearly as elevated as the high plains in the Sierra Madre and Andean mountain ranges.
5   Timothy Morton, *The Ecological Thought* (Cambridge, MA: Harvard University Press, 2010), 92.
6   Antonio Cornejo Polar, 'Prólogo', in *El mundo es ancho y ajeno*, by Ciro Alegría (Caracas: Biblioteca Ayacucho, 1978), xviii.
7   Raúl Botelho Gosálvez, *Altiplano* (La Paz: Editorial Juventud, 1982), 7.
8   Aníbal Vargas-Barón, 'Altiplano: Novela india', *Hispania* 39, no. 1 (1956): 77.
9   Gosálvez, *Altiplano*, 12–20.
10 Ciro Alegría, *El mundo es ancho y ajeno* (Caracas: Biblioteca Ayacucho, 1978), 5.
11 Polar, 'Prólogo', xv.
12 Ibid., xviii; Carlos Villanes, 'Introducción', in *Los perros hambrientos*, by Ciro Alegría (Madrid: Cátedra, 1996), 54.
13 See Jorge Marcone, 'De retorno a lo natural: La serpiente de oro, "la novela de la selva" y la crítica ecológica', *Hispania* 81, no. 2 (1998): 299–308.
14 Ibid., 299.
15 Ibid., 300.
16 Carlos Villanes, 'Introducción', *Los perros hambrientos*, by Ciro Alegría (Madrid: Cátedra, 1996), 74–9; Manuel Larrú, 'Oralidad y representación. La otra voz en la narrativa de Ciro Alegría', *Letras* 80, no. 115 (2009): 53; Armando Zubizarreta, 'Realidad y ficción en *Los perros hambrientos*, de Ciro Alegría', *Revista de Crítica Literaria Latinoamericana* 24, no. 48 (1998): 162.

17 Ciro Alegría, *Los perros hambrientos* (Lima: Zig-Zag, [1939] 1968), 7.
18 Pontalti, *Diccionario Enciclopédico Quechua-Castellano del Mundo Andino*.
19 Alegría, *Los perros hambrientos*, 8.
20 Ibid., 10.
21 Ibid., 12.
22 Garrard, *Ecocriticism*, 35.
23 Alegría, *El mundo es ancho y ajeno*, 115.
24 *Diccionario de la Real Academia Española*, 23rd ed. (2014).
25 Alegría, *Los perros hambrientos*, 29.
26 Ibid., 149.
27 Ibid., 127.
28 Ibid.
29 Ibid.
30 Ibid., 135.
31 Ibid., 127.
32 Villanes, 'Introducción', 52.
33 According to Sergio López Mena, the title *El Llano en llamas* already contains a geographical reference. Notice that the word 'Llano' is capitalized, alluding to 'a place with that name south of Jalisco' (xxxii).
34 Francisco Antolín, *Los espacios en Juan Rulfo* (Mexico D.F.: Ediciones Universal, 1991), 15.
35 Carlos Blanco Aguinaga, 'Introducción', in *El Llano en llamas*, by Juan Rulfo (Madrid: Cátedra, 2014), 25.
36 Juan Rulfo, 'Luvina', in *Toda la obra*, ed. Claude Fell (Madrid: ALLCA XX, 1991), 103. My emphasis.
37 Elaine Gan, Anna Tsing, Heather Swanson and Nils Bubandt (eds.), *Arts of Living on a Damaged Planet: Ghosts of the Anthropocene* (Minneapolis: University of Minnesota Press, 2017), 2.
38 Rulfo, 'Luvina', 102.
39 Ibid., 104. My emphasis.
40 Ibid., 105. My emphasis.
41 Ibid., 111.
42 In *Radiografía de la pampa*, Ezequiel Estrada mentions this dichotomy when discussing the potential value of the Pampas grasslands. As the colonizers realized that there were hardly any riches to be found above ground after failing to find the mythical city of Trapalanda, they had to search for the 'hidden riches' in the ground itself (14). The plains have been a surface upon which to project the desire for capital since the Spanish Conquest, whether it be through the literal extraction of minerals or the intensive agriculture of vast estates.
43 Juan Rulfo, *Obra* (Mexico D.F.: Editorial RM-Fundación Juan Rulfo, 2017), 176.

44 Jean Franco, 'El viaje al país de los muertos', in *Toda la obra*, by Juan Rulfo (Madrid: ALLCA XX, 1991), 767.
45 Ana María López, 'Presencia de la naturaleza, protesta sociopolítica, muerte y resurrección en *El Llano en llamas*, de Juan Rulfo', *Anales de Literatura Hispanoamericana* 4 (1975): 173.
46 Franco, 'El viaje al país de los muertos', 767.
47 Rulfo, 'Luvina', 103.
48 Gustavo Martínez, *El Llano en llamas o la fatalidad hecha tierra* (Mexico D.F.: Rebeca Linke Editoras, 2010), 123.
49 Rulfo, 'Luvina', 102.
50 Carlos Huamán López, 'Los condenados de *Luvina*', in *Revisión crítica de la obra de Juan Rulfo*, ed. Sergio Lópes Mena (Mexico D.F.: Editorial Praxis, 1998), 59.
51 Lucy Bell, 'The Death of the Storyteller and the Poetics of (Un)Containment: Juan Rulfo's *El Llano en llamas*', *The Modern Language Review* 107, no. 3 (2012): 822.
52 See Luís Leal, 'El cuento de ambiente: "Luvina", de Juan Rulfo', in *Homenaje a Juan Rulfo*, ed. Helmy F. Giacoman (Mexico D.F.: Las Américas, 1974).
53 Rulfo, 'Luvina', 102.
54 Ibid.
55 Cynthia Deitering, 'The Postnatural Novel: Toxic Consciousness in Fiction of the 1980s', in *The Ecocriticism Reader: Landmarks in Literary Ecology*, eds. Cheryll Glotfelty and Harold Fromm (Athens, GA: University of Georgia Press, 1996), 201.
56 Elaine Gan, Anna Tsing, Heather Swanson, and Nils Bubandt (eds.), *Arts of Living on a Damaged Planet: Ghosts of the Anthropocene*, 3.
57 Tim Ingold, 'Whirl', in *Veer Ecology: A Companion for Environmental Thinking*, eds. Jeffrey Jerom Cohen and Lowell Duckert (Minneapolis: University of Minnesota Press, 2017), 431
58 Rulfo, 'Luvina', 102.
59 Ibid., 103.
60 Ibid., 104.
61 Ibid., 111.
62 Lucy Bell, 'Viscous Porosity: Interactions between Human and Environment in Juan Rulfo's *El Llano en llamas*', *Journal of Iberian and Latin American Research* 21, no. 3 (2015): 392.
63 Rulfo, 'Luvina', 107.
64 Charles Perrone, *Seven Faces: Brazilian Poetry since Modernism* (Durham, NC: Duke University Press, 1996), 22.
65 Candido, *A educação pela noite e outros ensaios*, 161.
66 Caroline LeFeber Schneider, 'The Prose of Place in *Grande Sertão: Veredas* and *Pedro Páramo*', *Luso-Brazilian Review* 53, no. 2 (2016): 32.
67 Ibid., 38.

68 Jon Vincent, *João Guimarães Rosa* (Woodbridge, CT: Twayne Publishers, 1978), 63.
69 Although this distinction is no longer widely used in Portuguese, the term 'estória' corresponds to the fictional sense of a story and the term 'história' refers to the factual dimension of 'history'.
70 Vincent, *João Guimarães Rosa*, 135.
71 Ibid.
72 Schneider, 'The Prose of Place in *Grande Sertão: Veredas* and *Pedro Páramo*', 38.
73 Ibid.
74 *Diccionário Priberam da Língua Portugesa*.
75 Marli Fantini, *Guimarães Rosa: Fronteiras, Margens, Passagens* (Rio de Janeiro: Ateliê Editorial, 2004), 45.
76 João Guimarães Rosa, 'Páramo', in *Estas Estorias* (São Paulo: Editora Nova Fronteira, 2015), 211.
77 Ibid., 223.
78 Ibid., 225.
79 Ibid., 213.
80 Ibid., 212.
81 Ibid., 213.
82 Ibid., 217.
83 Ibid., 221.
84 Ibid.
85 Ibid., 212.
86 Ibid., 213.
87 Ibid., 218.
88 Ibid., 211.
89 Ibid., 225.
90 Ibid., 224.
91 Ibid., 234.

Chapter 3

1 Sergio Balaguera-Reina, Ariel Espinosa-Blanco, Mónica Morales-Betancourt, Andrés Seijas, Carlos Lasso, Rafael Antelo, and Llewellyn Densmore, 'Conservation Status and Regional Habitat Priorities for the Orinoco Crocodile: Past, Present, and Future', *PLoS ONE* 12, no. 2 (2017): 2.
2 Vladimir Dinets, *Dragon Songs: Love and Adventure among Crocodiles, Alligators, and Other Dinosaur Relations* (New York: Arcade Publishing, 2013), 65.
3 Andrés Seijas, Rafael Antelo, John Thorbjarnarson and María Cristina Ardila Robayo, 'Orinoco Crocodile *Crocodylus Intermedius*', in *Crocodiles. Status Survey*

and Conservation Action Plan, eds. S. C. Manolis and C. Stevenson (Darwin: Crocodile Specialist Group, 2010), 60.

4 Antonio Castro Casal, Manuel Merchán Fornelino, Mario Fernando Garcés Restrepo, Miguel Andrés Cárdenas Torres and Fernando Gómez Velasco, 'Uso histórico y actual del caimán llanero (*Crocodylus intermedius*) en la Orinoquia (Colombia-Venezuela)', *Biota Colombiana* 14, no. 2 (2013): 71.

5 Moore, *Capitalism in the Web of Life,* 26.

6 Ursula K. Heise, *Imagining Extinction: The Cultural Meanings of Endangered Species* (Chicago: University of Chicago Press, 2016), 8.

7 Donna Haraway, *When Species Meet* (Minneapolis: University of Minnesota Press, 2008), 15.

8 Javier Uriarte and Felipe Martínez-Pinzón, 'Introduction. Intimate Frontiers: A Literary Geography of the Amazon', in *Intimate Frontiers: A Literary Geography of the Amazon*, eds. Felipe Martínez-Pinzón and Javier Uriarte (Liverpool: University of Liverpool, 2019), 17.

9 For a nuanced discussion on the theme of madness and jungle environments in José Eustasio Rivera's *La vorágine*, see Charlotte Rogers, *Jungle Fever: Exploring Madness and Medicine in Twentieth-Century Tropical Narratives* (Nashville: Vanderbilt University Press, 2012).

10 Sergio Balaguera-Reina, Ariel Espinosa-Blanco, Mónica Morales-Betancourt, Andrés Seijas, Carlos Lasso, Rafael Antelo and Llewellyn Densmore, 'Conservation Status and Regional Habitat Priorities for the Orinoco Crocodile: Past, Present, and Future', *PLoS ONE* 12, no. 2 (2017): 2.

11 Heise, *Imagining Extinction*, 4.

12 Barney Nelson, *The Wild and the Domestic: Animal Representation, Ecocriticism, and Western American Literature* (Reno: University of Nevada Press, 2000), 137.

13 Moore, 'The Rise of Cheap Nature', 87.

14 Brians R. Langerhans, 'Evolutionary Consequences of Predation: Avoidance, Escape, Reproduction, and Diversification', in *Predation in Organisms: A Distinct Phenomenon*, ed. Ashraf M. T. Elewa (New York: Springer, 2007), 177.

15 Robert Taylor, *Predation* (London: Chapman and Hall, 1984), 3–4.

16 Langerhans, 'Evolutionary Consequences of Predation: Avoidance, Escape, Reproduction, and Diversification', 180.

17 Carlos Cosentino and Declan Bates, *Feedback Control in Systems Biology* (London: CRC Press, 2011), 3.

18 Peter Chesson and Jessica J. Kuang, 'The Interaction between Predation and Competition', *Nature* 456 (2008): 235.

19 Morton, *Dark Ecology*, 6.

20 Morton, *The Ecological Thought*, 39.

21 Invasive species do alter food chains in given ecosystems, although we should not be quick to dismiss their role as detrimental. Such a position is often dualistic

in its approach to the conservation of native species against the dangers of alien species that have accompanied humans in their commercial routes throughout the planet. There is no such thing as static, pristine biome that remains untouched. A radically conservationist approach ends up repeating the trope of an idyllic nature that is opposed to society. It is far more helpful to think of invasive species as a manifestation of the capitalist world ecology that distributes species throughout the world in its production through nature. Fred Pearce begins *The New Wild: Why Invasive Species Will Be Nature's Savior* by explaining that these species 'are travelling the world in ever greater numbers, hitchhiking in our hand luggage, hidden in cargo holds, stuck to the bottom of ships and migrating to keep up with climate change' (1). Although Pearce continues to reframe the discussion in dualistic terms – invasive species are the saviours of nature, not a part of the web of life – his contribution raises important questions as to the preconceived notions latent in the conservation of native species.

22 Consentino and Bates, *Feedback Control in Systems Biology*, 1.
23 Morton, *The Ecological Thought*, 40.
24 Bruno Latour, *We Have Never Been Modern*, trans. Catherine Porter (Cambridge, MA: Harvard University Press, 1993), 99.
25 Garrard, *Ecocriticism*, 140.
26 Haraway, *When Species Meet*, 9.
27 Ibid., 10.
28 John Berger, *About Looking* (London: Penguin, 1980), 3.
29 Haraway, *When Species Meet*, 4.
30 Ibid., 35.
31 Levi Bryant, 'Black', in *Prismatic Ecology: Ecotheory beyond Green*, ed. Jeffrey Jerome Cohen (Minneapolis: University of Minnesota Press, 2013), 303.
32 Ibid.
33 Ibid.
34 Gallegos, *Doña Bárbara*, 204.
35 Montserrat Ordóñez, 'Introducción', *La vorágine,* by José Eustasio Rivera (Madrid: Cátedra, 2012), 51.
36 José Eustasio Rivera, *Obra literaria* (Bogotá: Editorial Pontificia Universidad Javeriana, 2009), 282.
37 Gallegos, *Doña Bárbara*, 5.
38 Sharon Magnarelli, *The Lost Rib: Female Characters in the Spanish-American Novel* (Lewisburg, PA: Bucknell University Press, 1985), 38.
39 Alonso, *The Spanish American Regional Novel*, 66.
40 French, *Nature, Neo-Colonialism, and the Spanish American Regional Writers*, 132.
41 Ibid.
42 Alonso, *The Spanish American Regional Novel*, 109.

43 Germán Bula and Ronal Bermúdez, *Alteridad y pertenencia: Lectura ecocrítica de María y La vorágine* (Bogotá: Editora Universidad de la Salle, 2009), 91–6.
44 The plains that surround the Orinoco river basin encompass both the region of Casanare depicted in *La vorágine* and that of Apure in *Doña Bárbara*.
45 Gallegos, *Doña Bárbara*, 12.
46 Rivera, *Obra literaria*, 296–7.
47 Ibid., 374.
48 Ibid., 373.
49 Greg Garrard, 'Ferality Tales', in *The Oxford Handbook of Ecocriticism*, ed. Greg Garrard (Oxford: Oxford University Press, 2014), 242.
50 Nelson, *The Wild and the Domestic*, 6.
51 Rivera, *Obra literaria*, 370–1.
52 Gallegos, *Doña Bárbara*, 121.
53 Ibid., 212.
54 Ibid., 183.
55 Ibid., 193.
56 Haraway, *When Species Meet*, 287.
57 Alison N. P. Stevens, 'Predation, Herbivory, and Parasitism', *Nature Education Knowledge* 3, no. 10 (2010): 36.
58 Rivera, *Obra literaria*, 579.
59 Ibid., 303.
60 Ibid., 379.
61 Ibid., 296.
62 Ibid., 366.
63 Ibid., 580.
64 Ibid., 387–90.
65 Ibid., 296.
66 Ibid., 297.
67 Ordóñez, 'Introducción', 94.
68 Rivera, *Obra literaria*, 388.
69 French, *Nature, Neo-Colonialism, and the Spanish American Regional Writers*, 143.
70 Rivera, *Obra literaria*, 380.
71 Ibid., 381.
72 Gallegos, *Doña Bárbara*, 14.
73 Ibid., 24.
74 Ibid., 85.
75 Alonso, *The Spanish American Regional Novel*, 139.
76 Gallegos, *Doña Bárbara*, 4.
77 Ibid., 12.
78 Ibid., 131.

79 Casal, Fornelino, Restrepo, Torres and Velasco, 'Uso histórico y actual del caimán llanero (*Crocodylus intermedius*) en la Orinoquia (Colombia-Venezuela)', 77.
80 Gallegos, *Doña Bárbara*, 132.
81 Ibid., 212.
82 Casal, Fornelino, Restrepo, Torres and Velasco, 'Uso histórico y actual del caimán llanero (*Crocodylus intermedius*) en la Orinoquia (Colombia-Venezuela)', 74.
83 Ibid.
84 Ibid., 75.
85 Gallegos, *Doña Bárbara*, 132.
86 Ibid., 133.
87 Ibid., 25.
88 Ibid., 24.
89 Ibid.
90 Ibid., 44.
91 Ibid., 196.
92 Magnarelli, *The Lost Rib*, 39.
93 Ibid., 38.
94 Haraway, *When Species Meet*, 10.
95 Ibid.
96 Rivera, *Obra literaria*, 310.
97 Gallegos, *Doña Bárbara*, 82.
98 Ibid., 46.
99 Ibid., 20.
100 Aaron Moe, *Zoopoetics: Animals and the Making of Poetry* (New York: Lexington Books, 2014), 15.
101 Magnarelli, *The Lost Rib*, 45.
102 Gallegos, *Doña Bárbara*, 120.
103 Ibid., 117.
104 Ibid., 72.
105 Sommer, *Foundational Fictions*, 264.
106 Ibid.
107 Magnarelli, *The Lost Rib*, 55.

Chapter 4

1 José Luiz de Andrade Franco, *Biodiversidade e ocupação humana do Pantanal mato-grossense: Conflitos e oportunidades* (São Paulo: Editora Grammond, 2013), 21.
2 Cristina Campos, *Manoel de Barros: O demiurgo das terras encharcadas: educação pela vivência do chão* (Cuiabá: Carlini & Caniato, 2010), 68.

3 Franco, *Biodiversidade e ocupação humana do Pantanal mato-grossense*, 32.
4 Abilio Leite de Barros, *Gente pantaneira: Crônicas de sua história* (Campo Grande: Instituto Histórico e Geográfico de Mato Grosso do Sul, 2012), 21.
5 Malcolm McNee, *The Environmental Imaginary in Brazilian Poetry and Art* (New York: Palgrave Macmillan, 2014), 40.
6 Francisco Aquino Corrêa, *Obras* (Campo Grande: Comemorativa do Centenário de Nascimento do Autor, 1985), 23.
7 McNee, *The Environmental Imaginary in Brazilian Poetry and Art*, 38.
8 Ibid.
9 João Guimarães Rosa, 'Entremeio—Com o vaqueiro Mariano', in *Estas Estórias* (São Paulo: Nova Fronteira, 2015), 103.
10 Manoel de Barros, *Poesia completa* (São Paulo: LeYa, 2013), 202.
11 Ibid., 7.
12 Rosa, 'Entremeio', 117.
13 Barros, *Poesia completa*, 189.
14 Judith Bronstein, *Mutualism* (Oxford: Oxford University Press, 2015), 3.
15 Corrêa, *Obras*, 90.
16 Thacker, *The Great Prairie Fact and Literary Imagination*, 14.
17 Ibid., 51.
18 Ibid., 86.
19 Ibid., 54.
20 Ibid., 55.
21 Ibid., 90.
22 The resemblance between Dom Aquino's stanza and a passage from James Fenimore Cooper's *The Prairie* is striking: 'The earth was not unlike the ocean, when its restless waters are heaving heavily, after the agitation and fury of the tempest have begun to lessen. There was the same waving and regular surface, the same absence of foreign objects, and the same boundless extent to the view [. . .] *Here and there a tall tree rose out of the bottoms, stretching its naked branches abroad, like some solitary vessel*; and, to strengthen the delusion, far in the distance, appeared two or three round thickets, looming in the misty horizon like islands resting on the waters' (my italics 13).
23 Corrêa, *Obras*, 23.
24 Ibid., 22.
25 Ibid., 26.
26 Buell, *The Environmental Imagination*, 78.
27 Corrêa, *Obras*, 90.
28 McNee, *The Environmental Imaginary in Brazilian Poetry and Art*, 1.
29 For a complete bibliographic register of publications by Guimarães Rosa, the Universidade de São Paulo maintains the online database *Banco de dados bibliográficos João Guimarães Rosa*.

30 Rosa, 'Entremeio', 93.
31 Maria Esther Maciel, 'Paisagens zooliterárias. Animais na literatura brasileira moderna', *Revista de Crítica Literaria Lationamericana* 79 (2014): 267.
32 Rosa, 'Entremeio', 93.
33 Ibid., 96.
34 Ibid., 94.
35 Ibid., 102.
36 Ibid.
37 Ibid., 103–4.
38 Marianne Soisalo and Sandra Cavalcanti, 'Estimating the Density of a Jaguar Population in the Brazilian Pantanal Using Camera-Traps and Capture-Recapture Sampling in Combination with GPS Radio-Telemetry', *Biological Conservation* 129 (2006): 487.
39 Kevin Seymour, 'Panthera onca', *Mammalian Species* 340 (1989): 1.
40 Soisalo and Cavalcanti, 'Estimating the Density of a Jaguar Population in the Brazilian Pantanal Using Camera-Traps and Capture-Recapture Sampling in Combination with GPS Radio-Telemetry', 488.
41 Rosa, 'Entremeio', 94.
42 Ibid., 119.
43 Maciel, 'Paisagens zooliterárias. Animais na literatura brasileira moderna', 266.
44 Rosa, 'Entremeio', 103.
45 Ibid., 113.
46 Ibid., 114.
47 Ibid., 124.
48 Ibid., 114–15.
49 Ibid., 124.
50 Barros seems to allude to this episode in 'Entremeio' when in *Livro de pré-coisas* he describes the *quero-quero* bird in the following manner: 'If the cattle herder is preparing the lasso nearby, in an improper place, he complains. If a child is hunting insects in the swamp, he screams in that scratched sound that is similar to that of the *arara*. He defends himself like a bull' (214).
51 Rosa, 'Entremeio', 112.
52 Adalberto Müller, *Encontros Manoel de Barros* (Campo Grande: Azougue Editorial, 2016), 20.
53 Barros, *Poesia completa*, 186.
54 Barros, *Arranjos para assobio* (São Paulo: Alfaguara, 2016), 7.
55 Barros, *Poesia completa*, 202.
56 Ibid., 183.
57 Ibid., 191.
58 *Dicionário Ilustrado Tupi Guarani*.

59 Ruth Albernaz-Silveira and Carolina Joana da Silva, 'Rede Alimentar de Aves: Conexões Ecológicas em Território Pantaneiro', *Profiscientia* 5 (2013): 73.
60 Barros, *Poesia completa*, 211–16.
61 Ibid., 215.
62 Paulo Eduardo Benites de Moraes and Josemar de Campos Maciel, 'Cultura híbrida no cerrado: Práticas sociais do discurso literário e a construção da identidade nos poemas de Manoel de Barros', *Todas As Letras* 15, no. 2 (2013): 86.
63 Barros, *Poesia completa*, 216.
64 Ibid., 375.
65 Ibid., 183.
66 Ibid., 188.
67 Ibid., 189.
68 Ibid.

Conclusion

1 Jonathan Lash, 'Foreword', in *Pilot Analysis of Global Ecosystems: Grasslands Ecosystems*, by Robin White, Siobhan Murray and Mark Rohweder (Washington, DC: World Research Institute, 2000), viii.
2 See, for example, the book-length report of grasslands under the auspice of the Food and Agriculture Organization of the United Nations in J. M. Suttie, S. G. Reynolds and C. Batello, *Grasslands of the World* (Rome: Food and Agriculture Organization of the United Nations, 2005).
3 White, Murray and Rohweder, *Pilot Analysis of Global Ecosystems*, 7.
4 Estrada, *Radiografía de la pampa*, 9.
5 Quantic, *The Nature of Place*, xvi.
6 Lash, 'Foreword', viii.
7 See Boaventura de Sousa Santos, *O fim do império cognitivo: A afirmação das epistemologias do Sul* (Belo Horizonte: Autêntica, 2019).
8 See Adriana López, *De mitos, estrellas y cosmogonías en las tierras del cóndor* (Córdoba, Argentina: Editorial Brujas, 2008), 49–56. See also Eduardo Galeano, *Memoria del fuego I: Los nacimientos* (Mexico D.F.: Siglo XXI, [1982] 1991), 29.
9 Benson, 'The Lord, the Ruler', 54.
10 Ibid., 62.
11 Many canonical fictions throughout Latin America incorporate predation into their narratives. In Brazil, for example, writer José de Alencar introduces the jaguar in his regionalist novel *O sertanejo* (1875) as a wild predator that the protagonist Arnaldo manages to tame in a show of mastery and courage to the landowner. Modernist writer Mario de Andrade also incorporates predation in his novel *Macunaíma*

(1928) via the metaphor of cultural anthropophagy that is also present in his fellow writer Oswald de Andrade's *Manifesto Antropófago* (1928).

12 See the collection of essays in Monica Gagliano, John C. Ryan and Patricia Vieira (eds.), *The Language of Plants: Science, Philosophy, Literature* (Minneapolis: University of Minnesota Press, 2017) and Jeffrey Nealon, *Plant Theory: Biopower and Vegetable Life* (Stanford: Stanford University Press, 2015).

13 See Gustavo Giberti, 'Bonpland's Manuscript Name for the Yerba Mate and Ilex Theezans C. Martius ex Reisseck (Aquifoliaceae)', *Taxon* 39, no. 4 (1990): 663–5.

14 Another important documentary on these grasslands is *Sertão Serrado* (2016) by flimmaker Dagmar Talga.

15 Guilherme de Oliveira, Miguel Bastos Araújo, Thiago Fernando Rangel, Diogo Alagador and José Alexandre Felizola Diniz-Filho, 'Conserving the Brazilian Semiarid (Caatinga) Biome Under Climate Change', *Biodiversity and Conservation* 21, no. 11 (2012): 2914.

16 Ibid.

References

Adamson, Joni. *American Indian Literature, Environmental Justice, and Ecocriticism: The Middle Place*. Tucson: University of Arizona Press, 2001.

Aguinaga, Carlos Blanco. 'Introducción'. In *El Llano en llamas*, by Juan Rulfo, 1–32. Madrid: Cátedra, 2014.

Albernaz-Silveira, Ruth and Carolina Joana da Silva. 'Rede Alimentar de Aves: Conexões Ecológicas em Território Pantaneiro'. *Profiscientia* 5 (2013): 61–77.

Alegría, Ciro. *El mundo es ancho y ajeno*. Caracas: Biblioteca Ayacucho, [1941] 1978.

Alegría, Ciro. *Los perros hambrientos*. Lima: Zig-Zag, [1939] 1968.

Alonso, Carlos. *The Spanish American Regional Novel: Modernity and Autochthony*. Cambridge: Cambridge University Press, 1990.

Alpers, Paul. *What Is Pastoral?* Chicago: University of Chicago Press, 1996.

Antolín, Francisco. *Los espacios en Juan Rulfo*. Mexico D.F.: Ediciones Universal, 1991.

Arguedas, Alcides. *Raza de bronce*. Caracas: Biblioteca Ayacucho, [1919] 2006.

Balaguera-Reina, Sergio, Ariel Espinosa-Blanco, Mónica Morales-Betancourt, Andrés Seijas, Carlos Lasso, Rafael Antelo, and Llewellyn Densmore. 'Conservation Status and Regional Habitat Priorities for the Orinoco Crocodile: Past, Present, and Future'. *PLoS ONE* 12, no. 2 (2017): 1–20.

Barbas-Rhoden, Laura. *Ecological Imaginations in Latin American Fiction*. Gainesville: University Press of Florida, 2012.

Barros, Abilio Leite de. *Gente pantaneira: Crônicas de sua história*. Campo Grande: Instituto Histórico e Geográfico de Mato Grosso do Sul, 2012.

Barros, Manoel. *Arranjos para assobio*. São Paulo: Alfaguara, [1982] 2016.

Barros, Manoel. *Poesia completa*. São Paulo: LeYa, 2013.

Bate, Jonathan. *Romantic Ecology: Wordsworth and the Environmental Tradition*. London: Routledge, 2013.

Beckman, Ericka. 'Troubadours and Bedouins on the Pampas: Medievalism and Orientalism in Sarmiento's *Facundo*'. *Chasqui: Revista de literatura latinoamericana* 38, no. 2 (2009): 37–46.

Bell, Lucy. 'The Death of the Storyteller and the Poetics of (Un)Containment: Juan Rulfo's *El Llano en llamas*'. *The Modern Language Review* 107, no. 3 (2012): 815–36.

Bell, Lucy. 'Viscous Porosity: Interactions between Human and Environment in Juan Rulfo's *El Llano en llamas*'. *Journal of Iberian and Latin American Research* 21, no. 3 (2015): 389–404.

Bennet, Jane. *Vibrant Matter: A Political Ecology of Things*. Durham, NC: Duke University Press, 2010.

Benson, Elizabeth P. 'The Lord, the Ruler: Jaguar Symbolism in the Americas'. In *Icons of Power: Feline Symbolism in the Americas*, edited by Nicholas J. Saunders, 53–76. London: Routledge, 1998.

Berger, John. *About Looking*. London: Penguin, 1980.

Blaser, Mario. *Storytelling Globalization from the Chaco and Beyond*. Durham, NC: Duke University Press, 2010.

Blaser, Mario and Marisol de la Cadena. 'Pluriverse: Proposals for a World of Many Worlds'. In *A World of Many Worlds*, edited by Marisol de la Cadena and Mario Blaser, 1–22. Durham, NC: Duke University Press, 2018.

Boixo, José Carlos González. 'Introducción'. In *Pedro Páramo*, by Juan Rulfo, 9–62. Madrid: Cátedra, 2012.

Bronstein, Judith. *Mutualism*. Oxford: Oxford University Press, 2015.

Bryant, Levi. 'Black'. In *Prismatic Ecology: Ecotheory beyond Green*, edited by Jeffrey Jerome Cohen, 290–310. Minneapolis: University of Minnesota Press, 2013.

Buell, Lawrence. *The Environmental Imagination: Thoreau, Nature Writing, and the Formation of American Culture*. Cambridge, MA: Belknap Press, 1995.

Buell, Lawrence. *The Future of Environmental Criticism: Environmental Crisis and Literary Imagination*. London: Blackwell Publishing, 2005.

Bula, Germán and Ronal Bermúdez. *Alteridad y pertenencia: Lectura ecocrítica de María y La vorágine*. Bogotá: Editora Universidad de la Salle, 2009.

Bury, Jeffrey and Anthony Bebbington. 'New Geographies of Extractive Industries in Latin America'. In *Subterranean Struggles: New Dynamics of Mining, Oil, and Gas in Latin America*, edited by Anthony Bebbington and Jeffrey Bury, 27–66. Austin: University of Texas Press, 2013.

Campos, Cristina. *Manoel de Barros: O demiurgo das terras encharcadas: educação pela vivência do chão*. Cuiabá: Carlini & Caniato, 2010.

Candido, Antonio. *A educação pela noite e outros ensaios*. São Paulo: Editora Ática, 1989.

Cardenal, Ernesto. *Versos del Pluriverso*. Madrid: Trotta, 2005.

Casal, Antonio Castro, Manuel Merchán Fornelino, Mario Fernando Garcés Restrepo, Miguel Andrés Cárdenas Torres and Fernando Gómez Velasco. 'Uso histórico y actual del caimán llanero (*Crocodylus intermedius*) en la Orinoquia (Colombia-Venezuela)'. *Biota Colombiana* 14, no. 2 (2013): 65–82.

Chesson, Peter and Jessica J. Kuang. 'The Interaction between Predation and Competition'. *Nature* 456 (2008): 235–8.

Cohen, Jeffrey Jerome and Lowell Duckert. 'Introduction: Eleven Principles of the Elements'. In *Elemental Ecocriticism: Thinking with Earth, Air, Water, and Fire*, edited by Jeffrey Jerome Cohen and Lowell Duckert, 1–26. Minneapolis: University of Minnesota Press, 2015.

Cohen, Jeffrey Jerome and Lowell Duckert. 'Introduction: Welcome to the Whirled'. In *Veer Ecology: A Companion for Environmental Thinking*, edited by Jeffrey Jerome Cohen and Lowell Duckert, 1–15. Minneapolis: University of Minnesota Press, 2017.

Cooper, James Fenimore. *The Works of J. Fenimore Cooper*. Vol. 8. New York: George P. Putnam, 1851.

Corrêa, Francisco Aquino. *Obras*. Campo Grande: Comemorativa do Centenário de Nascimento do Autor, 1985.

Cosentino, Carlos and Declan Bates. *Feedback Control in Systems Biology*. London: CRC Press, 2011.

Crosby, Alfred W. *Ecological Imperialism: The Biological Expansion of Europe, 900-1900*. Cambridge: Cambridge University Press, 1986.

Cvitanovic, Dinko. 'Radiografía de la pampa en la historia personal de Martínez Estrada'. In *Radiografía de la pampa*, by Ezequiel Martínez Estrada, 327–48. Madrid: ALLCA XX, 1991.

Dabove, Juan Pablo. *Nightmares of the Lettered City: Banditry and Literature in Latin America 1816–1929*. Pittsburgh: University of Pittsburgh Press, 2007.

Dean, Warren. *With Broadax and Firebrand: The Destruction of the Brazilian Atlantic Forest*. Berkeley: University of California Press, 1995.

Deitering, Cynthia. 'The Postnatural Novel: Toxic Consciousness in Fiction of the 1980s'. In *The Ecocriticism Reader: Landmarks in Literary Ecology*, edited by Cheryll Glotfelty and Harold Fromm, 196–203. Athens, GA: University of Georgia Press, 1996.

DeVries, Scott. *A History of Ecology and Environmentalism in Spanish American Literature*. Lewisburg, PA: Bucknell University Press, 2013.

Dinets, Vladimir. *Dragon Songs: Love and Adventure among Crocodiles, Alligators, and Other Dionosaur Relations*. New York: Arcade Publishing, 2013.

Dussel, Enrique. *Ética de la liberación en la edad de la globalización y de la exclusión*. Madrid: Trotta, 1998.

Dussel, Enrique. *Polítical de la liberación I: Historia mundial y crítica*. Madrid: Trotta, 2007.

Dussel, Enrique. *Polítical de la liberación II: Arquitectónica*. Madrid: Trotta, 2009.

Dussel, Enrique. *Siete ensayos de filosofía de la liberación: Hacia una fundamentación del giro decolonial*. Madrid: Trotta, 2020.

Echevarría, Roberto González. *Modern Latin American Literature: A Very Short Introduction*. Oxford: Oxford University Press, 2013.

Escobar, Arturo. *Designs for the Pluriverse: Radical Interdependence, Autonomy, and the Making of Worlds*. Durham, NC: Duke University Press, 2017.

Estrada, Ezequiel Martínez. *Los variantes históricos en el Facundo*. Buenos Aires: Casa de Pardo, [1947] 1974.

Estrada, Ezequiel Martínez. *Radiografía de la pampa*. Madrid: ALLCA XX, [1933] 1991.

Estrada, Ezequiel Martínez. *Sarmiento*. Buenos Aires: Argos, 1946.

Fantini, Marli. *Guimarães Rosa: Fronteiras, Margens, Passagens*. Rio de Janeiro: Ateliê Editorial, 2004.

Feustle, Joseph. 'Sarmiento and Martínez Estrada: A Concept of Argentine History'. *Hispania* 55, no. 3 (1972): 446–55.

Franco, Jean. 'El viaje al país de los muertos'. In *Toda la obra*, by Juan Rulfo, 763–74. Madrid: ALLCA XX, 1991.

Franco, Luiz de Andrade. *Biodiversidade e ocupação humana do Pantanal matogrossense: Conflitos e oportunidades*. São Paulo: Editora Grammond, 2013.

French, Jennifer L. *Nature, Neo-Colonialism, and the Spanish American Regional Writers*. Hanover: Dartmouth College Press, 2005.

Gagliano, Monica, John C. Ryan and Patricia Vieira (eds.). *The Language of Plants: Science, Philosophy, Literature*. Minneapolis: University of Minnesota Press, 2017.

Galeano, Eduardo. *Memoria del fuego I: Los nacimientos*. Mexico D.F.: Siglo XXI, [1982] 1991.

Gallegos, Rómulo. *Doña Bárbara*. Caracas: Biblioteca Ayacucho, [1929] 1977.

Gan, Elaine, Anna Tsing, Heather Swanson and Nils Bubandt (eds.). *Arts of Living on a Damaged Planet: Ghosts of the Anthropocene*. Minneapolis: University of Minnesota Press, 2017-

Garrard, Greg. 'Ferality Tales'. In *The Oxford Handbook of Ecocriticism*, edited by Greg Garrard, 241–59. Oxford: Oxford University Press, 2014.

Garrard, Greg. *Ecocriticism*. London: Routledge, 2004.

Gillis, John R. 'Not Continents in Miniature: Islands as Ecotones'. *Island Studies Journal* 9 (2014): 155–66.

Gómez-Barris, Macarena. *The Extractive Zone: Social Ecologies and Decolonial Perspectives*. Durham, NC: Duke University Press, 2017.

Gosálvez, Raúl Botelho. *Altiplano*. La Paz: Editorial Juventud, 1982.

Grusin, Richard. 'Introduction'. In *The Nonhuman Turn*, edited by Richard Grusin, viii–xxix. Minneapolis: University of Minnesota Press, 2015.

Haberly, David T. 'Francis Bond Head and Domingo Sarmiento: A Note on the Sources of *Facundo*'. *MLN* 120, no. 2 (2005): 287–93.

Haraway, Donna. *Staying with the Trouble: Making Kin in the Chthulucene*. Durham, NC: Duke University Press, 2016.

Haraway, Donna. *When Species Meet*. Minneapolis: University of Minnesota Press, 2008.

Heise, Ursula. *Imagining Extinction: The Cultural Meanings of Endangered Species*. Chicago: University of Chicago Press, 2017.

Hermida, Carola. 'Ver el esqueleto de la tierra: *Radiografía de la pampa* de Ezequiel Martínez Estrada'. *CELEHIS - Revista del Centro de Letras Hispanoamericanas* 12 (2000): 99–114.

Herrera, Lorena, Malena Sabatino, Aitor Gastón and Santiago Saura. 'Grassland Connectivity Explains Entomophilous Plant Species Assemblages in an Agricultural Landscape of the Pampa Region, Argentina'. *Austral Ecology* 42 (2017): 486–96.

Horcasitas, Fernando. 'La Danza de los Tecuanes'. *Estudios de Cultura Náhuatl* 14 (1980): 239–319.

Hudson, Rex. *Peru: A Country Study*. Washington, DC: Library of Congress, 1993.

Humboldt, Alexander von. *Views of Nature*. Translated by Mark W. Person. Chicago: Chicago University Press, [1808] 2014.

Ingold, Tim. 'Whirl'. In *Veer Ecology: A Companion for Environmental Thinking*, edited by Jeffrey Jerome Cohen and Lowell Duckert, 421–33. Minneapolis: University of Minnesota Press, 2017.

Kelly, William. *Plotting America's Past: Fenimore Cooper and The Leatherstocking Tales*. Carbondale: Southern Illinois University Press, 1983.

Krenak, Ailton. *Ideias para adiar o fim do mundo*. São Paulo: Companhia das letras, 2019.

Langerhans, Brians R. 'Evolutionary Consequences of Predation: Avoidance, Escape, Reproduction, and Diversification'. In *Predation in Organisms: A Distinct Phenomenon*, edited by Ashraf M. T. Elewa, 177–220. New York: Springer, 2007.

Larrú, Manuel. 'Oralidad y representación. La otra voz en la narrativa de Ciro Alegría'. *Letras* 80, no. 115 (2009): 47–62.

Lash, Jonathan. 'Foreword'. In *Pilot Analysis of Global Ecosystems: Grassland Ecosystems*, by Robin White, Siobhan Murray and Mark Rohweder, viii–ix. Washington, DC: World Research Institute, 2000.

Latour, Bruno. *We Have Never Been Modern*. Translated by Catherine Porter. Cambridge, MA: Harvard University Press, 1993.

Leal, Luís. 'El cuento de ambiente: "Luvina", de Juan Rulfo'. In *Homenaje a Juan Rulfo*, edited by Helmy F. Giacoman, 91–8. Mexico D.F.: Las Américas, 1974.

León-Portilla, Miguel. *Aztec Thought and Culture*. Norman: University of Oklahoma Press, 1963.

Levinas, Emmanuel. *The Levinas Reader*. Edited by Seán Hand. Oxford: Blackwell, 1989.

Lowenthal, David. 'The American Scene'. *Geographical Review* 58 (1968): 61–88.

Ludmer, Josefina. *The Gaucho Genre*. Translated by Molly Weigel. Durham, NC: Duke University Press, 2002.

Lynch, Tom, Cheryll Glotfelty and Karla Armbruster (eds.). *Bioregional Imagination: Literature, Ecology and Place*. Athens, GA: University of Georgia Press, 2012.

Machado, Juliana Medianeira, Marta Gomes da Rocha, Fernando Luiz Ferreira de Quadros, Anna Carolina Cerato Confortin, Aline Bosak dos Santos, Maria José de Oliveira Sichonany, Laila Arruda Ribeiro, and Aline Tatiane Nunes da Rosa. 'Morphogenesis of Native Grasses of Pampa Biome under Nitrogen Fertilization'. *Revista Brasileira de Zootecnia* 42, no. 1 (2013): 22–9.

Maciel, Maria Esther. 'Paisagens zooliterárias. Animais na literatura brasileira moderna'. *Revista de Crítica Literaria Latinoamericana* 79 (2014): 265–76.

Madan, Aarti. *Lines of Geography in Latin American Narrative: National Territory, National Literature*. New York: Palgrave Macmillan, 2017.

Madan, Aarti. 'Sarmiento the Geographer: Unearthing the Literary in *Facundo*'. *MLN* 126, no. 2 (2011): 259–88.

Maestri, Mário. *Breve história do Rio Grande do Sul: da Pré-História aos dias atuais*. São Paulo: Editora Universidade de Passo Fundo, 2010.

Magnarelli, Sharon. *The Lost Rib: Female Characters in the Spanish-American Novel*. Lewisburg, PA: Bucknell University Press, 1985.

Maher, Susan Naramore. 'Literature of the Great Plains: Nature, Culture, and Community'. In *A History of Western American Literature*, edited by Susan Kollin, 129–44. Cambridge: Cambridge University Press, 2015.

Marcone, Jorge. 'De retorno a lo natural: La serpiente de oro, "la novela de la selva" y la crítica ecológica'. *Hispania* 81, no. 2 (1998): 299–308.

Martínez, Gustavo. *El Llano en llamas o la fatalidad hecha tierra*. Mexico D.F.: Rebeca Linke Editoras, 2010.

Marx, Leo. *The Machine in the Garden: Technology and the Pastoral Ideal in America*. Oxford: Oxford University Press, 2000.

McMahon, Elizabeth. *Islands, Identity and the Literary Imagination*. London: Anthem Press, 2016.

McNee, Malcolm. *The Environmental Imaginary in Brazilian Poetry and Art*. New York: Palgrave Macmillan, 2014.

Mena, Sergio López. 'Nota filológica préliminar'. In *Toda la obra*, by Juan Rulfo, xxxi–xxxix. Madrid: ALLCA XX, 1991.

Merrill, Tim and Ramón Miró. *Mexico: A Country Study*. Washington, DC: Library of Congress, 1997.

Mignolo, Walter. *Local Histories/Global Designs: Coloniality, Subaltern Knowledges, and Border Thinking*. Princeton: Princeton University Press, 2000.

Mignolo, Walter and Catherine E. Walsh. *On Decoloniality: Concepts, Analytics, Praxis*. Durham, NC: Duke University Press, 2018.

Mitchell, Lee Clark. *Witnesses to a Vanishing America*. Princeton: Princeton University Press, 1981.

Moe, Aaron. *Zoopoetics: Animals and the Making of Poetry*. New York: Lexington Books, 2014.

Moore, Jason W. *Capitalism in the Web of Life: Ecology and the Accumulation of Capital*. New York: Vintage, 2015.

Moore, Jason W. 'The Rise of Cheap Nature'. In *Anthropocene or Capitalocene? Nature, History, and the Crisis of Capitalism*, edited by Jason W. Moore, 78–115. Oakland: PM Press, 2016.

Moraes, Paulo Eduardo Benites de and Josemar de Campos Maciel. 'Cultura híbrida no cerrado: Práticas sociais do discurso literário e a construção da identidade nos poemas de Manoel de Barros'. *Todas As Letras* 15, no. 2 (2013): 81–90.

Morton, Timothy. *Dark Ecology: For a Logic of Future Coexistence*. New York: Columbia University Press, 2016.

Morton, Timothy. *The Ecological Thought*. Cambridge, MA: Harvard University Press, 2010.

Müller, Adalberto. *Encontros Manoel de Barros*. Campo Grande: Azougue Editorial, 2016.

Nealon, Jeffrey. *Plant Theory: Biopower and Vegetable Life*. Stanford: Stanford University Press, 2015.

Nelson, Barney. *The Wild and the Domestic: Animal Representation, Ecocriticism, and Western American Literature*. Reno: University of Nevada Press, 2000.

Neruda, Pablo. *Canto General*. Buenos Aires: Editorial Losada, [1950] 1955.

Nixon, Rob. *Slow Violence and Environmentalism of the Poor*. Cambridge, MA: Harvard University Press, 2011.

Oliveira, Guilherme de, Miguel Bastos Araújo, Thiago Fernando Rangel, Diogo Alagador and José Alexandre Felizola Diniz-Filho. 'Conserving the Brazilian Semiarid (Caatinga) Biome under Climate Change'. *Biodiversity and Conservation* 21 (2012): 2913–26.

Ordoñez, Montserrat. 'Introducción'. *La vorágine*, by José Eustasio Rivera, 11–58. Madrid: Cátedra, 2012.

Pearce, Fred. *The New Wild: Why Invasive Species Will Be Nature's Salvation*. London: Icon Books, 2015.

Pengue, Walter. 'The Impact of Soybean Expansion in Argentina'. *Seedling* 18, no. 3 (September 2001): 1.

Perrone, Charles. *Seven Faces: Brazilian Poetry since Modernism*. Durham, NC: Duke University Press, 1996.

Polar, Antonio Cornejo. 'Prólogo'. In *El mundo es ancho y ajeno*, by Ciro Alegría, ix–xxxii. Caracas: Biblioteca Ayacucho, 1978.

Pollman, Leo. 'Génesis e intención de Radiografía de la pampa'. In *Radiografía de la pampa*, by Ezequiel Martínez Estrada, 445–60. Madrid: ALLCA XX, 1991.

Pollman, Leo. 'Introducción del Coordinador'. In *Radiografía de la pampa*, by Ezequiel Martínez Estrada, xix–xxii. Madrid: ALLCA XX, 1991.

Pontalti, Adalberto A. Rosat. *Diccionario Enciclopédico Quechua-Castellano del Mundo Andino*. Lima :Grupo Editorial Verbo Divino, 2009.

Quantic, Diane Dufva. *The Nature of the Place: A Study of Great Plains Fiction*. Lincoln: University of Nebraska Press, 1995.

Quantic, Diane D. and P. Jane Hafen. 'Foreword: What Is in This Reader'. In *A Great Plains Reader*, edited by Diane D. Quantic and P. Jane Hafen, xi–xvi. Lincoln, NE: University of Nebraska Press, 2003.

Rama, Angel. *The Lettered City*. Translated by John Charles Chasteen. Durham, NC: Duke University Press, 1996.

Reiter, Bernd (ed.). *Constructing the Pluriverse: The Geopolitics of Knowledge*. Durham, NC: Duke University Press, 2018.

Rivera, José Eustasio. *Obra literaria*. Bogotá: Editorial Pontificia Universidad Javeriana, 2009.

Rivera-Barnes, Beatriz. *Reading and Writing the Latin American Landscape*. New York: Palgrave Macmillan, 2009.

Roberts, Brian Russell and Michelle Ann Stephens. 'Archipelagic American Studies: Decontinentalizing the Study of American Culture'. In *Archipelagic American Studies*, edited by Brian Russell Roberts and Michelle Ann Stephens, 1–54. Durham, NC: Duke University Press, 2017.

Rodríguez, Fermín. 'Martínez Estrada, Macedonio Fernández: Una ficción para el desierto argentino'. *Hispamérica* 95 (2003): 85–91.

Roesch, Luiz Fernando Wurdig, Frederico Costa Beber Vieira, Vilmar Alves Pereira, Adriano Luis Schünemann, Italo Filippi Teixeira, Ana Julia Teixeira Senna, and Valdir Marcos Stefenon. 'The Brazilian Pampa: A Fragile Biome'. *Diversity* 1, no. 2 (2009): 182–98.

Rogers, Charlotte. *Jungle Fever: Exploring Madness and Medicine in Twentieth-Century Tropical Narratives*. Nashville: Vanderbilt University Press, 2012.

Rosa, João Guimarães. 'Entremeio—Com o vaqueiro Mariano'. In *Estas Estórias*, 91–124. São Paulo: Nova Fronteira, [1969] 2015.

Rosa, João Guimarães. 'Páramo'. In *Estas Estorias*, 211–34. São Paulo: Editora Nova Fronteira, [1969] 2015.

Roscio, Francisco João. *Compendio noticiozo do Continente do Rio Grande de S. Pedro até o destricto da Ilha de St. Caterina: extraido dos meus diarios, observações, e noticias, que alcancey nas jornadas, que fez ao ditto continente nos annos 1774, e 1775*. Rio de Janeiro: Biblioteca Nacional do Brasil, 1781.

Rose, Deborah Bird. 'Shimmer: When All You Love Is Being Trashed'. In *Arts of Living on a Damaged Planet*, edited by Anna Lowenhaupt Tsing, Heather Anne Swanson, Elaine Gan and Nills Bubandt, 51–63. Minneapolis: University of Minnesota Press, 2017.

Ruffato, Luiz. 'Prefácio: O arquipélago Erico Veríssimo'. In *O Arquipélago*, by Érico Veríssimo, 7–11. São Paulo: Companhia das Letras, 2018.

Rulfo, Juan. 'Luvina'. In *Toda la obra*, edited by Claude Fell, 102–13. Madrid: ALLCA XX, 1991.

Rulfo, Juan. *Obra*. Mexico D.F.: Editorial RM-Funadación Juan Rulfo, 2017.

Sá, Lúcia. 'Endless Stories: Perspectivism and Narrative Form in Native Amazonian Literature'. In *Intimate Frontiers: A Literary Geography of the Amazon*, edited by Felipe Martínez-Pinzón and Javier Uriarte, 128–49. Liverpool: University of Liverpool Press, 2019.

Sá, Lúcia. *Rain Forest Literatures: Amazonian Texts and Latin American Culture*. Minneapolis: University of Minnesota Press, 2004.

Santos, Boaventura de Sousa. *Epistemologies of the South: Justice against Epistemicide*. London: Routledge, 2014.

Santos, Boaventura de Sousa. *O fim do império cognitivo: A afirmação das epistemologias do Sul*. Belo Horizonte: Autêntica, 2019.

Santos, Hellen and Cristina Vieira. 'Pecuária ajuda e é ajudada pelo meio ambiente na região do Pampa, RS'. *Globo Rural* (13 August 2017).

Sarmiento, Domingo Faustino. *Facundo*. Madrid: Cátedra, [1845] 2008.

Schneider, Caroline LeFeber. 'The Prose of Place in *Grande Sertão: Veredas* and *Pedro Páramo*'. *Luso-Brazilian Review* 53, no. 2 (2016): 31–61.

Seijas, Andrés, Rafael Antelo, John Thorbjarnarson, and María Cristina Ardila Robayo. 'Orinoco Crocodile *Crocodylus intermedius*'. In *Crocodiles. Status Survey and*

Conservation Action Plan, edited by S. C. Manolis and C. Stevenson, 59–65. Darwin: Crocodile Specialist Group, 2010.

Seymour, Kevin. 'Panthera onca'. *Mammalian Species* 340 (1989): 1–9.

Soisalo, Marianne and Sandra Cavalcanti. 'Estimating the Density of a Jaguar Population in the Brazilian Pantanal Using Camera-Traps and Capture-Recapture Sampling in Combination with GPS Radio-Telemetry'. *Biological Conservation* 129 (2006): 487–96.

Sommer, Doris. *Foundational Fictions: The National Romances of Latin America*. Berkeley: University of California Press, 1993.

Stevens, Alison N. P. 'Predation, Herbivory, and Parasitism'. *Nature Education Knowledge* 3, no. 10 (2010): 36.

Taylor, Robert. *Predation*. London: Chapman and Hall, 1984.

Thacker, Robert. *The Great Prairie and Literary Fact*. Albuquerque: University of New Mexico Press, 1989.

Thayer, Robert L. *Lifeplace: Bioregional Thought and Practice*. Berkeley: University of California Press, 2003.

Uriarte, Javier and Felipe Martínez-Pinzón. 'Introduction. Intimate Frontiers: A Literary Geography of the Amazon'. In *Intimate Frontiers: A Literary Geography of the Amazon*, edited by Felipe Martínez-Pinzón and Javier Uriarte, 1–22. Liverpool: University of Liverpool, 2019.

Vargas-Barón. 'Altiplano: Novela india'. *Hispania* 39, no. 1 (1956): 72–9.

Veríssimo, Érico. *O Continente*. Vol. 1. São Paulo: Companhia das Letras, [1949] 2004.

Veríssimo, Érico. *Solo de Clarineta: Memorias*. Vol. 1. Porto Alegre: Editora Globo, 1974.

Villanes, Carlos. 'Introducción'. In *Los perros hambrientos*, by Ciro Alegría, 11–108. Madrid: Cátedra, 1996.

Vincent, Jon. *João Guimarães Rosa*. Woodbridge, CT: Twayne Publishers, 1978.

Wald, Sarah D., David J. Vázquez, Priscilla Solí Ybarra and Sarah Jaquette Ray. 'Introduction: Why Latinx Environmentalisms?'. In *Latinx Environmentalisms: Place, Justice, and the Decolonial*, edited by Sarah D. Wald, David J. Vázquez, Priscilla Solí Ybarra and Sarah Jaquette Ray, 1–34. Philadelphia, PA: Temple University Press, 2019.

Weinberg, Gregorio. 'Liminar'. In *Radiografía de la Pampa*, by Ezequiel Martínez Estrada, xv–xviii. Madrid: ALLCA XX, 1996.

White, Robin, Siobhan Murray and Mark Rohweder. *Pilot Analysis of Global Ecosystems: Grasslands Ecosystems*. Washington, DC: World Research Institute, 2000.

Ybarra, Priscilla Solís. *Writing the Goodlife: Mexican American Literature and the Environment*. Tucson: University of Arizona Press, 2016.

Zubizarreta, Armando. 'Realidad y ficción en *Los perros hambrientos*, de Ciro Alegría'. *Revista de Crítica Literaria Latinoamericana* 24, no. 48 (1998): 159–72.

Index

Adamson, Joni   137 n.53
agency, of nature   46–7
Aguinaga, Carlos Blanco   48
Alegría, Ciro   16, 39, 40, 125
Alencar, José de   19, 138 n.60, 153 n.11
Alonso, Carlos   13, 14, 74, 75, 84, 133 n.19
Alpers, Paul   140 n.32
Altiplanicies. *See* Altiplanos
Altiplano (Gosálvez)   41, 42
Altiplanos   5, 6, 23, 39, 142–3 n.1
  Andean grasslands and drought in *Los perros hambrientos* and   41–8
  'Luvina' and   48–56
  'Páramo' and   56–63
  significance of   40
Amazon river basin   143 n.4
American landscape, contradiction between ideas of   25
anaconda   82
Andean condor (*Vultur gryphus*)   45–6
Andes (South American region)   8
Andes region   39, 143 n.4
Andrade, Carlos Drummond de   113
Andrade, Mario de   153 n.11
Andrade, Oswald de   154 n.11
anhuma (horned screamer)   108, 111–12, 115
animality, textual performance of   90
Anthropocene age   10, 11, 32
anthropocentrism   40, 70, 77, 78, 86, 105
anthropomorphism   68, 72, 73, 86, 88, 89, 116, 117
Apure plains   14, 65, 83, 89, 91, 149 n.44
Argentina   8, 19, 21, 23, 27, 30–2, 37
  extension problem and   32
  plains as psychological space of   33
  X-ray metaphor and   32
Argentina (Martínez Estrada)   31
Argentine Desert Campaign (1833–4)   5
Arguedas, Alcides   6
Armbruster, Karla   134 n.25

Arts of Living on a Damaged Planet   49
Assis, Machado de   100
Atlantic Rainforest   131 n.8
autochthony, notion of   13–14, 119, 133 n.19
avifauna   98, 105, 110, 111, 112
Azores   131 n.8

Bachmann, Theresa Katarina   143 n.4
baguaris, significance of   116
Banco de dados bibliográficos João Guimarães Rosa (online database)   151 n.29
Barbas-Rhoden, Laura   136 n.42
Barros, Abílio Leite de   93
Barros, Manoel de   16, 93–8, 113–21, 139 n.10, 152 n.50
Bate, Jonathan   140 n.32
Batello, C.   153 n.2
Bebbington, Anthony   6, 134 n.23
Bell, Lucy   52, 56
Bennett, Jane   9
Berger, John   71
bioregionalism, significance of   134 n.25
black ecology   72
Blackfish (documentary)   70
Blaser, Mario   3, 132 n.10
Bolaño, Roberto   19, 20
Bolivia   40, 115, 116
Bonpland, Aimee   8, 126, 134–5 n.31
Borges, Jorge Luis   19
Brazil   8, 19, 21, 37, 93, 115, 128, 143 n.4
Brazilian Canudos Campaign (1896–7)   5
Bryant, Levi   72
Buell, Lawrence   3, 103, 140 n.32, 142 n.68
Bula, Germán   75
Bury, Jeffrey   6, 134 n.23

Caatinga biome   128
Cabellos, Ernesto   127, 142 n.1

Cadena, Marisol de la   132 n.10
Calibán (Fernández Retamar)   20
'Caminho do Cerrado' project   128
Canada   13
Canary Islands   131 n.8
Candido, Antonio   56, 138 n.60
Canto General (Neruda)   17
capitalism and nature, link between
    10–11, 35, 65, 67–8, 75,
    138 n.60
Cardenal, Ernesto   132 n.10
Casal, Castro   86, 87
Casanare   149 n.44
Central Mexican plateau (Mexican
    altiplanicie)   40
Cerrado biome   101, 128
cerro, notion of   52, 56
Chapada dos Veadeiros   128
chicalote plant, significance of   52–4,
    56, 63
civilization and barbarism, dichotomy of
    Pampas and   23, 25, 28, 32
    predation in Orinoco Llanos and   66,
    67, 72, 79, 91
Colombia   6
coloniality, of knowledge   7
condor, notion of   45–6
Confortin, Anna Carolina
    Cerato   141 n.51
continental imaginaries, significance
    of   1–2. *See also individual
    entries*
continentalism   2, 124–5. *See also
    individual entries*
Cooper, James Fenimore   5, 26, 36, 38,
    140 n.17, 151 n.22
    and Sarmiento
        comparison of   22, 23
        influence on   24
Coronado, Francisco   23
Corrêa, Francisco Aquino. *See* Dom
    Aquino
Correio da Manhã (newspaper)   94
cougar (Puma concolor), naming
    convention of   109–10
Cowperthwaite, Gabriela   70
crocodiles, significance of   65, 67, 72, 75,
    79, 82, 83, 85–7
    culling of   86–8, 92

Crosby, Alfred W.   131 n.8
Cvitanovic, Dinko   31

Dabove, Juan Pablo   30
da Cunha, Euclides   5, 100, 103
Daughter of the Lake
    (documentary)   142–3 n.1
Dean, Warren   131 n.8
decolonial, significance of   11
Deitering, Cynthia   53
'de la pampa', significance of   32
D'Elia, André   128
desolate landscape   23, 28, 37, 48, 52,
    53, 84
de Sousa Santos, Boaventura   4, 12
DeVries, Scott   136 n.42
de Waal, Franz   70
Díaz, Eduardo Acevedo   138 n.60
*Diccionario de la Real Academia
    Española*   45
*Diccionario Enciclopédico Quechua-
    Castellano*   43
Dicionário Priberam da Língua Portuguesa
    (DPLP)   58
difference and alterity, significance of
    132 n.12
Dom Aquino   94, 99–100, 151 n.22
Doña Bárbara (Gallegos)   5, 14, 125.
    See also Orinoco Llanos
Dussel, Enrique   7, 11, 132 n.12,
    136 n.47, 137 n.50

Echeverría, Esteban   19
ecocritical readings, significance of
    9–11, 16–17, 136 nn.41–2
ecological interdependence, significance
    of   72
'El gaucho insufrible' (Bolaño)   20
El Llano en llamas   40, 48, 56, 144 n.33
    translation of   143 n.4
El mundo es ancho y ajeno (Alegría)   41,
    42, 45
emptiness discourse, significance of   23
'ensayo de interpretación' genre
    142 n.61
'Entremeio–Com o vaqueiro Mariano'
    (Guimarães Rosa)   94, 97,
    104–12, 152 n.50
'epistemicide'   4

Epistemologies of the South (de Sousa Santos)   12
Escobar, Arturo   3, 132 nn.10, 12
Esso, Lucas van   127
established totality, moment of   11
  exteriority and   11–12
Estas estórias   58, 94
extractive zones   5

Facundo (Sarmiento)   5, 6, 10, 20, 32, 67, 126, 140 n.17
  grasslands in   38
  land possession in   35
  Pampas as desert in   21–30
feedback loops   69, 72, 85
feral animals   28, 55, 66, 68, 71
  anthropocentrism and   78
  predation and   73–9
Fernández Retamar, Roberto   20
Franco, Jean   50
French, Jennifer L.   74, 133 n.19, 136 n.42
Future of Ecocriticism, The (Buell)   142 n.68

Galeano, Eduardo   19
Gallegos, Rómulo   5, 14, 16, 66, 72, 75, 90, 107, 125
Gândavo, Pêro de Magalhães   118
Garrard, Greg   25–6, 78
gaucho literature, significance of   19, 21
gaze, idea of   28, 108, 117, 121
  between animals and humans   71
  masculine   14, 92, 103
  predation in Orinoco Llanos and   67, 70–1, 75, 76, 84, 88, 91–2
gendered predators   89–92
Gifford, Terry   140 n.32
Glotfelty, Cheryll   134 n.25
Gómez-Barris, Macarena   5
Gosálvez, Raúl Botelho   41
Gran Chaco (documentary)   127
Grande sertão: Veredas (Guimarães Rosa)   56, 57, 139 n.10
grasslands   32. *See also* plains
  abstract and geometric portrayal of   33
  abstraction of   31
  as barren   47–8

  devaluation, as desert   30, 38
  geometric wilderness of   38
  as immensity without limits   23, 29, 34
  infinite   23
  as obstacle to civilization   27
  as ocean   23
  PAGE report on   123–4
  portrayal of   20
  significance of   21
  as wasteland   23
Grasslands Ecosystems (report)   123
'Great Divides'   66, 69, 70, 78, 89, 91, 92, 125
Great Plains of North America   3
Great Plains Reader, A (Quantic and Hafen)   13, 139 n.7
Guimarães Rosa, João   16, 39, 40, 56, 94–8, 104, 121, 139 n.10, 151 n.29
Güiraldes, Ricardo   19, 138 n.60
Gutiérrez, Eduardo   19

Haberly, David T.   140 n.17
Hafen, Jane   13, 139 n.7
Haraway, Donna   9, 66, 71, 136 n.40
Heise, Ursula K.   67
Hermida, Carola   21
Hernández, José   19, 138 n.60
highlands, significance of   6
Hija de la Laguna (documentary)   127
Historia naturalis palmarium (Martius)   135 n.31
Hobbes, Thomas   70
horizon, significance of   49, 102
Houaiss, Antonio   113
human–animal binary   70–3
human exceptionalism   70, 71, 76, 78, 85, 92
Humboldt, Alexander von   22, 23, 29, 38, 126, 134 n.31, 135 n.34, 140 n.17

'ichu', notion of   43–4
idyll, notion of   44–5
imagined geography, significance of   23, 29, 98–9
Indigenous community, significance of   42–3, 45
infinitesimal, significance of   118–21

International Food Policy Research Institute   123
invasive species, significance of   147–8 n.21
island archipelagos   131–2 n.8

jaguar   110
João Roscio, Francisco   1, 2
jungle and political ecology   42

Kelly, William   27
Krenak, Ailton   137 n.53

La guerra del fracking (documentary)   127
Latour, Bruno   69
La vorágine (Rivera)   66, 68, 71–6, 78, 80–2, 89, 127, 147 n.9
Leatherstocking (Cooper)   26
Lefeber Schneider, Caroline   57, 58
Leviathan (Hobbes)   70
Levinas, Emmanuel   132 n.12
liberation, politics of   11–12
Literaturas da Floresta (Sá)   137 n.56
Livro de pré-coisas (Barros)   94, 97, 113–21, 152 n.50
Llanos   5, 6, 14. *See also* Orinoco Llanos
local knowledge, idea of   39, 41, 44, 81, 124–7, 135 n.34
    continental imaginaries of Latin America and   7–8, 12, 15–16
    Pampas and   30, 33, 34, 36
    Pantanal wetlands and   96, 99, 100, 104, 105, 111, 121
Lopes Neto, João Simões   19
López, Carlos Huamán   51
Los perros hambrientos (Alegría)   40, 41, 51–3, 55, 63, 125
    drought in Andean grasslands in   41–8
Lowenthal, David   19
Lugones, Leopoldo   19
'Luvina' (Rulfo)   40, 41
    and 'Páramo' compared   57, 58, 62–3
    windy summits in   48–56
Lynch, Tom   134 n.25

Machado, Juliana Medianeira   141 n.51
Maciel, Josemar de Campos   117
Maciel, Maria Esther   105, 110
McMahon, Elizabeth   2
McNee, Malcolm   96
Macunaíma (Andrade)   153 n.11
Madan, Aarti   22, 23, 29, 140 n.17
Magnarelli, Sharon   89
Manifest Destiny policy, significance of   5, 22, 33, 125
Manifesto Antropófago (Andrade)   154 n.11
Manuel de Rosas, Juan   21, 27
Marcone, Jorge   42
Mariátegui, José Carlos   142 n.61
'marketable geography', significance of   22–4, 36
Martínez Estrada, Ezequiel   15, 19, 20, 27, 30, 32–8, 102, 124, 139 nn.10, 13, 144 n.42
Marx, Leo   25
masculine gaze, significance of   14, 92, 103
Mato Grosso (Brazil)   94, 100, 103
Mato Grosso do Sul (Brazil)   93, 113, 116
Maurer, Melissa   128
Mena, Sergio López   144 n.33
messianic rupture, moment of   11
Mexico   39
Mignolo, Walter   7
Mitchell, Lee Clark   7
Moe, Aaron   90
monotony, significance of   43
Moore, Jason W.   10, 35
Moraes, Paulo Eduardo Benites   117
Morton, Timothy   41, 69, 135–6 n.40
mutualism
    ecological knowledge and naming and   96, 97, 99
    human and domestic animals and   108, 112
    non-human naming and   115, 116, 119, 121

nails, notion of   50
naming, colonial ecologies in   8–9
nature. *See also individual entries*
    agency of   46–7
    and capitalism, link between   10–11, 35, 65, 67–8, 75, 138 n.60
    as environment   33

personification of   37–8, 47, 51, 54, 102
negative feedback loops   69
Nelson, Barney   78
Neruda, Pablo   17
new order creation, moment of   11
New Wild, The (Pearce)   148 n.21
New World   25
new world pastoral   103
Nhecolândia (Pantanal)   106
Nietzsche, Friedrich   32
Nixon, Rob   11, 134 n.23
non-human, significance of   9–11, 66, 75, 91
   Altiplanos and   43, 48–51, 55, 56, 59, 62–3
   naming of   113–21
   predation and   79–89
novelas de la selva (Amazonian perspectivism), significance of   13, 66, 137 n.56
novelas de la tierra (regional novels), significance of   13–14, 66, 74, 133 n.19
Nuevo Álbum de Zoología (Pacheco)   127

O Arquipélago (Veríssimo)   1, 2
ocean of land metaphor, significance of   3
ocelot (*Leopardus pardalis*)   84
O Continente (Veríssimo)   1, 2
Odes (Corrêa)   100
ombú tree (*Phytolacca dioica*)   102, 127
   Pampas as deserts and   37
   personification of   37–8
   significance of   36–7
On the Genealogy of Morals (Nietzsche)   32
O Planalto em Chamas   143 n.4
Ordóñez, Montserrat   82
O Retrato (Veríssimo)   1
Orinoco crocodile (*Crocodylus intermedius*)   65, 67, 72, 86
Orinoco Llanos
   gendered predators in   89–92
   human and non-human predation in   79–89
   predation and ferality in   73–9
   predatory ecologies and   68–73
   significance of   65–8

Orinoco river basin   6, 14, 16, 65, 149 n.44
O sertanejo (Alencar)   153 n.11
Os sertões (da Cunha)   5, 100
O tempo e o vento trilogy (Veríssimo)   1–4, 94
outsider-insider knowledge binary, significance of   106, 108–9, 111

Pacheco, José Emilio   127
Pampas   1, 5, 6, 11, 141 n.51
   as desert   21–30, 37, 38
   ecological issues in   24–5
   significance of   8, 10, 19
Pantanal wetlands   5, 8, 16, 93–5, 143 n.4
   humans and domestic animals and   104–12
   naming, mutualism, and ecological knowledge and   95–9
   non-human naming and   113–21
   settler ecology and   99–104
   significance of   93–4
Paraguay   37, 103, 115, 116
'Páramo' (Guimarães Rosa)   40, 41
   and 'Luvina' compared   57, 58, 62–3
   suffocating highlands in   56–63
passion of Christ and land   55–6
pastoral and wilderness, link between   25–6
pastoral mode, definition of   140 n.32
Paz, Octavio   142 n.61
Pearce, Fred   148 n.21
Pedro Páramo (Rulfo)   50, 57, 58
personification
   of nature   37–8, 47, 51, 54, 102
   of times   90
Peru   40
Philipp von Martius, Carl Friedrich   8, 126, 135 n.31
Pilot Analysis of Global Ecosystems (PAGE)   123
plains. *See also* grasslands
   as abstract space   29
   autochthony of   13–14, 119, 133 n.19
   as barren desert   29–30
   as battlefield   24–5
   as cemetery   50
   civilization bringing to   6
   as desolate planet   23
   dominant image of   7, 10–11, 52, 65

as empty   4–7, 31, 35–6, 38, 52, 102
extension of   34–6, 38
as geometries of value   30–8
immensity of   100, 108
literature of Latin American   13–15
as metaphysical entity   139 n.10
modernity and   3
significance of   3–4
as sterile   6
as *terra nullius*   2
as threatening place   67
as vacant landscape   27, 36
vastness of   3, 5, 13–15, 23, 31, 35, 38, 144 n.42
as wasteland   57, 59
    irreversible   40
'planetary pampas'   17
pluriverse, significance of   2–3, 132 n.10
Polar, Cornejo   41
political ecology   42
Pollmann, Leo   30, 33
postcolonialism   11
Potosí   6
Prairie, The (Cooper)   5, 23, 26–7
prairie topography, significance of   20
predation
    and ferality   73–9
    gendered   89–92
    human and non-human   79–89
predatory ecologies   68–73
predatory relations, significance of   65–8
Primates and Philosophers (de Waal)   70
pumas (*Panther once palustris*)   110
Puna. *See* Altiplanos

Quadros, Fernando Luiz Ferreira de   141 n.51
Quantic, Dufva   8, 13, 124, 133 n.16, 139 n.7
quero-queros   112, 152 n.50
Quiroga, Facundo   21, 27

Radiografía de la pampa (Martínez Estrada)   20, 21, 124, 139 n.10, 144 n.42
    plains as geometries of value in   30–8
ranching   6, 16, 25, 38
    Pantanal wetlands and   94, 104–10, 112

predation in Orinoco Llanos and   65, 66, 72, 74, 76–80, 86–8, 91
Raza de bronce (Arguedas)   6
regional novels, significance of. *See novelas de la tierra* (regional novels), significance of
Reiter, Bernd   132 n.10
renewed life, significance of   26
Reyles, Carlos   138 n.60
Reynolds, S. G.   153 n.2
Ribeiro, Laila Arruda   141 n.51
Rio Grande do Sul   1, 19, 143 n.4
    significance of   1–2
Rivera, José Eustasio   16, 66, 72, 81, 127, 147 n.9
Rivera-Barnes, Beatriz   136 n.42
Rocha, Marta Gomes da   141 n.51
Rodó, José Enrique   142 n.61
Rogers, Charlotte   147 n.9
Rosa, Aline Tatiane Nunes da   141 n.51
Rose, Deborah Bird   10, 136 n.41
ruined landscape. *See* Altiplanos
Rulfo, Juan   16, 39, 40, 139 n.10

Sá, Lúcia   137 n.56
Santa Fé city   1
Santos, Aline Bosak dos   141 n.51
Sarmiento, Domingo   5, 6, 10, 15, 19, 20, 27, 32, 107, 140 n.17
    and Cooper
        comparison of   22–4
        influence of   24
Sater, Almir   93
screech owl   83–4
sea of grass metaphor   23
Serpiente de oro (Alegría)   42
Sertão Serrado (documentary)   154 n.14
Ser Tão Velho Cerrado (documentary)   128
settler ecologies, of Latin American plains   4–13
Sichonany, Maria José de Oliveira   141 n.51
Sierra Madre mountain range   39, 48, 143 n.4
Slow Violence and Environmentalism (Nixon)   134 n.23
Solanas, Fernando   127
Sommer, Doris   21, 140 n.17
soroche sickness, significance of   60

Spanish American Regional Novel, The (Alonso)   74
Staying with the Trouble (Haraway)   9, 136 n.40
Stevens, Alison N. P.   80
stork   88
subterranean, idea of   50, 52, 120, 124
super-regionalism   56
Suttie, J. M.   153 n.2

Talga, Dagmar   154 n.14
Taunay, Visconde de   103
Taylor, Robert   68
Terra-Cambará family, significance of (fictional family)   1, 2
Terra natal (Corrêa)   94, 95, 99, 100, 102
Thacker, Robert   3, 20
Thayer, Robert L.   134 n.25
totality and exteriority, relationship between   11–12
transnational ethics, of place   11
Tratado da Terra do Brasil (Gândavo)   118
Tratado geral das grandezas do ínfimo (Barros)   117–18
Treaty of Madrid (1750)   1
Tuana, Nancy   56
tuiuiú bird   93, 114

United States   13, 20
Universidade de São Paulo   151 n.29

Uriburu, José Felix   30
Uruguay   8, 19, 37

Venezuela   6, 65
Veríssimo, Érico   1–3, 19, 94
Viana, Javier de   138 n.60
'vibrant materialism', politics of   9
Views of Nature (Humboldt)   22–3, 135 n.34
Vincent, Jon   58
viscous porosity   56

When Species Meet (Haraway)   71
'Why Look at Animals?' (Berger)   71
Wild and the Domestic, The (Nelson)   78
wild-domestic binary   78
wilderness   28, 38
    asymmetry with city   30
    and pastoral, link between   25–6
    plains as geometric   36
wind
    as condor metaphor   46
    significance of   54–5, 61–2
World Research Initiative   123

yacabó. See screech owl
Ybarra, Priscilla Solís   137 n.53

Zagury, Eliane   143 n.4
'zero-degree of nature'   84, 86
zoomorphism   68, 72, 73, 83, 88–90
zoopoetics   90

www.ingramcontent.com/pod-product-compliance
Lightning Source LLC
Chambersburg PA
CBHW070641300426
44111CB00013B/2203